First published in Great Britain in 2008 by
University of Hertfordshire Press
Learning and Information Services
University of Hertfordshire
College Lane
Hatfield
Hertfordshire AL10 9AB

Designed by Tony McDermott for the University of Hertfordshire

© Copyright 2008 University of Hertfordshire
All rights reserved. No part of this book may be reproduced or uitlised in any form or by any means, electronic or mechanical, including photocopying, recording or by any information storage and retrieval system, without permission in writing from the School of Education, University of Hertfordshire.

British Library Cataloguing in Publication Data
A catalogue record for this book is available from the British Library

ISBN 978-1-905313-52-5

Printed in Great Britain by 4edge, Hockley, Essex

University of Hertfordshire

Children's Literature ANNUAL No. 2

The Story and The Self
Children's Literature: Some Psychoanalytic Perspectives

Papers and presentations from conference 2007

Contents:

1	**Jenny Plastow** An invitation from the Editor	07
2	K E Y N O T E : **Rosemary Stones** Stories We Tell Ourselves	10
3	**Alison Waller** Re-reading Children's Literature: Memory and Emotion	20
4	**Rebecca Butler** The Scholar, the Hero and Their Faithful Friend	29
5	**Rebecca-Anne C. Do Rozario** Mirrored: The Self and Inheritance as seen in Children's Narrative	46
6	**Debbie Hindle and Sylvia Wilson** Dialogues with Literature and Psychoanalysis	58
7	**Debbie Hindle** Ethical Space in the Island of Struay	60
8	**Sylvia Wilson** Children on the Edge: insights from Literature and Psychotherapy	68
9	**Andrea Peterson** The Representation of Shell Shock in Michael Morpurgo's *Private Peaceful*	76
10	**Jenny Plastow** Making the Man	86
11	**Pat Pinsent** The Theme of Facial Disfigurement in some recent books for young readers	98
12	**Jake Hope** Fairytale Heart: an exploration of memory, story and childhood through Philip Ridley's novels and plays.	110

13	**Conference 2007:** Photographs	**124**
14	**Nick Midgely** The Courage to be Afraid: Fearful encounters in the work of Neil Gaiman and Dave McKean	**128**
15	K E Y N O T E : **Margaret Rustin and Michael Rustin** The Regeneration of *Doctor Who*	**142**
16	**Peter Bramwell** Pagan Themes: The Green Man	**160**
17	**Madelyn Travis** Journey to the Self: Feminine Symbols and Archetypes in Lloyd Alexander's *The Chronicles of Prydain* and Susan Cooper's *The Dark is Rising* sequence.	**171**
18	**John Burton** Pattern-Matching and Childhood Stories	**186**
19	**David Rudd** Holed and Porous, but not Impossible: Children's Literature, Psychoanalysis and Constructions of the Child	**191**
20	**Diane Duncan** Love, Loss and Magic: connecting author and story	**202**
21	**Gerry Byrne** The Evocation of Mystery in the Art of Anthony Browne	**219**
22	**Victoria de Rijke and Howard Hollands** The Thing that is not There: A Psychoanalytic Reading of Mervyn Peake's *Captain Slaugterboard Drops Anchor*	**236**
23	**Antony Lishak** The Story of the Story of the Story	**249**
24	**Cast in order of appearance**	**256**
25	**Acknowledgements**	**260**
26	**2008 Conference:** Further details	**261**

Jenny Plastow

An invitation from the Editor

TO THOSE ADULTS who love reading children's literature, it has always been something of a private passion. Whether re-reading known favourites, aloud to children or privately by the fire during influenza, or discovering a new and astonishing piece of work, we tend at the back of our minds always to have the image of the raised eyebrow on the face of a colleague, the question as to the validity of children's literature as a genre. 'What is there to research about children's literature? Does that *really* belong in Humanities?' In many a department – though luckily not mine - the eyebrow raises even higher if we request funding to attend, or worse to stage, a conference.

> 'Something to do with one of those Potters? Harry, is it? Or Beatrix?'

For those dealing with cynics and doubters, this collection is a gift. Within these pages, as at the conference itself, a wide range of thinkers, from varying disciplines, schools and fields have given their attention to psychoanalytic considerations of children's text and media, and anyone dipping into the book will experience a deepening of their understanding and compassion in the analysis of issues which beset us all. Here are our reasons for reading children's literature. As Philip Pullman has stated, adult literature – especially at the best selling end of the market – often concerns itself with trivia. Children's literature deals with the deep issues – what is my identity? where am I going? how can I make sense of this experience called life? There is *play* here – that function too much neglected in today's society, through which we rehearse, examine and overcome, building confidence, managing doubts, trying out alternatives – and the light touch of many of our writers invites and encourages us to play too. Engaging in the game will enrich and intrigue you – considering the role of Story here, you will not leave these pages without a change in your understanding of the Self. As for the Potters, well, it is something to do with both. Harry Potter is called to witness here, in an engrossing study of the developing psyche. And Beatrix's Mr McGregor gets a justified citation as one of the representations of childhood's deep fears.

As the passion for reading, re-reading and re-interpreting our readings of children's literature increases, psychoanalysis has an important part to play. Children's literature is by its very nature transgressive as well as seminal; it is the place we start, the place we aspire to, the place we explore and eventually, rest and find comfort. Not only the literature itself but the changing ways in which we read the literature and in which we revisit our own memories are part of the kaleidoscope – the patterning - of our experience.

The tone for the conference was set by Rosemary Stones' elegant and delicate opening address, in which she invited us to consider how a children's book can express the transformative experience of becoming aware of the feelings of another. Because this talk so beautifully encapsulated the mood of the conference, in demonstrating a sensitivity to the complexity of the experience of self-hood, I have kept it here in its initial position. The other papers, however, noting the prismatic cross-referencing and glancing at main themes, I have not grouped, though at the conference main themes were stated to help listeners choose. As a reader you can easily sample; and two papers of real quality which could not be delivered at the time have been included here.

This collection is an extraordinary reading experience in itself, each essay a distinctive and piquant contribution to the whole, to be selectively unwrapped and thoughtfully savoured. Some essays – such as David Rudd's unpacking of Louis Sachar's *Holes*, will challenge you. Some, such as Madelyn Travis's feminist reading of Susan Cooper, will fill in gaps in your own thinking. Some may shock – Jake Hope's exploration of Philip Ridley's work was delivered at the conference with a health warning which I repeat here – where others, such as John Burton's meditation on the timelessness of pattern, will soothe and beguile. Other papers, such as Margaret Rustin and Michael Rustin's keynote delivery on *The Regeneration of Doctor Who*, trace the psychoanalytic significance of events in popular culture, while the playful approach of Victoria de Rijke and Howard Hollands to Mervyn Peake's *Captain Slaughterboard Drops Anchor* combines the insightful with the carnivalesque. Rebecca Butler's fascinating consideration of the developing strength of the self through relationship to others throughout the *Harry Potter* series reveals the psychological underpinning of the series' construction, while Pat Pinsent offers an unusual and thought-provoking reading of stories of psychological adjustment to facial disfigurement. Rebecca do Rozario and Alison Waller explicitly develop the title theme of the conference, grounding understanding of the developing self in the theories of Lacan and Winnicott.

Many papers, inevitably, make reference to war and the challenging times in which we, and children, live. Beth Lockwood, Andrea Peterson and throughout the collection several others refer to the use of psychoanalytic theory in the task of managing what must be managed. But magic and its uses also appear as a continual theme; the link between magic and the work of the subconscious in adjusting to loss and change are addressed by Diane Duncan and Gerry Byrne. The atmosphere of magic also pervades the tenderly transformative accounts of children's psychoanalytic work presented by Debbie Hindle and Sylvia Wilson, while Peter Bramwell considers the subconscious links between natural processes and the child's experience of taking control of the environment. Transformation in a different sense is considered by Nick Midgely in his analysis of the role of fear, also considered in the *Dr Who* paper by the Rustins.

Give a copy of this book to your sceptical colleagues, and banish the raised eyebrow for ever.

Enjoy!

Rosemary Stones

Stories We Tell Ourselves (and how they can get stuck)

WHAT I WANT to start with today is something about story and the links between the relationship of the writer to their book and the relationship of the patient to the therapist. I also want to talk about misunderstanding and the way that some stories can get stuck.

I guess that some of you are very familiar with psychoanalytic concepts, some of you are somewhat familiar and perhaps some people aren't familiar at all. I hope you will excuse me if you experience the approach in this paper as too unfamiliar or conversely, too basic.

Children's literature centralises childhood – its preoccupations and themes, even when the central character is not a child. Psychoanalytic theory also centralises childhood. It was Freud's great discovery of the unconscious mind and of the transference as the central element in the psychoanalytic situation that revealed how our earliest relationships, both real and fantasised, lay down inside us general tendencies, repeated in our relationships with other people. We thus relate to others not just in terms of their reality but in line with unconscious expectations, and fantasies of our own. In the consulting room, the transference gradually reveals to the analyst what Freud described as the 'kernel of (the patient's) intimate life history'.

This 'intimate life history' or, in other words, the patient's story, is differently described by Winnicott as 'the line of life'. Winnicott continues:

> 'The basis for all theories about human personality development is continuity of the line of life, which presumably starts before the baby's actual birth; continuity which carries with it the idea that nothing that has been part of an individual's experience is or can ever be lost to that individual, even if in various complex ways it should and does become unavailable to consciousness'. (Davis and Wallbridge, 1981)

Even when, or perhaps especially when, these experiences are preverbal their unconscious influence will shape how a person negotiates relationships, events and difficulties. Individuals will be seen and experienced in ways that are shaped by these early experiences. We might say that an unconscious authorial perspective is in place.

So already, as Freud and Winnicott search for ways to convey the inner experience of the mind, we have in place words like 'history' and 'line of life'. Charles Rycroft (Rycroft) extends this 'literary' vocabulary to include 'metaphor':

> 'I should like to open by asserting dogmatically that we inevitably use metaphor when talking about mental activity. Thoughts and feelings, the raw material of psychology, or at least of subjective psychologies such as psychoanalysis, are experiences which people have, not phenomena which people observe, but when we try to describe them we are compelled to use analogies derived from phenomena which we do observe. We talk of thoughts flowing freely or otherwise, of our seeing the point of an argument or failing to do so; we attribute warmth to our affectionate emotions and coldness to hate; at every turn we are compelled to draw on our knowledge of the physical world in which to describe our subjective experiences.'

Writers use metaphor in their fictions. Patients use metaphors of all kinds to convey what is going on in their psychic worlds. They use verbal metaphors, of course, but there will also be metaphors that take other forms – they may have a headache, for example, or leave their umbrella behind. A patient recently complained to me how hard he found it to put his feelings into words. How he felt that something always 'got lost in translation'. And indeed, while it is necessary for both writer and patient to put things into words in order to communicate with the intended audience, it can be a distancing from primary experience. Metaphor allows associative links and helps to minimise language's reduction of the complexity of primary experience. Through metaphor, as through dreams (those complex metaphors which are both visual and verbal) unconscious meanings move towards consciousness, without diminution or destruction of their vitality.

There is another parallel to be drawn between the world of psychoanalysis and that of literary endeavour. Both are about couples – the patient and therapist is a couple relationship, as is the relationship between an author and the book that is being written. In both cases it is a relationship that can go well and one that can go badly – at times there may be surges of creativity when the unconscious mind is somehow released to offer up its unexpected insights and stimulus; at other times there is frustration and blockage. In both situations there is interplay between conscious and unconscious processes.

When we write fiction we create an imagined world in which there are characters who relate to each other in particular ways. We do this by drawing on our imagination and on our experiences of people, relationships and events in the external world and in our inner world (writing is essentially about internalised relationships). When we enter therapy, the consulting room becomes crowded with characters from our past and current relationships. And, as the transference develops, the therapist begins to occupy a space amongst these dramatis personae along the lines prescribed by the patient's inner authorial voice. Thus, a patient whose mother used to get angry when she looked sad, is wary about telling me about pain and difficulty in her life, assuming that I too will become angry. The central element of the therapeutic relationship which enables emotional restructuring (we could think of it as the story being rewritten or given different emphases) is the transference (a metaphor in itself). The patient projects onto the therapist as the writer projects into his/her characters.

But I don't want to overdo the parallel – in the consulting room, as I have said, there are many different levels of metaphor as well as the actual metaphors the patient uses. Therapist and patient enter into a special kind of relationship that allows a deep emotionality to surface and bring about change.

Psychoanalysis is known as the talking cure. Language is its pre-eminent tool as it is that of the writer. The writer has to create the kind of language that will meet the requirements of the particular book. Within the consulting room, therapist and patient evolve a shared language in order to conduct what Meltzer calls 'conversations between internal objects', a language that is cognisant of the meaning for the patient of the experiences and relationships that are brought.

In psychoanalytic writings, the word 'object' is nearly always used to denote a person, parts of a person or symbols of one or the other while in everyday speech, 'object' is used to denote a 'thing', ie that which is not a person. The book is a 'thing', a concrete object yet it can also become a symbolic object for the writer as they create.

Part of my theme today is misunderstanding, how stories can get stuck. I want to start with a fictional story, Oliver Jeffers' *Lost and Found*. This picture book encompasses many important themes. Loneliness, separation, friendship are among them, but for me the theme that resonates the most is Jeffers' exploration of misunderstanding and how understanding emerges.

A boy meets a penguin and concludes that he is lost and wants to go home. The boy thinks of a way to get the penguin back to the South Pole, for he has discovered that that is where penguins come from, and the pair set off on an epic voyage in the boy's tiny rowboat through waves sometimes as big as mountains. However, once at the South Pole, the penguin looks sad rather than happy. An illustration shows us the boy waving goodbye to the penguin. We see the penguin's back as he watches the boat sailing away. He is clutching a yellow umbrella and there is something enormously poignant about this stocky, solitary little figure. Turn the page and the next double page spread presents a tremendously exciting (and unusual) sequence – we are actually shown the boy's inner process. We are told the boy feels strange to be on his own. It seems that this feeling of strangeness enables him to identify empathically with the penguin for the first time. He is then able to think about the feeling and in so doing he realises that he has made a mistake. The penguin is not lost – he is lonely.

It is extraordinary how Jeffers uses the minimalist elements with which he creates the boy (dots for eyes, matchstick legs, a square torso, shadow) to convey inner workings so eloquently. First the boy's hands are clasped behind his back as he gazes downwards, then one hand moves up to scratch his head, letting us know that he is beginning to reflect in a different way. The hand moves to his chin as the boy realises that he has misunderstood. Then both arms are flung wide, the matchstick legs move and a mouth opens in astonishment as he finally understands what the penguin has been trying to convey to him. The images of the boy become gradually larger. The reader is initially presented with a rather remote, emotionally cut off-boy alone in his boat, but is then moved closer and closer into contact with the boy, just as he is able to bring together in his mind the elements of his interaction with the penguin and see their significance. This sequence is the emotional climax of the book and while Jeffers keeps us on our toes as the boy searches for the penguin, who seems to have disappeared, we know that the pair must somehow be reunited, as indeed they are.

Now I would like to turn to an example of stuckness from my own clinical practice. One of the difficulties of talking about or writing about what happens in the consulting room is patient confidentiality. In this case I have my patient's permission to describe how he made use of particular fictional characters. All the other details about the patient have been changed. For the purposes of this paper I have called him 'Philip'.

Philip grew up with an absent father and an overburdened, anxious mother. From an early age he kept difficulties from her and tried to be cheerful and self-reliant. Inside, he felt overwhelmed by his inability to manage and to make his mother happy. There was an absence of the kind of maternal attention, understanding and comfort he needed and a paternal absence. Philip turned to fictional characters to fill the gap. These characters were profoundly significant for him, constantly revisited and they appeared in the

The boy said goodbye...

and floated away. But as he looked back, the penguin looked sadder than ever.

It felt strange to be on his own...

and the more he thought...

...the more he realised he was making a big mistake.

The penguin wasn't lost. He was just lonely.

consulting room when Philip came into psychotherapy.

Two of these characters were Calvin and Hobbes. Calvin and Hobbes is a humorous comic strip by American Bill Watterson which was syndicated in newspapers from 1985 to 1995. There are also eighteen Calvin and Hobbes books. Calvin is an imaginative and adventurous six year-old boy and Hobbes his sardonic toy tiger. Interestingly these characters are named after John Calvin, a leader of the Protestant Reformation in France and Switzerland in the 16th century and Thomas Hobbes, the 17th century English political philosopher.

The themes of the strips deal with Calvin's misadventures, his friendship with Hobbes, his relationships and interactions with his parents, teachers and friends and his views on a range of social and political topics. The dual nature of Hobbes is a recurring motif. To everyone else, Hobbes is a toy, a stuffed tiger. To Calvin, however, Hobbes is an anthropomorphic tiger with his own thoughts, ideas and wisdom. For Calvin, the child who is 'forming' himself, Hobbes is his alter ego, his philosopher as well as a representation of his potential confidence and maturity. The comic strips play with the notion of 'me' and 'part of me'.

For Philip, the lonely and deprived child, there was a deep craving for, as it were, 'reformation', however unaware he was of what was missing, what it was that he craved. The aesthetic experience of reading this comic strip about the relationship between Calvin and Hobbes became a medium in which his unconscious desires could be safely explored in the hope of reformation. By coming into psychotherapy as an adult, he was again pursuing an experience that he hoped would offer reformation, hopefully this time of a more solid and durable kind.

Philip described one of the stories to me:

> 'It is raining and Calvin goes to the bus stop for the school bus. Hobbes holds an umbrella over him. Calvin gets on the bus and waves goodbye. At school Calvin is sad without Hobbes. Mum sees Hobbes in the garden with the umbrella and brings him inside. Hobbes is sad without Calvin.'

From this account, it seemed that Philip identified deeply with Calvin. He longs to have a Hobbes part which would protect him as Hobbes protects Calvin from the rain. Calvin and Hobbes are parted as the bus drives away. How is this separation to be managed? Calvin waves goodbye cheerfully enough but Hobbes's absence, the absence of the protector, then hits him and he is sad. In the same way Philip was unable, at this point in the analysis, to keep alive inside him a sense of being internally protected. In Calvin's absence, Hobbes becomes an inert stuffed toy once again. Mum sees Hobbes in the garden and brings him inside but Philip's account has a rather dismissive feel as if Mum is tidying up rather than looking after Hobbes and what Hobbes means to Calvin. The lively (alive) part of Hobbes is missing and he is sad without Calvin. Each is depleted without the other. Philip's account of the story is bleak: Calvin is sad without Hobbes and Hobbes is sad without Calvin. This is a powerful communication of Philip's inner state of being.

Another important fictional character for Philip since his days at Primary school was Dr Who. Philip's obsession with this character was such that he read nothing but Dr Who to the point where his mother and his school insisted that he also read other things. For Philip, Dr Who was the hero who endlessly saved the world from monsters and from faceless oppression, the man who knew how to do everything because he'd lived for hundreds of years and had done it all before. Dr Who provided Philip with an idealized version of the father he had never had. Philip's identification with Dr Who appeared to have enabled him to lead an alternative existence in fantasy by providing him with a space for his own discoveries, even if it was a tiny, Tardislike one.

Dr Who as a replacement for a father, however helpful it may have been at a young age, proved problematic in several ways as Philip grew older. While day-dreaming can be important and creative it can also become a defence against feeling. Life in a fantasy world that the day-dreamer can control can be a retreat from pain of reality. Then, if Dr Who is an idealised father and role model, logically his son has to live up to the ideal. Philip felt that he too had to be endlessly available to save the world for everyone. The boundary between fantasy and reality failed and for Philip, Dr Who became more than a character in a drama. Thus the ideal combined with the harsh superego and Philip was left feeling that he could never get it right, could never be perfect like his role model. This is not to say that a liking for Dr Who will inevitably lead to children feeling obliged to save the world. In Philip's case it seems that such a conclusion about the way to live was rather confirmed by his identification with Dr Who. Philip had already concluded that it was his job to be responsible for his mother's happiness.

One of the attractions of Dr Who to Philip as a young child may have been Dr Who's androgynous nature. While Dr Who is not a castrated male he is certainly not a phallic, genitally-driven one. He has a constant female companion but this relationship never develops. It too remains constant, series after series after series. Dr Who thus represents the unawakened, unthreatening male, arrested in time. The image of Dr Who thus came to serve as a part of a defence against oedipal conflict.

Philip eventually became disillusioned with Dr Who. This was in part prompted by a new actor being found to play the character. It seemed that on this occasion a change of actor interfered with Philip's fantasising in a way that had not previously occurred. The break brought home to him that he was dealing with actors, not fantasy figures. There was an interruption between the text and what went on in his fantasy by the intermediary of the television show with its concrete need for a change of cast. Philip began to develop his own story away from the confined space of the Tardis where he had been stuck.

In *Lost and Found*, Oliver Jeffers' picture book, as the boy rows to the South Pole with the penguin we are told that he tells stories and the penguin listens to everything he says. Later in the narrative when the penguin is nowhere to be found the boy sets off for home alone, feeling sad and in silence. Jeffers comments: 'There was no point telling stories because there was no one to listen except the wind and the waves.' So I return to the relationship between the writer and the book and the way it parallels the relationship between patient and therapist.

Anxiety is aroused for the patient in the encounter with the therapist as it can be for the writer in the encounter with the blank page. Thomas Ogden has described (Ogden, 1989) how, within the analytic hour patients sometimes try to allay their anxiety by reconstituting what he calls a sensory 'floor', some kind of bounded sense of themselves. They may do this by stroking their face, tapping a foot, humming and so forth. Something similar can happen for the writer trying to allay the anxiety of putting words on the page so that the creative process can begin or be rediscovered – there are the rituals that involve a particular kind of notebook or pen, the arranging of the writing materials on the desk, the cup of coffee in the usual mug, and so on.

In the process of writing there is the possibility for the writer to move beyond where they started from just as the patient may surprise himself with where he arrives. As we have seen, sometimes the evolution of the narrative gets stuck or blocked in some way. In the consulting room the patient has available an independent mind, hopefully chugging along empathically to help with the endeavour. For the writer who is stuck, it is, hopefully, the process of writing that can allow problems to be challenged so that the book can move forward and the writer with it.

In the consulting room the patient has stories to tell and the therapist stands in for the missing book. For the writer the book may serve as the object listening to him or the object that enables him to listen to himself externalising. When it goes well, the book can offer its writer a dynamic exploration of blocks, of being stuck. At other times it may fail to offer that possibility.

REFERENCES

Sigmund Freud, 'The question of lay analysis', in S. Freud, *Two Short Accounts of Psychoanalysis*. Harmondsworth: Penguin, 1962.

M. Davis and D. Wallbridge, *Boundary and Space*. Harmondsworth: Penguin,1981.

Charles Rycroft, *Viewpoints*. London: The Hogarth Press, 1969.

Oliver Jeffers, *Lost and Found*. London: HarperCollins, 2005.

Thomas H. Ogden, *The Primitive Edge of Experience*. London: Karnac, 1989.

Alison Waller

Rereading Children's Literature: Memory and Emotion

> *Whatever people read or played with in their childhood not only seems in memory to have been the most beautiful and best thing possible, it often, wrongly, seems unique.*
> Walter Benjamin

THERE IS NO doubt that our relationship with books from our past is a complex and bittersweet one. Walter Benjamin argues that by the time we reach adulthood the magic of books and toys from our own childhood is lost, partly because the stuff of childhood is ephemeral and easily eradicated, and partly because adults lack the ability to notice new sources of magic in contemporary objects. Thus, that book we read and adored as a child (or even the one that terrified us, bored us, or reminds us of sad times) becomes untouchable, wrapped up in nostalgia and memory, and irrevocably bound to our youthful emotional responses to the joys of reading.

For most, perhaps, this is not a serious problem, although many adults (often now parents themselves) attempt to return to a childhood favourite only to discover it no longer sparks the precious feelings it did when they first read it as a youngster. But here I am not concerned with general re-readings and those pleasures and disappointments. I want to ask, what of the student or scholar of children's literature who is obliged to return to childhood favourites with a critical, rather than a sentimental, eye? In studying the books of our youth, must we avoid our memories at all costs in order to maintain a professional objectivity, or is it possible and desirable to access our original reactions to texts without reverting to simple reminiscence?

There are certainly critics who think we must turn away from our original, immature readings. Critic Judith Armstrong tackles this question in a retrospective reading of her own childhood favourite, *The Children who Lived in a Barn*, by Eleanor Graham. Armstrong returns to a text that she remembers to be thrilling and wholly enjoyable only to find that it now appears shockingly limiting: the heroine is the heroine because, like any number of female protagonists from the first half of the twentieth century, she delights in practical, domestic skills and has low expectations for real agency. Armstrong is dismayed that her childhood self was so enchanted by what she now sees is an ideologically suspect book: 'Why did [I] have to love this book in particular? Why, with [my] passion for freedom and adventure, did [I] not suspect that there was something undermining going on here?' (Armstrong, 2003). Armstrong's solution to this quandary is to reject her previous childish

self with a wistful sigh, and celebrate the fact that this naïve young girl is now 'grown up' enough to understand the problems in Graham's text.

This response seems inadequate in many ways, and it keys into a tradition in children's literature criticism which several voices have attacked for revealing more about the adult's idealised version of childhood than about real children (Rose, 1984; Lesnik-Oberstein, 1994). In particular, it rather unhelpfully disregards any previous interaction with a text that does not correspond with our current critically aware and politically astute interpretation. I would like to suggest that there is, rather, value to be found in trying to access and retain a sense of that initial engagement.

The story and the self are closely entwined, and although I will not draw directly on psychoanalytical theory in this discussion, I am concerned with the relationships between remembered childhood and active adulthood, between memory and rereading, and between emotional and critical responses to texts.

Emotion and Reading

Feminist critic Lynne Pearce endeavours to forge a meaningful connection between her powerful and intricate emotional reactions to literature and her professional and political urge to understand and explain texts. In *Feminism and the Politics of Reading*, she states that her interest is 'not the mechanics of interpretation (how meaning is made) but the process of reading, which results in a text-reader relationship that I have described as implicated' (Pearce, 1997). That is to say, she actively embraces the fact that reading is never a simple matter of decoding the content of a text, or even of interacting with that text in a process of interpretation and revelation; instead it is a fraught process akin to a lover's relationship, where emotion and circumstance play a part alongside scholarly meaning-making. Here is her account of reading and rereading Olive Schreiner's *Story of an African Farm*:

> ...I succumb to a complicated sequence of emotions that represent my relationship to the text and its characters. Longing, loss, pride and regret crowd in upon one another in rapid succession, as all my past readings and revisitings collapse together. It is in not simply that this is a text that, upon one reading, will produce a roller-coaster of emotional affect (though, of course, it is,) but the fact that the different emotions are associated with different hauntings. And this, now, is part of the pain and the confusion as well as the fascination of my return. To return to this text is to return to the ghosts of all my former intra-textual selves...
> (Pearce, 1997)

Pearce uses terms we are unused to in literary criticism – pride, regret and pain – and allows extra-textual considerations (such as specific moments of reading and the self-knowledge of her own reading position) to play a part in understanding the text and her reactions to it. She deconstructs her past readings as we might deconstruct a long-lost affair.

Can we, then, consider our relationship with past childhood texts as a kind of early romantic entanglement or friendship? Are these books like lost friends or ex-lovers? At first, this terminology appears unseemly in an academic context, where by and large the imperative is to overcome or neutralise emotional responses to the books we read (repulsing phrases like 'the story made me feel sick with terror' or 'I fell in love with it' and replacing them with expressions like 'its narrative draws on traditions of the gothic...' or 'the text appeals to a child at the phallic stage...'). Discussing what we feel about, and for, books seems at first glance to return us to the cosy, non-theoretical criticism children's literature is often condemned for: simple personal responses to simple frivolous texts.

Yet in other disciplines the importance of emotion and memory is taken for granted, and Pearce's emotive language masks the complexity of affective experience. It is not only Psychoanalysis which recognises this significance; Philosophy, Anthropology, Cognitive Psychology and Socio-biology are all interested in what and why we feel, and whatever scholarly imperatives dictate our work in literary studies, very few would refute the fact that mostly we read because texts provoke an emotional reaction. Much has been written in the past about the pleasures of reading, from the satisfaction of interpretation (e.g. Iser, 1974) to readerly delight in anticipating or reworking narrative patterns (e.g. Radway, 1984) (of course, there is also a whole theoretical discourse about jouissance in textual interplay, pointing us towards more complicated ideas of pleasure, mixed in with pain (e.g. Barthes, 1975). Other emotions have encouraged fewer theoretical debates; as if pleasure can be understood as part of the intellectual game of literary criticism but anger, boredom, fear or disgust cannot or will not be integrated. Although we might plan to read for pleasure, it is inevitable that sometimes we will be disappointed or frustrated: the story does not fulfil exactly the role we hoped it might. Sometimes pleasure will be intermingled with other feelings that might be connected to the text itself: anger on behalf of a heroine who is about to be split from her daemon, for example (Pullman, 1995). Feelings might also be associated more closely with our personal situation: the Dementors in stories of Harry Potter might be terrifying, but the text may still induce feelings of comfort and calm if it is read to us by a parent or other loved one (Rowling, 1999). It is certainly well recognised that a text like Judy Blume's Forever provokes a whole range of feelings, from fear, embarrassment and disgust, to excitement, desire, amusement and regret; all depending on how the novel positions us as individual reader in time (Blume, 1975).

Pleasure and other Emotions

In using terms like 'pleasure', 'anger', 'desire', 'amusement' it is easy to accept that they are concepts both equal and self-evident. However, there are degrees of affective states of being and anthropologists identify a range of emotional types. It is useful to imagine a spectrum ranging from basic emotions, which are universal and innate, to higher cognitive emotions, which are often learned and more likely to exhibit cultural variations. Generally included in the first category are joy, distress, anger, fear, surprise and disgust, whilst love, guilt, shame, embarrassment, pride, envy and jealousy can be explained as emotions that are less essential to basic states of being and survival. Moods offer an even more nuanced understanding of the affective universe: these are less immediate emotional states, ones not triggered by specific events but emerging instead from indistinct origins. As well as categorising emotions in this way, conventional psychologists argue (developing an Aristolean idea) that emotions are dependent on beliefs. To feel fear, for example, we must belief ourselves (or someone close to us) to be in danger (Dalgleish & Power, 1999; Evans, 2001).

The implications of these different emotional conditions and their foundations for the process of reading are considerable. Even a brief knowledge of the science of emotions indicates how far from simple and indulgent nostalgia a consideration of affective qualities in literature could be. Furthermore, there are a range of germane theoretical questions thrown up by an examination of emotions and reading: what kinds of emotions are commonly generated in our contact with texts; how might different types of literature provoke different degrees of affective state; and, most interestingly, how can readers exhibit emotional reactions (based on beliefs) to literary events or characters that are entirely fictional (and therefore are not believed to be real)? This last question suggests that if we feel fear while reading a terrifying story we are, in many ways, demonstrating irrationality since neither we nor anyone close to us is truly threatened: after all, characters in the book we are reading are not real and cannot be harmed. Several critics have engaged with this problem (Boruah, 1988; Feagin, 1996; Lamarque, 1981; Radford, 1975) but none make use of Pearce's idea that the emotional connection during the reading process is not entirely concerned with a relationship between reader and character or even reader and event. At times – according to Pearce and according to thinkers like Benjamin who understand the material influence of books, particularly books for children – readers can feel emotional responses to a text because they believe something about their relationship to it as text and as experience: not simply because they believe in the reality of the content. These are crucial ideas when it comes to children's literature, but existing criticism on fiction and emotion on the whole relies on a conventional understanding of rational adulthood. In questioning the problem of cognitive dissonance underlying emotional responses to literature, for example, Peter Lamarque maintains 'it is assumed that as reasonably sophisticated adults, we are not taken in by fiction' (cited in Boruah, 1988). Is it assumed, just as confidently, that children can be taken in and taken over by fiction, so that their response to reading is purely, and problematically, emotional? The sense that children have inferior reactions to literature remains a strong notion in children's literature criticism, as we have seen in Armstrong's anxious attempt to revisit her childhood favourite.

Emotion and Memory

The whole matter of the story and the emotional self is complicated when we, as critics of children's literature, consider books to which we can attach emotions from long ago. Matei Calinescu suggests that all critical reading is rereading, because when we have a scholarly interest in literature we look for meaning in each text we encounter, and treat the words as we have seen them before and can make connections and judgements, rather than reading with a naive, linear approach (Calinescu, 1993). But surely there is a marked difference between responses to a fresh new text and an old remembered one, particularly if the distance between reading and rereading is very great, and even more so if that distance involves the difference between a child reader and an adult one. As critics, perhaps we do approach all texts with a critical, rereading eye, but emotional reactions will be different on a first encounter and on a return to the text for the umpteenth time. A novel such as Peter Dickinson's *Eva* might engender surprise and fear on a first read, since the opening chapters deal with a teenage girl's discovery that her conscious self has been transplanted into the body of a chimp; on a reread, the strong emotions are likely to shift to moods of apprehension as we remember the key plot point. Without wishing to generalise about childhood and adult responses, there is also the chance that as a child we might experience a certain joyful emotion towards the concept of being at one with a wild animal, a sensation which, as an adult, might metamorphose into more ambivalent feelings of anxiety and guilt about modern issues surrounding animal testing and genetic engineering. Nonetheless, these differing responses are not completely separate; after all, they originate from the same human consciousness even if they are accessed differently, through memory and direct experience.

Personal emotions and memory are strongly linked in understanding reading processes and experiences. Psychologists argue that memories are stored and retrieved via emotional "tags". This process, known as "mood congruent recall", means that memories linked to our feelings of sadness – such as the day our cat died – are most likely to re-emerge when we experience sadness in the present. If we feel joyful, we are most likely to have flashbacks to previous moments of great happiness. Moreover, our strongest emotions evoke our most intense memories: that violent guilt we felt making our sister cry, when we were aged eight, will reappear powerfully in our memories, although peripheral details of place or dress are often lost. It is little wonder then, that books from our childhood provoke strong reactions however much our opinions and attitudes have changed as adults and literary professionals. Memories of books from our past are imbued with dramatic emotional energy and are not easily wrenched away from reconstructions of our youthful days.

Rereading Children's Literature

There are many reasons for studying children's literature. The books we give to young people have an important effect on their psyches and social awareness and should be carefully scrutinised; the body of work for young people reveals a great deal about changing attitudes towards childhood, education, family structures, gender roles, race relations and the future of humanity; examining the juvenile publishing industry most obviously engenders enquires into the role of author, reader, publisher and others in the production and consumption of literature; children's books freely address complex concerns about human psychology and the future of the world in ways that adult literature often shies away from. An equally important justification is the fact that as critics we are led back to the books that affected us most deeply as children in an attempt to discover why seemingly slight textual encounters maintain a strong hold over our readerly psyches. Part of our job is to discover if and how readers change emotionally and intellectually over time, and a valuable way of achieving this knowledge is to examine our own journeys across memory and emotion. Personal criticism in this vein has already established itself as popular and useful. Most recent and perhaps best known is Francis Spufford's memoir, *The Child that Books Built*, in which the author rereads the books that carried him 'from babyhood to the age of nineteen,' using this process to explore and analyse his own childhood but also producing 'the story (I hope) of the reading my whole generation of bookworms did' (Spufford, 2002). His reading of his early encounter with *The Lion, the Witch and the Wardrobe* recall is less theorised than Pearce's recollections of *Story of an African Farm*, but has a very similar agenda and effect:

> The book in my hand sent jolts and shimmers through my nerves. It affected me bodily. In Narnia, C. S. Lewis invented objects for my longing, gave forms to my longing, that I would never have thought of, and yet they seemed exactly right: he had anticipated what would delight me with an almost unearthly intimacy. (Spufford, 2002)

Spufford's response is physical and emotional, as well as intellectual (he writes of the Narnia books becoming the Platonic Book to his eight-year-old self). It also relates the individual experience to the collective, not producing self-indulgent nostalgia, but rather forming an interior cultural history of the 60s and 70s.

As part of the presentation of this paper at The Story and the Self conference, I outlined an exercise I use in the classroom to begin this process of reconnecting emotional responses and critical readings amongst students. I start by asking them to choose a book that figures significantly in their memories of childhood reading, disregarding whether that book evokes positive or negative feelings, recollections of excitement or safety, fear, disgust or boredom. I then use a technique borrowed from Pearce. Her main concern is to examine the shifts between professional feminist and non-professional personal readings, but the method adapts well to concepts of reading, rereading and remembering children's literature. In order to access and analyse emotional responses to literature, Pearce employs what she calls "re-memory", explaining this as 'my practice of writing down my "memory" of the texts I had read/viewed previously in advance of re-reading them' (Pearce, 1997). Accessing some of these memories accurately and without damaging a sense of self has its own problems, of course, and the practice is not supposed to be a form of psychotherapy; but through prompts and interviews students are able to produce a version of the text through the lens of their remembered emotional connection with it, including extra-textual information such as the location of the reading experience and recollections of the material reality of the book. Then they are asked to trace and revisit their chosen book.

Having already expressed what they can of their original strong emotional bond with this text, the intention is now to lay claim to, and explore, these initial reactions as well as to understand why current responses might be quite different, and possibly disappointing. By considering the way that emotions function – particularly in terms of reading and of memory – students (and more established scholars) can start to understand why certain texts remain important despite, or even because of, dramatically different feelings towards them in adulthood. This is a remarkably useful introduction to the theoretical problems of adults evaluating books for children. Of course, it also helps to bring to attention the fact that childhood itself is fictionalised and endowed with emotional meaning through constructed and reconstructed memory.

REFERENCES

Judith Armstrong 'New anticipations of the past', *Children's Literature in Education* 34:3, 249-255, 2003.

Roland Barthes, *The Pleasure of the Text*, trans. Richard Miller. New York: Hill and Wang, 1975.

Walter Benjamin, *Selected Writings, Volume 2:* 1927-34, ed. Michael W. Jennings, Howard Eiland, & Gary Smith, trans. Rodney Livingstone. Cambridge, Mass. & London: Belknap Press, 1999.

Judy Blume, *Forever*. London: Victor Gollancz, 1975.

Bijoy H. Boruah, *Fiction and Emotion: a study in Aesthetics and the Philosophy of Mind*. Oxford: Clarendon Press, 1988.

Matei Calinescu, *Rereading*. New Haven & London: Yale University Press, 1993.

Tim Dalgleish & Mick J. Power (Eds), *Handbook of Cognition and Emotion*. Chichester & New York: John Wiley & Sons, 1999.

Peter Dickinson, *Eva*. London: Victor Gollancz, 1988.

Dylan Evans, *Emotion: a very short introduction*. Oxford: Oxford University Press, 2001

Susan L. Feagin, *Reading with Feeling: the Aesthetics of Appreciation*. Ithaca & London: Cornell University Press, 1996.

Wolfgang Iser, *The Implied Reader: patterns in communication in prose fiction from Bunyan to Beckett*. Baltimore: Johns Hopkins University Press, 1974.

Peter Lamarque (1981) 'How can we fear and pity fictions?' *British Journal of Aesthetics*, 21, 291-304.

Karin Lesnik-Oberstein, *Children's Literature: criticism and the fictional child*. Oxford: Clarendon, 1994.

Lynne Pearce, *Feminism and the Politics of Reading*. London & New York: Arnold, 1997.

Philip Pullman, *Northern Lights*. London: Scholastic, 1995.

Colin Radford (1975) 'How can we be moved by the fate of Anna Karenina?' *Proceedings of the Aristotelian Society*, 49, 67-80.

Janice Radway, *Reading the Romance: women, patriarchy, and popular literature*. London & New York: Verso, 1984.

Jacqueline Rose, *The Case of Peter Pan: or the impossibility of children's fiction*. London: Macmillan, 1984.

J. K. Rowling, *Harry Potter and the Prisoner of Azkaban*. London: Bloomsbury, 1999.

Francis Spufford, *The Child that Books Built*. London: Faber & Faber, 2002.

'Rereading Children's Literature', Case Study for Northumbria University's MEDAL project [http://medal.unn.ac.uk] 2007.

Rebecca R. Butler

The Scholar, the Hero and Their Faithful Friend

Introduction

IN THE SIX *Harry Potter* books published to date J.K. Rowling has assembled a large cast of characters, some human and others not, some alive and some ghostly presences, some benign and some malign. At different points of the narrative, centre stage is occupied by different characters. But at critical points three figures dominate the scene, Harry himself and his two friends Hermione Granger and Ron Weasley. Rowling has said that triadic relationships have played an important part in her own personal history. But the significance of the Potter/Granger/Weasley nexus goes far beyond a borrowing from personal authorial experience. I will argue that this triadic structure is the main narrative driving force of the books and also that it generates relationships that lie close to the heart of the whole saga.

Fragmentation versus Integration

Splitting and fragmentation versus integration and unification are, I will argue, the keys to understanding the *Harry Potter* books. Harry is initially split, the bifurcation being between his mundane, slave-like existence as an unwanted orphan and his initially unknown potential as a world famous wizard. Harry must try – against the odds – to make himself a whole person. His attempt is made by integrating himself into the triad. Voldemort in contrast fractures himself in the quest for immortality, eventually even embodying fragments of his very soul into external objects known as Horcruxes.

If any fictional hero ever had a traumatic childhood, it is Harry. As a one year old he witnessed the violent death of both parents, victims of the Unforgivable Curse of Lord Voldemort, the Dark Lord. Harry's aunt and uncle the Dursleys treat Harry with a degree of negligence and contempt that is so exaggerated as to verge at times on the farcical: he sleeps in the cupboard under the stairs while his cousin has two bedrooms. His transformation at the age of eleven was total, when he learned that he was not only a wizard but a famous one, the only person ever to survive the killing curse. The curse left a lightning scar on Harry's forehead. But the scar was much more than just a superficial wound. During the attack, as we learn from Harry's headmaster Dumbledore and from Voldemort himself, some attributes passed from the Dark Lord to Harry, and some also in the opposite direction. Here is Dumbledore's explanation.

'Unless I am much mistaken, [Voldemort] transferred some of his own powers to you the night he gave you that scar.' (CS 245)

If we examine Harry as he stands immediately before he is transported to Hogwarts, we can assess the psychic fragmentation to which he has been subjected, and establish a baseline against which to measure his subsequent progress. With monumental cruelty, Harry was given a distorted picture of the deaths of his parents. His father, unemployed and probably drunk, had involved himself and his wife in a fatal road accident. Much to his uncle's displeasure, Harry recalled in a dream the journey on a flying motor cycle which brought him to their house. Even before he learned of his true nature, Harry was aware that there was something abnormal about him. We learn of unlikely encounters. "A tiny man in a violet top hat had bowed to him while out shopping with Aunt Petunia and Dudley." (PS 27) "A bald man in a very long purple coat had actually shaken his hand in the street the other day and then walked away without a word." (ibid) These strange people, as Harry observed, seemed to disappear the moment he tried to get a closer look at them. When Dudley and his friends chased Harry (PS 23) he suddenly found himself transported to the roof of the school kitchens. He was unaware that he shared the same teleportation skills as the strange people he met: he attributed his escape to a gust of wind. On a visit to the zoo Harry managed to cause the glass in a snake enclosure to vanish, allowing a boa constrictor to escape and terrify his pudgy cousin. The explanation for these unusual events is offered when the keeper of the keys, Rubeus Hagrid, appears (PS 39 ff). There was, Harry learned, a massive and perhaps unbridgeable gap between the two worlds of which he had been part: the ordinary everyday world of the Dursleys and the magical world of which he had been unaware. That unbridgeable gap also existed between the two halves of Harry's psychic reality.

Hagrid assumed that Harry would know that his parents were of the wizarding world, where they were educated and how and why they died. The shocking truth was that in the wizarding world every child knew more about Harry than he did about himself. What we see here is a portrait of a child whose persona is split; there is the mundane Harry and the magical Harry co-existing in one eleven year old frame. This bifurcation takes fewer than forty pages to establish. Yet it is fundamental to much that will follow, and requires careful analysis before we proceed.

Theoretical background: the Kleinian model

The significance of splitting in the human psyche was suggested by Melanie Klein. Klein's work helped to postulate an Object Relations Theory, a way of classifying the relations that a child establishes with objects – people included – in the external world. An essential tool for dealing with these external objects was splitting, the separation of good and bad objects and feelings. Splitting is not necessarily a negative function; it is the means by which feelings are classified. Projection and introjection are the names Klein gave to the processes of interaction – outward and inward respectively – between the inner and outer worlds.

Klein argued that the infant's inner world was primarily defensive, protecting the self from pain, frustration, aggression. The key defensive position was postulated as the paranoid schizoid position, based on part object relationships. The part object is what the child perceives while still incapable of introjecting whole objects. The most famous Kleinian example of part object perception is the 'good breast, bad breast'. The good breast gives comfort and sustenance, the bad breast takes them away when the child is frustrated. As the child matures, good and bad experiences are seen to flow from the same external object. The mother embodies both the good and bad breast. These perceptions lead the child to the depressive position, characterized by guilt and the fear of rejection. Eventually the depressive position will lead to a more integrated psyche, capable of introjecting positive attitudes and abilities from others as well as a desire to make reparation.

My hypothesis is that the *Harry Potter* books revolve around the concept of fragmentation versus integration. Harry begins the story as a deeply fragmented child. The succeeding volumes of the saga show him trying, slowly and against the odds, to build an integrated psyche by acquiring attributes from and learning lessons from and with his two closest friends. Voldemort progresses along the opposite path of bifurcation that will in the end lead to his very soul being fragmented and embodied in seven external objects known as Horcruxes. This is a battle between fragmentation and integrity. This is, let me make clear, certainly not to argue that J.K. Rowling had in mind a Kleinian model when she took up her pen. She may, for all I know, never have studied Klein. What I argue is that adding a Kleinian dimension to our critical apparatus adds depth to our reading of these multi-faceted novels. In the remainder of this paper I will collect examples of these processes at work, Harry's integration, Voldemort's fragmentation.

Harry Potter and the Philosopher's Stone

As already mentioned, Harry and Voldemort share certain attributes. These common attributes have, we learn, the capacity to shape Harry's entire destiny. As with all newcomers, the Sorting Hat must decide which House Harry will join, Gryffindor – traditionally the home of the brave – or Slytherin, the home of the cunning and ruthless, Voldemort's House. 'There's not a single witch or wizard who went bad,' says Hagrid, 'who wasn't in Slytherin.' (PS 61/2) When the Hat came to place Harry, it faced a dilemma. Slytherin was an attractive choice. 'You could be great, you know, it's all here in your head, and Slytherin will help you on the way to greatness, no doubt about that.' (PS 91) The reader learns from this passage that there is a conflict in Harry's psyche between the desire for success and the path of courage and honour, that Harry is split. Honour won a narrow but decisive victory.

The character of Harry's fragmented psyche is revealed when he comes across the mirror of Erised. The mirror reflects whatever its observer most deeply desires. When Harry stands in front of the mirror he sees his parents smiling and waving. Ron in contrast sees himself as Head Boy of Hogwarts and winner of the Quidditch cup. (PS 152 ff) What Rowling here shows the reader is that Harry yearns to be a member of a family, something that is beyond his current realm of possibilities, though the embrace of the Weasleys takes him some way towards it. Ron desires achievements to redeem him from his own self-deprecation and give his ambitious mother reason to be proud of him. Thus each boy has an aching void where the other has assets. Each yearns for what the other has – or will soon acquire. There is fertile ground here for the exchange of powers that will build the triad. This is the point of the story at which Klein's projective identification will enable the members of the triad to share and unify their capabilities. Dumbledore warns Harry not to spend too much time gazing into the mirror. (PS 156) He is thereby urging Harry not to spend too long contemplating an imaginary world but to get on building the triad.

Hermione Granger makes her entrance upon the scene in a manner that is far from promising. Neville Longbottom's toad has been lost and Hermione comes looking for it into the railway carriage occupied by Ron and Harry. In a short space of time Hermione manages to make herself objectionable in several different ways. She pours scorn on Ron's attempt to turn his pet rat yellow and claims that the spells she has tried ("just for practice") have all worked perfectly. (PS 79) Before she has even disclosed her name, she reveals that she has learned all the set books off by heart. She also appears to know from her reading far more about Harry than he knows about himself. She concludes by instructing the boys to get changed soon since they are nearing their destination, sounding more like a matron than a fellow-pupil. Hermione's capacity to irritate Harry and Ron rises to a peak when she demonstrates the levitation spell that Ron has been getting so wrong: of course it works perfectly for her.

> Ron was in a very bad temper by the end of the class.
> 'It's no wonder no one can stand her,' he said to Harry as they pushed their way into the crowded corridor. 'She's a nightmare, honestly.'
> Someone knocked into Harry as they hurried past him. It was Hermione. Harry caught a glimpse of her face – and was startled to see that she was in tears.
> 'I think she heard you.'
> 'So?' said Ron, but he looked a bit uncomfortable. 'She must've noticed she's got no friends.' (PS 127)

What the reader has so far learned about Hermione is that she has – at least by her own account – formidable intellectual capability that might prove a useful weapon in the imminent battle against the Dark Lord. But the reader has also learned that there is a serious obstacle impeding Hermione's ability to contribute. The obstacle combines Hermione's lack of awareness or sensitivity and the boys' lack of tolerance. She is the traditional classroom know-all and the boys have no patience with her. In Kleinian terms, Hermione's classroom supremacy is in danger of driving the boys into the key defensive psychic position, the paranoid schizoid. Hermione is isolated from them. The reader therefore finds that fragmentation has already raised its ugly head. What will become the triad is here divided – and bitterly divided too, as Hermione's tears testify.

Hermione hides in a girls' lavatory to come to terms with her unpopularity, and fails to hear the alarm raised when a troll enters Hogwarts. Harry and Ron set off without hesitation to rescue her. They manage to stun the troll and save Hermione. There are two highly significant points about this episode. First it marks the turning point in the consolidation of the triad.

> But from that moment on, Hermione Granger became [Ron's and Harry's] friend. There are some things you can't share without ending up liking each other, and knocking out a twelve-foot mountain troll is one of them. (PS 132)

It is also true that the spell Ron used to stun the troll was the same one Ron was trying to perfect when Hermione upset him. Her lesson may have irritated him, but it may also have saved their lives. For the very first time, a member of the triad brings into action a skill acquired from one of the others, and saves the day.

An important event in the story occurs in the Forbidden Forest. A significant process of fragmentation, of splitting, began at the same moment for Harry and Lord Voldemort, the moment when Harry survived the *Avada Kedavra* curse. Harry was split off from the parents who would have loved him and provided him with a healthy psychic development. Any chance he might have had of such development is thwarted by his cruel and unloving aunt and uncle. Voldemort, according to Hagrid, became 'too weak to carry on... somethin' about you finished him, Harry.' (PS 47) When Voldemort appears in the first *Harry Potter* book he is compelled to do so in disguise, occupying the body of the nervous Professor Quirrell. The reader understands just how fragmented Voldemort has become when Dumbledore explains the Dark Lord's position.

> 'He [Voldemort] is still out there somewhere, perhaps looking for another body to share... not being truly alive, he cannot be killed. He left Quirrell to die; he shows just as little mercy to his followers as his enemies.' (PS 216)

The life that Voldemort could support, inhabiting another body, is tenuous enough. It can only be sustained by desperate measures. Hagrid discovers that something is killing magical creatures in the Forbidden Forest. Harry, Neville Longbottom and Draco Malfoy are sent into the forest with Hagrid for a detention. There Harry encounters a shadowy figure, not recognised as Quirrell, drinking the blood of a newly slaughtered unicorn. The wise centaur Firenze explains why.

> '...it is a monstrous thing, to slay a unicorn.... The blood of a unicorn will keep you alive, even if you are an inch from death, but at a terrible price. You have slain something pure and defenceless to save yourself and you will have but a half life, a cursed life, from the moment the blood touches your lips' (PS 118)

If the Dark Lord was to be prevented from attaining immortality by means of the philosopher's stone, the triad would have to reach the stone before him. They find themselves (PS 197 ff) confronted by a series of obstacles designed to protect the stone, created by Hagrid and various Hogwarts professors. The first obstacle is recognizable as Cerberus, the three-headed dog, playfully called 'Fluffy' by Hagrid. Next comes Devil's Snare, a kind of bindweed that entangles them. Lighting a fire would dispel the weed. Hermione momentarily forgot that she could light a magical fire. Next they encounter the flying keys, from which they must select and trap the one that opens the door ahead. Harry's flying skill is paramount. In the chess game that follows, Ron is the leader. He is the best player and is willing to play himself as a chess piece and be knocked cold when he is taken. Finally the triad encounter the seven bottles, together with the logical puzzle that told them what each bottle contained, poison or protection. Hermione unravels this mystery by the exercise of pure logic – a skill the others signally lack. Harry exercises his own most potent talent – courage – by drinking the potion Hermione chose and walking through the wall of flame on Hermione's promise that all would be well.

Both Harry and Voldemort begin the series as fragmented beings. Voldemort is moving further in the direction of fragmentation, because he has no healthy relationships from which to draw integrating features. Harry turns to his friends for intellectual capability and steadfast dedication. The hero has found the scholar and their faithful friend. From a Kleinian viewpoint it is important that each member of the triad has shortcomings; Hermione's intellectual arrogance, Harry's heroic complex and Ron's lack of self confidence. The shortcoming in each enables the others to perceive good and bad objects and thus to develop differentiation.

Just how far these two processes had advanced was demonstrated at the end of Rowling's first volume. When Voldemort failed to kill Harry he had at least left on him the mark of his ordeal, the lightning-shaped scar on Harry's forehead. But when the opportunity arises for Quirrell, possessed by Voldemort, to kill Harry, he finds that he cannot bear to touch the boy. His skin burns and blisters wherever there was contact. At the moment when Voldemort failed to kill Harry, we understand, some attributes were conveyed in a two-way exchange between them. Harry, being set on a course towards integration and supported by his two friends, has the power to resist those evil elements conveyed to him. He is offered a place in Slytherin house, but chooses Gryffindor. Voldemort in contrast has no integral psyche with which to absorb what was transmitted from Harry. If Voldemort is to prevail, he will have to develop more powerful ways of being fragmented, not set off on a hopeless quest for integration.

Harry Potter and the Chamber of Secrets

In Rowling's second volume (CS) Voldemort has advanced the process of fragmentation. His psyche is embodied as Tom Riddle in the mysterious diary which falls into the possession of both Harry and Ginny Weasley. A manifestation of Voldemort's teenage self (a memory, not a ghost insisted Dumbledore) reveals to Harry carefully selected scenes from a fifty-year old past, and induces Ginny to act as Voldemort's surrogate. Not only is Voldemort splitting his own psyche between a seemingly healthy teenage boy and his own body, near death. He is also trying to split the ranks of his enemies, notably the triad, by convincing them that Hagrid has opened the Chamber of Secrets and released the monster, and by using Ginny as his unwilling vessel. The growing strength of the triad and of their links to their allies ensure that they never seriously believe Hagrid to be guilty.
Under the circumstances, with animals and students falling victim to the monster, there is feverish speculation about who might be the heir of

Slytherin. The triad suspect Draco Malfoy and mount their dangerous experiment with polyjuice, only to find they are mistaken. Harry, however, casts himself in the role of prime suspect during the dueling scene when a snake is conjured by Draco Malfoy. (CS 145) Harry instructs the snake not to harm a pupil, only to find that he has spoken in Parseltongue, a language known only to wizards on the dark side. This incident marks the point at which Voldemort's attempts to divide the triad seem closest to success. Even Hermione admits that for all they know Harry might be Slytherin's heir. (CS 147)

The ending of the second Potter volume, however, marks a triumphant stage in the building of the triad. It is Hermione who works out from the clues that the monster in the Chamber of Secrets is a basilisk. However, she also demonstrates one of the triad's weaknesses; instead of discussing her finding with Ron and Harry, she rushes off to put it to the test and gets petrified. Once it becomes known that a student of Hogwarts has been captured, that her skeleton will 'lie in the Chamber for ever' (CS 217), and that the victim is Ginny Weasley, Harry immediately decides to rescue her and Ron hesitates not for a second in accompanying him. This was the first manifestation of what Hermione would later call Harry's hero fixation. Although the victim is Ron's sister, it was Harry who takes the lead and would have done so alone if Ron had not instantly volunteered to be his companion. We can now see that when the members of the triad work together they can achieve their joint aims even when they succumb to their individual weaknesses – Hermione's tendency to keep her speculations to herself, Harry's tendency to cast himself in the role of the universal champion, and Ron's inclination to devalue everything about himself, from his pet rat to his beautifully eccentric home.

What Harry achieves in the Chamber, confronted by the fragmented image of the younger Voldemort and the deadly basilisk, is to introject Hermione's intelligence and Ron's loyalty, thus countering his own tendency towards solitary self-glorification. The loyalty is enough to summon the sword of Gryffindor and the healing powers of Dumbledore's phoenix, Fawkes. Otherwise all would have been lost.

Harry Potter and the Prisoner of Azkaban

It has been widely remarked that the tone of the Potter novels darkens from the third book (PA) onwards. The members of the triad face mounting challenges. Harry is confronted by the Dementors, whose presence evokes the screams of his dying mother. He also learned that Sirius Black, the wizard convicted of betraying his parents, has escaped from prison with the sole aim of finishing his work and killing Harry. Hermione, magically enabled to turn back time, attends so many classes that even her intellectual resources are drained to the limit. Ron is destined to learn that his harmless pet rat Scabbers is a dark wizard in animal form, the very man who had in fact betrayed Harry's parents. Yet at the same time the triad finds itself no longer so isolated. During the course of the novel it acquires two powerful and attractive allies, the dashing, somewhat reckless but heroic Sirius, revealed as Harry's godfather, and the calm, reflective, considerate Remus Lupin, who happens to be a werewolf. If Remus encourages Harry to be more thoughtful, however, it must be admitted that Sirius still favours action over thought. Confronted by Peter Pettigrew, the wizard who actually betrayed the Potters, Remus is in favour of hearing the full truth, while Sirius's reaction is to kill Pettigrew at once. (PA 269) This tendency to unthinking action, common to Harry as well as Sirius, will remain a crucial weakness of the triad, proving that they can introject dangerous elements as well as useful. In the case of Pettigrew, Remus's calm advice prevailed.

The members of the triad also acquire impressive new magical instruments during PA, and the skills to use them. From Professor McGonagall Hermione acquires the time-turner, the device that is to save the lives of Sirius and the hippogriff. From the Weasley twins they acquire the Marauder's Map. Remus also trains Harry in the ability to produce a corporeal Patronus, the magical creature which can dispel Dementors. His Patronus is a stag, commemorating his father's animagus form. This is one of the most significant introjections of the whole saga: part of his dead father's psyche is integrated into Harry. Indeed when Harry's Patronus intervenes to save Sirius, Harry mistakes the figure generating the Patronus for his father. It was in fact himself in a different time frame.

The effect of these changes is to cast the triad even more firmly into the front line of the battle against the Dark Lord and his forces. As the series approaches its midpoint, the lines of battle are being drawn up. The centaurs tell Harry that what the world was currently witnessing was a lull between two wars. The next one would be a fight to the death. It was not possible that Harry and the Dark Lord would both survive.

Harry Potter and the Goblet of Fire

In the fourth book of the series (GF) Voldemort employs a different form of fragmentation. The Dark Lord separates Barty Crouch junior from his own independent freedom of action by means of the Imperius Curse, then causes him by means of the polyjuice potion to become a replica of the teacher and auror, Mad-Eye Moody. This is a highly effective use of fragmentation. As a famous auror, an implacable enemy of the Dark Lord, the pseudo-Moody would never be suspected of working for Voldemort.

This stratagem succeeds in posing the most serious threat so far to the unity of the triad. Attending the World Cup of Quidditch (GF 87 ff) the triad and their circle are closely bonded by a memorable event and by its sinister aftermath, the appearance of the Dark Mark in the sky. But the announcement of the Triwizard tournament (GF 152 ff) tears the triad to pieces. When Harry's name is added to the three contestants envisaged by the rules, Ron becomes furious. He believes that Harry must have entered his own name

surreptitiously in the Goblet of Fire, and bitterly resents Harry's unwillingness to confess. Hermione understands where the problem lay, and puts her finger on a potentially fatal weakness.

> 'Oh, Harry, isn't it obvious?' Hermione said despairingly. 'He's jealous.'
> 'Jealous?' Harry said incredulously. 'Jealous of what? He wants to make a prat of himself in front of the whole school, does he?'
> 'Look,' said Hermione patiently, 'it's always you who gets all the attention, you know it is. I know it's not your fault...' (GF 254)

The virtues of the triad here both work and fail. Hermione's intelligence tells her that Harry could not have entered his name in the Goblet: its magical defences are too strong for that. Ron's greatest virtue, however, his loyalty to Harry and Hermione, is stretched beyond breaking point because he can conceive of himself as a possible candidate for the contest. Voldemort's divisive tactics are cunning in the extreme. It is also clear that Cedric Diggory, the legitimate Hogwarts' representative, did not accept Harry's protestations either. (GF 248) When the Slytherins organise the POTTER STINKS campaign, they seem to have plenty of support. Voldemort's campaign is splitting Harry from his natural supporters and giving opportunities to his enemies.

The plan of the Dark Lord now begins to unravel. Hagrid shows Harry the dragons the champions will have to face. He also allows Beauxbatons' teacher Madame Maxime to see them, so that the Beauxbatons champion Fleur Delacourt will also know. Voldemort's plan demands that Harry should win the contest and put his hand on the cup that is a portkey. But Hagrid's affection for Maxime has now given Fleur Delacourt an equal chance. And Harry's decency prompts him to share the information with Cedric too. Human decency is too difficult a factor for Voldemort to incorporate in his plans. Even with a role model like Dumbledore, Tom Riddle fails to introject any sense of humanity. Ron finally realizes that his suspicions have been misplaced when he sees how dangerous the contest really is.

> [Harry] was looking at Ron, who was very white and staring at Harry as though he was a ghost.
> 'Harry,' he said very seriously, 'whoever put your name in that Goblet – I – I reckon they're trying to do you in!'
> 'Caught on, have you?' said Harry coldly. 'Took you long enough.' (GF 313)

Rowling now makes clear a default in Harry that will later have serious consequences, both for him and for those opposing the Dark Lord. The second task for the Triwizard champions is to rescue someone prized from capture underwater. When Harry has secured the release of Ron and should be heading for home, he lingers to rescue the sister of Fleur Delacourt, assuming Fleur to have failed. This is a violation of the rules of the contest and should strictly have been punished. Dumbledore insists that Harry's action showed 'moral fibre' (GF 440) and awards him high marks. Yet this is another manifestation of Harry's unthinking reflex, to be the saviour and take the whole burden of responsibility on himself. It worries Hermione, and will later cost a precious life.

By this point in the narrative, the contrasting intentions of Harry and Voldemort are clear. Harry is seeking to reach out and share, taking attributes from his allies and introjecting them: Voldemort is set on his solitary path, isolating himself from enemies and allies alike. Yet the climax of this book reveals that these intentions could still have effects the exact opposite of what was intended. When Harry and Cedric Diggory reach the Triwizard cup (GF 548 ff) Cedric is within easy reach of the cup while Harry is partly immobilized by his injured leg. The two boys then have an old-fashioned decent-chap conversation about who has truly merited the victory, leading to the decision to share the trophy and lay hands on it simultaneously. The portkey transports both of them to the graveyard where Voldemort casually dispatches Cedric: *'Kill the spare.'* (GF 553) Thus Harry's desire to act in a spirit of unity has led directly to Cedric's death. Voldemort in turn sees this confrontation as an opportunity not only to renew his own corporeal existence but also to finish what he started and kill Harry in a duel. Yet the conjunction of the Dark Lord's wand and Harry's, both wands incorporating a feather from the same phoenix, produces the *Priori Incantatem* spell that reveals simulacra of the last victims Voldemort has killed, including Harry's parents. (GF 576 ff) These simulacra advise Harry how to defeat the Dark Lord and survive. Thus Voldemort's solitary plan, pitting himself alone against the undefended boy, has also misfired. For the first time Harry has the opportunity to speak to and draw sustenance from his dead parents. What Harry had hoped to gain from the mirror of Erised and failed, is delivered to him by his nemesis, contrary to the Dark Lord's intentions.

Harry Potter and the Order of the Phoenix

When we turn to the fifth book in the *Harry Potter* saga (OP) we find the triad placed in an almost impossible position. Up to now the triad has played a leading role in the struggle against the Dark Lord. Now a major clash has arisen between the adults opposing Voldemort, with Dumbledore and his allies re-forming the Order of the Phoenix and the Ministry of Magic pretending that nothing has happened. The triad, along with the other Weasley juniors, is excluded on grounds of age from participating in the work of the Order. A further obstacle is placed in the triad's way when a Ministry spy, Dolores Umbridge, is inserted into the management of Hogwarts. In desperation, and at Hermione's prompting, Harry forms and leads a resistance group known as Dumbledore's Army ('the DA'). Though Harry believes he is strengthening the resistance to the Dark Lord, he is further fragmenting the resistance in a way that leads to Dumbledore's suspension from the school. Other efforts are also being made to undermine the triad. Ron's brother Percy, once the favourite of his parents, has now become estranged. He is an officer of the Ministry of Magic, committed to the policy that Voldemort's supposed return is nothing but a scheme of Dumbledore's to usurp the Minister. Percy sees fraternisation with Harry as a danger to Ron's career.

> 'Seriously, Ron, you do *not* want to be tarred with the same brush as Potter, it could be very damaging to your future prospects, and I am talking here about life after school, too.' (Author's italics OP 267)

The triad and its handful of supporters in the DA are now being opposed not only by Voldemort and his supporters, the Death Eaters, but also by the official opposition to Voldemort as embodied at the Ministry. The odds are stacked heavily against the triad. We know from what Ron saw in the mirror of Erised – himself receiving public plaudits – that personal ambition matters to Ron. It is a tribute to his steadiness under fire that he never wavers in his support for Harry.

All the way through the books, the reader has been aware that at the moment when Voldemort failed to kill Harry, a strange link was established between them. Attributes passed in both directions between them – though the reader was not wholly certain to what effect. Rowling is here advancing beyond the point reached by Klein in her analysis. Klein was interested largely in the child and placed more emphasis on the impressions absorbed by the child. Later theorists such as Winnicott and Andre Green have placed more emphasis upon the two-way exchange.

The significance of that link now becomes explicit. When the giant snake Nagini attacks Mr Weasley, Harry witnesses the attack. And he witnesses it through the eyes of the snake, as Voldemort is also able to see. (OP 408 ff) Harry's ability to raise the alert saves Mr Weasley's life but it also warns Dumbledore that Voldemort is reaching deep into Harry's mind. Dumbledore's response to this crisis is baffling in the extreme. He cuts off personal communication with Harry, refusing even to look Harry in the eye. He also decides that Harry should have lessons in occlumency, the art of closing one's mind to external penetration, only to entrust these lessons to Professor Snape. Severus Snape had been, by his own admission, a Death Eater and was regarded with deep suspicion even now by some of Dumbledore's followers. He was admitted to the Order of the Phoenix. Those who accepted him did so only because they had unquestioning faith in Dumbledore's judgment.

As housemaster of the Slytherins, Snape would have been suspect in the eyes of the triad anyway. But Snape had also been the sworn enemy of Harry's father and transferred that dislike undiluted to Harry. It must have been quite obvious that personal antipathy would block any benefit Harry might take from these lessons – and so it proved. It must also be admitted that Harry remained curious about what he might learn from Voldemort, and perhaps took a secret pleasure from being in contact with a brilliant if depraved mind. Just why Dumbledore acted in this way, guaranteeing that Harry would remain vulnerable to Voldemort's mental intrusion, the reader does not yet know. Perhaps the answer will be provided in the seventh and final book of the series, unpublished at the time of writing.

Voldemort has set a trap intended to lure Harry into the department of mysteries at the Ministry of Magic. In his dreams Harry had seen the corridor where the department was situated, and felt an insatiable curiosity to penetrate the rooms. At the time of Harry's birth there had been a prophecy linking his destiny with that of Voldemort. Voldemort was desperate to retrieve this prophecy, but had learned that it could be retrieved only by one of the two people it concerned. Since Voldemort could hardly risk being apprehended in the Ministry, he must lure Harry into retrieving it. Voldemort used his access to Harry's mind – unblocked since the Occlumency had failed – to plant in Harry's mind an image of Sirius Black being held and tortured within the Ministry by the Death Eaters.

Rowling chooses at this point to illustrate just how far Harry still had to go before he could shake off his heroic obsessions. Before Harry witnesses the vision of Sirius captured by Death Eaters, Sirius has actually foreseen that such a situation might arise. He gives Harry a mysterious package. It turns out to be mirror: in a crisis Harry could contact Sirius by looking into the mirror. Harry's reaction is significant.

> [Harry] knew he would never use whatever it was. It would not be he, Harry, who lured Sirius from his place of safety... (OP 462)

Instead of using the mirror to communicate with Sirius, Harry talks to Sirius's treacherous house-elf, who plays his part in luring Harry into the trap. Rashly, Harry hastens off to the Ministry. Sirius of course is not there. But the Death Eaters are, waiting to force Harry to retrieve the orb in which the prophecy is contained. The Order of the Phoenix is compelled to invade the Ministry to save the day, and Sirius Black, Harry's devoted godfather, pays the price with his life. Harry's fixation with his own heroic status has cost him the most precious thing in his life. Significantly, Hermione had tried to alert Harry to the danger.

> 'You... this isn't a criticism, Harry! But you do... sort of...I mean – don't you think you've got a bit of a – a – saving people thing?' she said.
> He glared at her.
> 'And what's that supposed to mean, a "saving people thing"?' (OP 646)

Hermione gives the example of Harry's attempt to save Fleur's sister during the underwater Triwizard task, which Ron at the time had described as acting the hero. (OP 647) Hermione and Ron are combining forces to try to help Harry. But he has not yet reached that point of self-awareness where he could accept their guidance. The triad is still too weak. Even after Sirius's death, Harry does not learn the most important lesson; Sirius had given Harry a two-way mirror which would have enabled him to speak to his godfather wherever he was. Harry does not think of using this device to check on Sirius's whereabouts before rushing off to the Ministry of Magic. And when Harry does remember that he had the mirror (OP 756) his only thought was that he might use the mirror to talk to Sirius beyond the grave, not that due to Harry's forgetfulness Sirius had died an avoidable death.

Harry Potter and the Half-Blood Prince

In the sixth book of the series (HBP) the reader is introduced to the notion that has been awaited for so long, the device by which Voldemort hopes to render himself practically immortal – the Horcrux. A portkey is an ordinary object – a kettle, a shoe or a cup – invested with the magical ability to transport whoever touches it to a specific destination. A Horcrux is an ordinary object into which a wizard can project a part of his soul. Anyone who wishes to kill an individual so protected must find and destroy every Horcrux into which a fragment of the soul has been inserted. Professor Slughorn, the reluctant expert on the Horcrux, is seen in memory explaining the Horcrux for the first time to Tom Riddle, the young Voldemort. This is a key passage in the whole series, since it records Voldemort's acquisition of the skills that will enable him to lock himself for ever into the Kleinian paranoid schizoid position, beyond reach of projection or introjection.

> *'How do you split your soul?' [asked Riddle.]*
> *'Well,' said Slughorn uncomfortably, 'you must understand that the soul is supposed to remain intact and whole. Splitting it is an act of violation, it is against nature.'*
> *'But how do you do it?'*
> *'By an act of evil – the supreme act of evil. By committing murder. Killing rips the soul apart. The wizard intent upon creating a Horcrux would use the damage to his advantage: he would encase the torn portion...'*
> *'Encase? But how – ?'*
> *'There is a spell, do not ask me, I don't know!'* (HBP, 465)

Voldemort is clearly formulating a plan of his own, even at this early stage.

> *'What I don't understand, though – just out of curiosity – I mean, would one Horcrux be much use? Can you only split your soul once? Wouldn't it be better, make you stronger, to have your soul in more pieces? I mean, for instance, isn't seven the most powerfully magical number, wouldn't seven – '*
> *'Merlin's beard, Tom... Seven? Isn't it bad enough to think of killing one person? And in any case... bad enough to divide the soul ... but to rip it into seven pieces...'* (HBP 465/6)

And so Voldemort's plan is devised. In my opinion, this plan of the Dark Lord embodies perfectly the fragmentation that Klein envisaged, the splitting that exemplifies the paranoid schizoid position. The seven Horcruxes are judged to be: Voldemort's own body, in which some remnant of his psyche must remain; the Tom Riddle diary, now destroyed; the Slytherin ring, now in the possession of Dumbledore with its magical qualities removed; the locket that belonged to Voldemort's mother Merope; the Hufflepuff cup; perhaps the giant snake Nagini; and one or perhaps two more objects as yet unidentified but conjectured to have links to Ravenclaw and Gryffindor. (HBP 474/5)

At the end of this sixth book the reader encounters a stunning event, the death of Albus Dumbledore. Dumbledore has been weakened, his hand withered and blackened, by the act of retrieving the Slytherin ring. Just why Dumbledore's killer turns out to be Snape is a question to be answered in the final Potter book. The triad is now left without its guiding figure, facing the final challenge with Voldemort without him. The reader recalls what Hagrid said of Dumbledore when first meeting Harry.

> *'Reckon Dumbeldore's the only one You-Know-Who was afraid of.'* (PS 45)

This deadly challenge also obliges Harry to break off his burgeoning relationship with Ginny Weasley. She must not be implicated in the final deadly struggle, in which either Harry or the Dark Lord must perish. Left to his own devices, Harry's hero complex would have taken control, he would have faced the final challenge without even Ron or Hermione at his side.

> 'We'll be there, Harry,' said Ron.
> 'What?'
> 'At your aunt and uncle's house,' said Ron. 'And then we'll go with you, wherever you're going.'
> 'No – ' said Harry quickly: he had not counted on this, he had meant them to understand that he was undertaking this most dangerous journey alone.
> 'You said to us once before,' said Hermione quietly, 'that there was time to turn back if we wanted to. We've had time, haven't we? We're with you whatever happens.' (HBP 607)

Conclusion

On the surface Rowling's *Harry Potter* books demonstrate expert plotting. A minor detail mentioned in passing in one book turns out to have monumental consequences several books later. The books also deploy impressive imagination and a memorable cast of characters. Yet these are just the superficial attractions of the books. Beneath the surface is a deep and bitter psychological struggle. On one side is a boy from a hopelessly fragmented background, fighting against the odds to introject attitudes and skills that will lead him to an integrated personality, relying heavily on a precociously intelligent girl and a fiercely loyal boy. On the other side is a man from a very similar background – an orphan brought up without love, guidance or affection – who is determined to seek power and some kind of immortality, using murder to fragment his soul. The struggle between integration and fragmentation – which Melanie Klein saw as the primal contest for the human soul – is seen to run all through this complex work, and to be its underlying theme.

REFERENCES

J.K.Rowling, *Harry Potter and the Philosopher's Stone*. London: Bloomsbury, 1997

J.K.Rowling, *Harry Potter and the Chamber of Secrets*. London: Bloomsbury, 1998

J.K.Rowling, *Harry Potter and the Prisoner of Azkaban*. London: Bloomsbury, 1999

J.K.Rowling, *Harry Potter and the Goblet of Fire*. London: Bloomsbury, 2000

J.K.Rowling, *Harry Potter and the Order of the Phoenix*. London: Bloomsbury, 2003

J.K.Rowling, *Harry Potter and the Half-Blood Prince*. London: Bloomsbury, 2005

For ease of reference the Potter books are cited as follows:
Harry Potter and the Philosopher's Stone, 1997 (PS);
Harry Potter and the Chamber of Secrets, 1998 (CS);
Harry Potter and the Prisoner of Azkaban, 1999 (PA);
Harry Potter and the Goblet of Fire, 2000, (GF);
Harry Potter and the Order of the Phoenix, 2003, (OP);
Harry Potter and the Half-Blood Prince, 2005, (HBP).

My list of examples is not exhaustive. In books of such scope and detail I am sure readers will find many other instances of fragmentation and integration.

Rebecca-Anne C. Do Rozario

MIRRORED: The Self and Inheritance As Seen In Children's Narratives

SCENES IN *Harry Potter and the Prisoner of Azkaban* (book published 1999, film released 2004), *The Lion King* (film, 1994) and *The Empire Strikes Back* (film, 1980) all feature a young male who is confronted with an image of himself in which he sees that of his father, a father he believes to have been unjustly killed. That these scenes occur in three of the most seminal popular culture phenomena of the late twentieth century suggests that such correlation is noteworthy. In the juxtaposition of these scenes with the mirror images presented to heroines in fairy tale and popular culture, different experiences of inheritance and power are revealed, suggesting increasing divisions in the patriarchal legacy and a recollection of innate female power.

These three scenes occur in three pivotal narratives. Using a little imagination, one can say that the children who saw *The Empire Strikes Back* in 1980 grew up to have the children who saw *The Lion King* in 1994 and then went on to read *Harry Potter and the Prisoner of Azkaban* in 1999. It is appropriate to consider why, in some of the most culturally defining entertainment phenomena of recent years, these young male heroes 'find their selves' through images of their dead or lost fathers.

Luke Skywalker, the young protagonist of *The Empire Strikes Back*, is training to be a Jedi Knight, like his father before him. He believes this father to have been murdered by Darth Vadar, the – literally – black villain. One of Luke's training exercises, performed under the auspices of his wise mentor, Yoda, is to enter a cave and embark upon what is, to all intents and purposes, a dream quest. Luke encounters the image of Darth Vadar there and they battle. Luke takes off Vadar's head; and Vadar's mask then splits open to reveal Luke's own face. Luke is unaware that in confronting this image of himself in the mask of Darth Vadar, he is confronting the as yet unknown truth: Darth Vadar is his father. He is, in fact, seeing himself literally in the image of his father.

This is much what Simba in *The Lion King* sees. The young lion has gone into exile, blaming himself for the death of his father. His wise mentor, Rafiki, locates the exile and promises to take him to his father: "Your father is alive and I'll show him to you!" He takes him to a pool of water, instructing him to look. Simba retorts, "That's not my father. That's just my reflection." "No, look harder," Rafiki insists and the reflection ripples to become that of Mufasa, Simba's father. "You see?" Rafiki explains. "He lives in you" (Mecchi et al

1994). In this case, it is the image of the son that encapsulates the image of the father, the two images conflating in the rippling water.

In *Harry Potter and the Prisoner of Azkaban*, Harry thinks he sees his father from across another body of water. In a somewhat complex narrative sequence in which time repeats, he learns that the image was actually that of himself. Professor Dumbledore, the school's headmaster and Harry's guide and mentor, explains Harry's bewildered response to this occurrence: "You think the dead we have loved ever truly leave us? [...] Your father is alive in you, Harry [...] So you did see your father last night, Harry... you found him inside yourself" (Rowling 1999, 312). Dumbledore and Rafiki's words are uncannily similar, reinforcing the presence/likeness of the father in the son's image.

Joseph Campbell's examination of the hero's journey provides some insight into the fundamental narrative of these scenes. Luke, Simba and Harry are all heroes and their narratives are consistent with the cycles of the hero's journey. All have a wise mentor: Yoda, Rafiki, Dumbledore. These wise mentors have distinctive aspects in common, embodying a mix of childlike whimsy, nonsense and tough-minded wisdom. These particular scenes are explained by Campbell's reference to the myth of Narcissus: "What is the core of us? What is the basic character of our being?" (1949, 385). The gaze into one's reflection is interpreted as meditation: "This is the stage of Narcissus looking into the pool [...] The aim is not to see, but to realize what one is" (1949, 386). In both *Harry Potter* and *The Lion King*, pools of water are literally involved, whether the hero gazes into or across them. Luke's experience in a cave provides a likely equivalent.

Campbell's explanation is, of course, also consistent with the mirror stage identified by Lacan, which places emphasis upon identity as a social representation of the self.

Karen Coats argues that those children's books that describe a Lacanian growth into the Symbolic, a character separating from the Mother to 'become his own cause' (2004, 7) can be active in that very same process: "They provide the signifiers that we perform. We use them in much the same way the infant uses the mirror image – to reflect back to us our own idealized image that we then identify with and attempt to become" (2004, 33). The commonalities in these scenes, although including film, and their unusual international success, suggest that they provide specific signifiers that recent generations of children may, and in fact most likely do, perform.

If we deal with the concept of the mirror image, however, it is worth noting that these heroes are all adolescent males. Yet, in many respects, they haven't obtained their literally Symbolic identity, whether as Jedi Knight, King or Great Wizard, partly because their progress has been disrupted by prolonged mourning for their fathers, who 'died' in their infancy. The mirror stage also most often involves the mother. Coats argues that it is "inevitable that the mother will always stand alongside any Symbolic representation the child makes for himself" (2004, 20). In each case here, it is not a mother, but a Wise Mentor who assists the hero in viewing his image, in effect reinforcing the double reflection of the father and son. This seems to suggest that the Wise Mentor, a venerable patriarch, replaces the mother. However, the position is complicated by the nature of these Wise Mentors.

The Wise Mentors, all wearing robes, are not aggressively gendered; Rafiki became a female shaman in the theatrical adaptation (1997) without any significant alteration to the character. What is notable about each of them is their nonsense: Yoda 'with strange grammar speaks', Rafiki sings "asante sante squash banana" (Mecchi et al, 1994), Dumbledore's welcome speech goes "Nitwit! Blubber! Oddment! Tweak!" (Rowling 1997, 92). Coats locates the linguistic importance of nonsense in childhood: "in learning to read nonsense, [the child] manages to hold on to that bit of outlaw jouissance – as it appears in the humour, music, and anarchy of the nonsense text – that has broken off from the mother and winds up circulating in language itself" (2004, 64). That is, while the son enters meaning through the Father's Law, the Wise Mentors' nonsense represents, to again quote Coats, "the site of the mother's exclusion, while at the same time holding open a place for her as nonmeaning" (2004, 65). Since the mentors represent a link to nonmeaning as the Mother, it is logical that they should assist at the Mirror Stage. Male they are, but their masculinity is subsumed by nonmeaning, the preserve of the Mother. The Mother thus breaks through – it is her wisdom that, at the site of her exclusion, and from beyond the Father's Law, authors the Wise Mentors and thus ultimately informs her sons.

The ideal self of these heroes, with a particularly strong ethic of responsibility and justice, is conversely constructed in terms of an inheritance of Symbolic patriarchal burden. Annette Wannamaker argues that the "ethical foundation" represented by *Harry Potter* – and she, significantly, mentions *Star Wars* in passing – "is the timely and complex concept of inheritance explained in Jacques Derrida's book *Specters of Marx: The state of the Debt, the Work of Mourning, and New International*" (2003, 47). As Wannamaker says, "We all inherit a world created by those who came before us" (2003, 49). Of specific interest is that we are dealing with Symbolic inheritance in these particular mirror images, one borne in mourning. Luke, Simba and Harry are all mourning sons who are confronted with spectres of the past in their idealised image – specifically, spectres of their fathers, figures of enshrined patriarchal power that has failed in their death. Anakin Skywalker, the heroic Jedi Knight, was turned to the dark side and died a symbolic death; Mufasa, king of his pride, was murdered by his brother, Scar; Harry's father, hero of the alliance against Lord Voldemort, died at Voldemort's hands. Since their deaths, the times have, to paraphrase Hamlet, been out of joint: in the case of Harry Potter, they are literally out of joint, due to the use of a Time-Turner.
Coats locates the importance of the dead father in a psychoanalytical reading. "As we know, the death of the father is the essential element for entry into the

Symbolic – as the necessary third term, the Name of the Father as the Symbolic function necessitates the death of the Real father" (2004, 113). To mix my theoretical approaches, the Name of the Father becomes here the spectre, referencing loss in the son's inheritance of what the father symbolised. Derrida, in quoting *Hamlet*, itself a significant influence in *The Lion King*, says: "The one who says 'I am thy Father's Spirit' can only be taken at his word. An essentially blind submission to his secret, to the secret of his origin" (1994, 7). This sense of secrecy, of origin, marries well to the general thrust of these narratives: the secret of the death of the father haunts the son's image/self. The confluence at the mirror stage actually highlights the ideal representation of patriarchal power the sons would inherit from their fathers: but it is fragmented and diminished by the secret of the father's untimely and unjust death. A loss or fragmentation of patriarchy resonates in the double image of son and dead father.

Wannamaker actually finishes her essay with the scene of my interest from *Harry Potter and the Prisoner of Azkaban*. "In this one crucial moment in the series, past, present, and future come together to illustrate the importance of inheritance, that fact that our future can only come to us when we are working to interpret and re-interpret the past, when we are able to come to terms with specters" (2003, 55). Significantly, Harry is with his friend Hermione when he faces this re-interpretation. It is she who wields the Time-Turner and thus brings Harry into the past. In *The Lion King*, it is Nala, a young lioness, who, while hunting to preserve the pride, discovers Simba and challenges him to take up his position in the Symbolic, giving up the imaginary jungle in which he has exiled himself. In the Star Wars trilogy, Luke turns to Leia, who is revealed as his twin sister and final hope of the Jedi tradition should he fail. These heroines, at least one an official Princess, do not represent the maternal. They are not the mother who positions the hero to see his mirror image or who represents the big other. They represent the potential heroines of the future.

Heroines have always been conscious of spectres. Gertrude Postl asks, "Why did Derrida make the ultimate patriarchal relationship, namely the one between father and son, the focal point of his investigation? Which other ghosts, besides Shakespeare and Marx, do we have to learn to live with?" (1999, 65). Postl, with reference to Luce Irigaray, argues that the woman's body has "vanished" from Derrida's scenario (1999, 63), that: "This woman commodity with her artificial body, this mirror who mimes the living is herself neither dead nor alive" (1999, 65). The reference to the mirror itself suggests the possibility of the mirror image and there is an alternate reading in terms of theorising female or even matriarchal power through that same mirror image, a power that appears passive, but is nevertheless authoritative.

Heroines have always interacted with mirrors and mirror images. One of the most ancient of tales that alludes to the mirror stage is that of Snow White. The queen has a magic mirror that can never lie. The mirror has a voice, one which articulates the ideal self being represented: "You, O Queen, are the fairest of all" (Grimm and Grimm 2004, 244). Some, including Sandra M. Gilbert and Susan Gubar, have argued that the mirror's voice is that of a male, namely the husband/father or king. Gilbert and Gubar propose that his is "the patriarchal voice of judgement" and that, consequently, "he need no longer appear in the story because, having assimilated the meaning of her own sexuality [...] the woman has internalised the King's rules: his voice resides now in her own mirror, her own mind" (1984, 38). This interpretation of the voice, and even of absence, rests upon patriarchal authority. I would argue that this passes over the essential mirror stage exchange between the queen and Snow White, an exchange coherent with D.W. Winnicott's assertion. "In individual emotional development *the precursor of the mirror is the mother's face*" (1971, 111). The queen's face, rather than the mirror, is the focus of the Snow White narrative.

Shuli Barzilai argues "every mother is also a daughter", situating the contention between the women/queens as they represent mother and daughter "simultaneously" (1990, 525). Elizabeth Bell goes further to argue that the Disney adaptation (1937) represents the two simultaneously as ages of womanhood: the queen and Snow White are animated mirror images, themselves, the queen simply a more mature version of the same red lipped, pale skinned, black haired woman (1995, 121). The mother and daughter are, in many respects, one. Barzilai references Nancy Chodorow's conclusions, Chodorow arguing that the mother's "sense of oneness and continuity with her infant" is actually "stronger, and lasts longer, vis-à-vis daughters" and is consequently "more likely to retain and emphasize narcissistic elements, that is, to be based on experiencing a daughter as an extension or double of a mother herself" (1978, 109). Since in the mirror stage the mother situates the child in the mirror or provides her own face as a mirror, this symbiosis makes sense in terms of the fairy tale's articulation of the mirror image, one at times also reversible. The step/mother also sees her idealised self in her own reflection, but this self becomes the daughter; as Barzilai argues, "a mother who cannot grow up and a daughter who must" (1990, 534).

Yet, the fairy tale has not just one, but many versions, and secreted away in this tale is the daughter's gaze into the mirror. The mirror in the tale skews this (the mirror stage of course doesn't require an actual mirror): the mirror is the mother's gaze. In Grimms' fairy tale, the queen's gaze follows and haunts Snow White. Neil Gaiman and Dean McKean's *MirrorMask* (2005) is a riff upon Snow White, elaborating on this aspect of the tale. The heroine, Helena, is tricked by her mirror self into taking her place as princess of the Dark Lands, daughter of the Dark Queen:

> "*In my bedroom – the princess's bedroom – was a looking glass, and it had two eyeholes in it, so that the Queen could watch me from her throne room when I was sitting on my bed. I was pleased she watched me. It made me feel loved*" (Gaiman 2005, 52).

This is the dyad that Coats refers to, the dangerous dyad of mother and child, dangerous "because it is built on an impossibility. In the dyad, there is an illusion of totality" (2004, 21). Helena accuses the Queen of overpowering mothering – of not letting the princess grow up and break that totality – just as Snow White's evil stepmother does not wish her to grow up as the fairest and will do anything, including killing her, to prevent it. The MirrorMask Queen's response – "absolutely out of the question" (Gaiman 2005, 66) – highlights the threat and prohibition imposed to maintain the dyad.

Helena escapes the imaginary dream world by taking control of the mirror, the MirrorMask, herself: "I could feel it forming itself to my face [...] I was wearing the MirrorMask. It was weird. I still remember how when I had the mask on I knew things" (Gaiman 2005, 62-63). In fact, the MirrorMask gives that same illusion of totality as experienced in the dyad: "With the MirrorMask on, I could see everything" (Gaiman 2005, 73). The mirror still gives her the illusion of totality and she isn't quite free yet; Gaiman and McKean situate the Symbolic in real life and the imaginary in the dream. It is her father who wakes her up, to quote Coats: "Thus the Name of the Father [...] separates the subject from the mother's desire" (2004, 21). And Helena also knows that now she is free to seek her future boyfriend, whom she has discovered in her dream. Like Snow White, she apparently seeks a prince's kiss to further secure her in the Symbolic, although this will make her vulnerable to patriarchal oppression. However, it is likewise notable that Helena views herself as the potential rescuer of her boyfriend:

> "But if I keep my eyes open, I know I'll bump into him one day. After all, he really doesn't want to be a waiter" (Gaiman 2005, 76).

The mirror stage offers a view of Self that is not Self – it exists separate and ideal, perhaps as Snow White, the fairest of them all. Derrida likewise points out that the spectre is "the body of someone as someone other" (1994, 7). Important, too, in understanding the experience of Snow White and Helena is Derrida's injunction that "this spectral someone other looks at us" (1994, 7). For Snow White and Helena, this spectral someone other is the Mother; the mother/other construction who provides a mirror for the daughter, one the daughter must, in effect, take control of or embody herself – "But the young queen is a thousand times more fair" (Grimm and Grimm 2004, 255), noting that Snow White has usurped the position of queen – and pass through – Helena's "window I'd charcoaled on the back of the door" (Gaiman 2005, 72) – to separate and enter the Symbolic.

Often, though, the gaze belongs to a male and is interpreted in patriarchal terms. Laura Mulvey is notable here in defining the subject position of the female: "pleasure in looking has been split between active/male and passive/female" (1975, 11). The gaze is that of the active male; the passive female is looked at. In the tales just described, the gaze belongs to the queen, a woman who embodies power often to the exclusion of a king. Gaiman's Queens have no Kings and even the Grimms' *"Snow White"* introduces the queen who daydreams of her child from what she observes (her gaze) and when the queen dies after Snow White's birth, "A year later, her husband, the king, married another woman" (2004, 244). The king is identified by his status as her husband and serves merely to mark the transfer of power between queens. Gilbert and Gubar's interpretation of his "absence" as "a fact that emphasizes the almost stifling intensity with which the tale concentrates on the conflict in the mirror between mother and daughter, woman and woman, self and self" (1984, 37), reinscribes patriarchal control through patriarchal absence, but fairy tale consistently places such conflicts in the preserve of the female.

This curious 'downgrading' of patriarchal power in fairy tale and folk lore is evident even in Vladimir Propp's morphology of the folktale. The category of 'princess and her father' clearly defines the father's role in relation to the princess's, just as the functions of the role clearly provide the princess with inherent power, in deliberate spite of apparent patriarchal laws of inheritance. Although often the princess appears to suffer in the binary – male is active, female is passive – passivity need not automatically equate to submissiveness. Passive power infers no requirement of action: the male must act to obtain power, the female already has it. Hence heroes don't become kings until they win a princess, but princesses quite often automatically attain status as queens. In Grimms' *"Snow White"*, the hero is a prince and takes Snow White to his father's castle and immediately, without any indication of the prince's ascension, Snow White becomes the "young queen" (2004, 255). She then effectively turns the gaze back on the queen, her stepmother, and, as the Grimms say, 'paralyses' her (2004, 255). Her stepmother is put in hot iron shoes and made to dance to death. Snow White is never seen to take action, for power, evident in the female gaze, is simply hers to employ.

This innate, if inert, power underwrites the film *Labyrinth* (1986). The Goblin King has keen sight and is male and Sarah, the young heroine, is constantly the object of his gaze. He calls her a "precious thing" (Dennis Lee et al, 1986) and his recurring references to her eyes eroticise his own look, itself heightened by theatrical make up. There are clear overtones of Mulvey's assertion of fetish looking: "turning the represented figure itself into a fetish so that it becomes reassuring rather than dangerous," thus it "builds up the physical beauty of the object, transforming it into something satisfying in itself" (1975, 14). The fetish, however, does not originate solely from the male gaze. Mulvey's specific assertion of the male gaze has, of course, been challenged, developed and altered over the last decades. In this analysis, the significance of the male gaze is not in its control or desire, but in its use as a mirror. The Goblin King's gaze provides Sarah with a mirror image. It is one, furthermore, constructed by Sarah herself, since she even constructs that gaze. The Goblin King is her fantasy, a glamorously fey figure inspired by the sculpture on her dressing table, which in turn projects the 'hers as his' fantasy back upon herself, and she identifies and becomes the powerful figure she sees there.

The Goblin King tries to restrict her by reflecting back to her, her idealised image of herself as a princess with very big hair and a puffy white dress at a masked ball. The image is actually satisfying to her imagination, mimicking as it does the figure on the music box she has in her bedroom, thus, like the Goblin King himself, originating from her own 'fetish.' She momentarily becomes the image, but it is Imaginary. She literally shatters her image within the crystal bubble the King has trapped her in, as she goes on to shatter the image of her 'Real' life and an Escher-inspired labyrinth. She continues to shatter the mirror image until she finds a meaningful place in the Symbolic by remembering words she has always forgotten, words with which she can confront and disempower the Goblin King: "My kingdom is great. You have no power over me" (Dennis Lee et al, 1986). The Goblin King insists that he has been "generous" – indeed, active – in pandering to her every desire: he has even been frightening in response to her cowering (Dennis Lee et al, 1986). In fact, Sarah's 'passivity,' or perhaps more accurately her steadfastness, is her power; he simply can not rule her unless she acts to allow him. She possesses her kingdom and, in many ways, the goblin king too, a figment of her unlimited imagination. Lacan alludes to this power of immoveable possession: "Women hold to the *jouissance* in question – none of them hold to being not all, and my God, and it would be wrong not to recognise that, contrary to what is said, it is none the less they who, for the most part, possess the men." (Mitchell and Rose 1982, 144-45).

The first season of the television series *Doctor Who* scripted by Russell T. Davies ended with Rose, another adolescent girl, discovering and remembering innate power. Faced with wide scale death threatened by the Dalek emperor, who has elevated himself to scary patriarchal godhood, the Doctor sends Rose home in the TARDIS. The TARDIS, an empathetic, seemingly-living, womb-like spaceship, appears to signify the feminine, even the Mother, and the TARDIS' gendering may well explain the popularity of a female companion for the regenerating male Doctor, the companion herself signifying the 'unacknowledged' female TARDIS. As we discover in Davies' first season, the TARDIS has left words spread across time and space: Bad Wolf. This is actually the TARDIS/Rose's message to herself, a textual manifestation of the mirror stage through which Rose literally tears open and looks into the soul of the TARDIS and takes that look/those words, with all the power of the totality of time and space, within herself. With just a look, she has power over life and death, is able to return to the Doctor, destroy a Dalek army and bring back to life Captain Jack. The totality is that of the dyad and subsequently dangerous, so the Doctor reasserts the Name of the Father – "I think you need a Doctor" (Davies 2005) – with a kiss in order to save her. Like Snow White or Sleeping Beauty or many of the other classic fairy tale heroines, the princess's power is so overwhelming, so 'everything,' it is difficult to contain even for her, necessitating fragmentation or division through the kiss, in spite or even because of its potential repression (although in differing contexts, such repression is neither total nor permanent). Her assertion of Bad Wolf even indicates that voracious, consuming power. She is able to eventually pass into the Symbolic, or at least a parallel world version, in the following series.

The Empire Strikes Back, *The Lion King*, and *Harry Potter* articulate the patriarchal burden that the son inherits through the idealised double image of dead father and son. Many stories conversely elaborate the innate female power that girls see in the mirror, a power so fixed and strong that heroines don't actually need to act to exercise it. Such tales of gazing into the mirror to seek idealised selves effectively provide insights into differing male and female experiences of the ideal self and their consequences for the understanding of patriarchal – and indeed matriarchal – power structures.

REFERENCES

Shuli Barzilai, "Reading 'Snow White': the mother's story", *Signs* 15, 3, 515-34, 1990.

Elizabeth Bell, "Somatexts at the Disney Shop: constructing the pentimentos of women's animated bodies." In *From Mouse to Mermaid: The Politics of Film, Gender, and Culture*, edited by Elizabeth Bell, Lynda Haas, and Laura Sells, 107-24. Bloomington: Indiana University Press, 1995.

Joseph Campbell, *The Hero with a Thousand Faces*, Princeton: Princeton University Press, 1949.

Nancy J. Chodorow, *The Reproduction of Mothering: Psychoanalysis and the Sociology of Gender*. Berkeley: University of California Press, 1978.

Karen Coats, *Looking Glasses and Neverlands: Lacan, Desire, and Subjectivity in Children's Literature*. Iowa City: University of Iowa Press, 2004.

Russell T. Davies, "The Parting of the Ways." *Doctor Who*, directed by Joe Ahearne. 2005.

Jacques Derrida, *Specters of Marx: The State of the Debt, the Work of Mourning, and the New International*. Trans. Peggy Kamuf. New York: Routledge, 1994.

Neil Gaiman and Dave McKean, *MirrorMask*. London: Bloomsbury, 2005.

Sandra M. Gilbert and Susan Gubar, *The Madwoman in the Attic: The Woman Writer and the Nineteenth-Century Literary Imagination*. New Haven: Yale University Press, 1984.

Jacob Grimm and Wilhelm Grimm. "Snow White." In *The Annotated Brothers Grimm*, 240-55, edited and translated by Maria Tatar. New York: W.W. Norton & Company, 2004.

Dennis Lee, Jim Henson and Terry Jones. *Labyrinth*, directed by Jim Henson, 1986.

George Lucas, Leigh Brackett and Lawrence Kasdan. *Star Wars: Episode V – The Empire Strikes Back*, directed by Irvin Kershner, 1980.

Irene Mecchi, Jonathan Roberts and Linda Woolverton. *The Lion King*, directed by Roger Allers and Rob Minkoff, 1994.

Juliet Mitchell and Jacqueline Rose (Eds), *Feminine Sexuality: Jacques Lacan and the école freudienne*. Trans. Jacqueline Rose. London: Macmillan Press, 1982.

Laura Mulvey, "Visual pleasure and narrative cinema." *Screen*, 16,3, 6-18, 1975.

Gertrude Postl, "Of ghosts, commodities, and women: Irigaray and Derrida." *Philosophy Today*, 43, 62-67, 1999.

Vladimir Propp, *Morphology of the Folktale*, Trans. Laurence Scott. Rev. and ed. Louis A. Wagner, Austin: University of Texas Press, 1968.

J.K. Rowling, *Harry Potter and the Phliosopher's Stone*, London: Bloomsbury, 1997.

J.K. Rowling, *Harry Potter and the Prisoner of Azkaban*. London: Bloomsbury, 1999.

Annette Wannamaker, "Specters of Potters: inheritance in the Harry Potter series." In *Elsewhere: Selected Essays from the "20th Century Fantasy Literature: From Beatrix to Harry" International Literary Conference*, edited by Deborah Bice. Lanham: University Press of America, 45-57, 2003.

D.W. Winnicott, *Playing and Reality*. London: Tavistock Publications, 1971.

I would like to thank the organisers of the conference, the presenters, and those participants who asked questions and provided feedback, all of which has proved so helpful in developing my initial ideas.

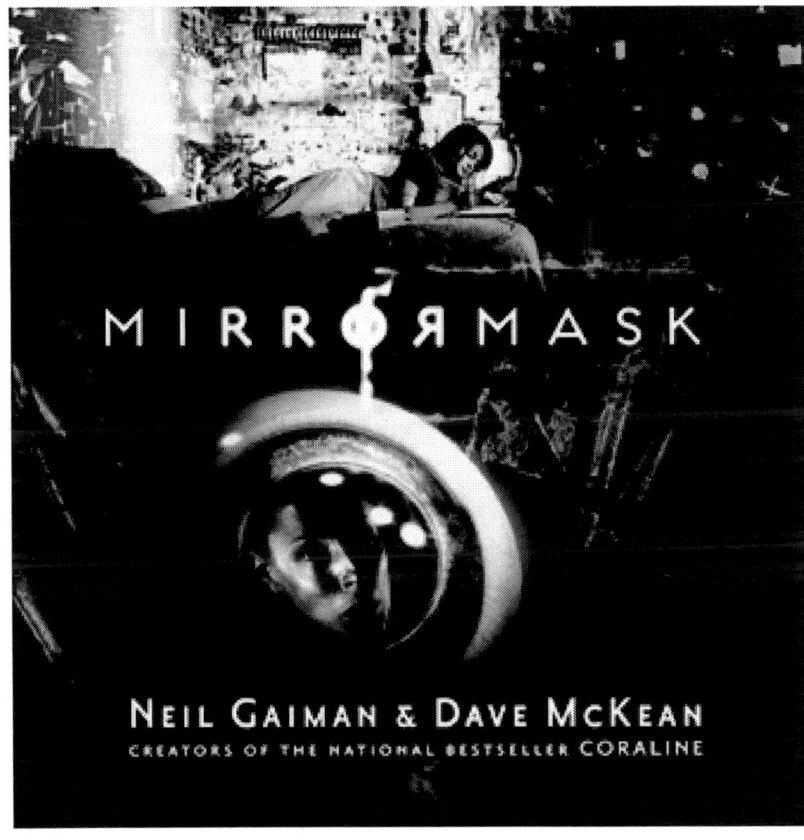

Debbie Hindle and Sylvia Wilson

Dialogues with Literature and Psychoanalysis

CHILDREN'S LITERATURE has the power to delight and inspire. But good literature, like fables and fairy tales, touches on universal themes – issues of separation, loss, fear, cruelty, regret, love – which are encountered in children's literature by the child as the central character, who is often also shown to be struggling internally with mixed emotions or real moral dilemmas. This is the stuff of internal conflict, of growth and development, which is also at the heart of psychoanalytic thinking and personality development.

From 2000-2002, at the Scottish Institute of Human Relations, we held two series of public lectures in Glasgow, bringing together contemporary Scottish children's writers in discussion with child and adolescent psychotherapists. The series was also supported by Glasgow City Libraries (who funded 10 places for children's librarians to attend) and by the Scottish Book Trust (who subsidised the authors' fees). The idea behind the series was also strongly influenced by Michael and Margaret Rustin's (2001) book *Narratives of Love and Loss*.

The series was aimed at parents, teachers, play therapists, psychotherapists, librarians – 'All those who work with children and those who are still children at heart!'

The first series, *Story and Imagination* was planned to follow the development of children from early childhood through to adolescence. The authors were chosen because they primarily (although not exclusively) wrote for a particular age group. The aim of this series was to explore the way in which books for children can enhance our understanding of the child's inner world and the way in which inner preoccupations change during the course of development.

The second series, *Childhood Past and Present* dealt with the struggles involved in the transition from late childhood to adolescence and the difficult issues involved in apprehending the world and in seeking independence.

In both series, the authors reflected on how they imaginatively re-created the world of childhood through the medium of fiction. From where did they draw their material? How did they enter the world of the child or young person? Many authors also talked about personal experiences that had a profound impact on them and had influenced their writing.

For the child and adolescent psychotherapists involved in this project, it opened the door to a different imaginative process – in linking the stories and the challenges the characters encountered with observational or clinical work and to an understanding of the inner world. Klein (1955) described what she meant by the inner world as follows:

'This inner world consists of innumerable objects taken into the ego, corresponding partly to the multitude of varying aspects, good and bad, in which the parents (and other people) appeared to the child's unconscious mind throughout various stages of development. Further they also represent all the real people who are continually becoming internalised in a variety of situations provided by the multitude of ever-changing external experiences as well as phantasised ones. In addition, all these objects are in the inner world in an infinitely complex relation both with each other and with the self.'

This definition captures the complexity of the process of internalisation, the 'aliveness' of the interactions within the inner world, and helps us to understand the way in which it both colours and shapes our experience of reality.

The material that follows was drawn from the first and second series of lectures and is linked to two central aspects of the training and work of child and adolescent psychotherapists – observational skills and clinical work.

Debbie Hindle

Ethical Space in the Island of Struay

Mairi Hedderwick is a very popular Scottish children's writer and illustrator best known for her Katie Morag stories set on the mythical Isle of Struay. For many years Mairi lived on the island of Coll and many of her stories and her drawings are a testimony to her involvement in and observation of island life. Hedderwick repeatedly locates her main characters in the context of their families, the community and the natural world that surrounds them. Her attention to detail, seen in her illustrations, has many parallels with her capacity to attend to the child's inner world and her understanding of a child's need for space, internal and external – space to find their own emotional truth.

Katie Morag and the Tiresome Ted

The story opens to great excitement with the birth of a new baby in her family – an excitement shared with and enjoyed by all the community. (Slide 6) Everyone seems delighted, except Katie, who complains that 'no one talks to me any more…or brings me presents.' But everyone says, 'Don't worry. Katie Morag will soon get over it.'

> 'But Katie could not and would not get over it. She kept doing naughty things, like stamping her feet and nipping her little brother….One day she was so cross that she stomped all the way down to the jetty and kicked her friendly old one-eyed teddy bear into the sea. 'Tiresome Ted!' she shouted, as he disappeared into the choppy waves.'

By now her mother said she couldn't cope – looking after the new baby, Liam her younger brother and Katie – who was 'too much of a handful!' and she was sent to her Grannie's for a few days. In Hedderwick's illustration, we see Katie trudging her way up a hill towards Grannie's, alone and buffeted by a gathering storm that mirrors the upset and conflict she seems to be experiencing internally.

But even before leaving her home and family, Katie was missing her Ted and regretted having thrown him away. In the illustrations, we see her tossing and turning in her bed, unable to sleep without him, eventually creeping to her brother's bed and taking his hot-water bottle – 'but even it didn't make her feel much better'. Several days later when the storm subsided and the sun came out, Katie took a walk along the shore in front of her Grannie's house and to her amazement, she found Ted washed up on the beach, soggy and torn, but unmistakably Ted. Her delight at finding him is beautifully portrayed.

What follows are scenes of her repairing him by sewing his torn tummy, sneaking the newly laundered baby-grow out of Grannie's washing basket, and returning to her mum and the new baby. In this illustration, Katie is seen holding Ted in her arms, now dressed in her baby brother's baby-grow, standing next to her mum who is nursing her baby in much the same way.

In this story, we see Katie's anger and upset. Her feelings of being excluded, her wish to get rid of the new baby and her anger towards her parents all seem to be projected into Ted, who is literally kicked into the sea (much as she too feels kicked out of her central position in the family). Yet, feelings of longing, regret and loneliness soon creep in. It is hard to feel only one way when feelings of love and the wish to be part of a family jostle with feelings of hate. Katie's attempts to repair Ted – externally – can be seen as having parallels with what seems to be going on inside – a process worthy of Klein's (1937) 'Love, guilt and reparation.' In Katie's use of the baby-grow, we see another parallel, her identification with her mother – both in terms of the care Katie's mother had given her (now also witnessed in relation to the new baby) and in relation to aspirations for her own future – the possibility of being a mother and having children of her own (seen also in her handling of Ted).

We can see that Katie doesn't just 'get over it' – rather the story describes 'something happening inside' which requires space, time and effort. In the lecture series, Mairi Hedderwick made specific reference to children's need for space in which to reflect on experience, an idea that has many parallels with Fonagy et al's (1991) 'reflective thinking' which he defines 'as that ability to think about one's own experience and the capacity to imaginatively see oneself from another point of view.'

In this story, we also see the importance of the availability of extended family members. In this case, it is the grandmother who seems to provide a containing function for Katie and facilitates her capacity to emotionally digest the changes she is faced with (Bion, 1962).

The birth of a new baby is an ordinary enough experience – and yet it requires enormous adjustments: for the parents – to manage the demands of more than one child and to hold them in mind; and for the children – to accommodate to what may feel like a betrayal or loss, perhaps most poignantly of their baby selves. In any ordinary family, there may also be considerable ambivalence about the new baby. In kicking 'Tiresome Ted' into the sea, might Katie also be acting out her own parents' unconscious wish, perhaps, in relation to the 'troublesome' new baby, displaced onto the 'troublesome' Katie? (It is a significant part of the story that the 'last straw' that made her mother so furious was when Katie wet the bed.)

Young Child Observation

Throughout the UK there are a numerous Observational Studies courses, based on the Tavistock course which include one module on Young Child Observation. This seminar offers the opportunity to study the emotional development of a child of between two and four years old, within the context of his/her family, the wider community and in nurseries, and the impact of group and peer relations and institutional dynamics. The learning outcomes of this course could be summarised:

- to develop a capacity to observe, to maintain an observational stance, and to be sensitive to issues that may have an impact on the task of observation
- to develop an awareness of the emotional impact on the observer and an understanding of this in relation to the concept of countertransference
- to develop the capacity to reflect on the interaction and relationship between the young child and others, with particular reference to the emotional qualities of these and to unconscious processes
- to develop an understanding of ordinary development of young children at this stage, including the significance of play, symbolisation and language

- to develop an awareness of the impact of family and the wider community at home, or the significance of peer relations and institutional dynamics at nursery

What follows are excerpts from two young child observations undertaken and written by Anne Hainan, who is a member of this seminar at the Scottish Institute of Human Relations in Glasgow. Both observations take place in the home of the A. family. Present in the observations are the mother Jenny, Jaimie aged 3 years 5 months and his younger brother, Jake, who is just six weeks old at the time of the first observation. Their father is at work during the observations, but had been involved in the initial discussions and negotiations in relation to the observation.

First Observation

'When I arrived, Jaimie answered the door. He was expecting my visit as Jenny, his mother, told me how she had reminded him that I was coming. In the living room, Jake was lying on a furry baby rug on the floor and appeared to be asleep. Jaimie remained near his mother at first, but then wanted to show me his bedroom. He took his mother's hand and led her to the room and I followed. After some discussion between them, Jaimie settled on a number and picture matching game which Jenny said he had never played before. We all returned to the living room.

Jaimie pulled the game on to the floor and then brought it to show me. As he and his mother began preparing to play the game, the cat jumped up onto my knee and wanted to be stroked and simultaneously, baby Jake woke up and began to cry softly. Jaimie said to me that he had a new baby. Jenny indicated that there had been some jealousy issues with Jaimie in relation to Jake, while picking the baby up and rocking him in her arms.

Jaimie insisted on asking his mother to help him put the pieces of the game together. Jenny encouraged him verbally whilst holding Jake who almost immediately responded to his mother's touch and became quiet. Jaimie then tried to show me the game, but appeared not quite able to focus on it. Jake began crying again and Jaimie told his mother that he needed a plaster and held his finger up for her to see. Jenny asked him what he had done, but Jaimie didn't appear to know, eventually saying she (mother) had done it! Jenny got a plaster and, after much searching, placed the plaster on Jaimie's finger.

Later, Jake became unsettled again and mother rocked and fed him. Jaimie went over to the sofa and tried to get under his mother's arm, attempting to kiss Jake, but in a way that was a bit too rough, making him cry. Jenny told Jaimie to be a bit gentler. He then started to hang on to his mother's arm and threatened to bite her to which she protested, 'don't do that!' Jaimie then tried to turn this into a kiss. His mother tried again to interest him in the game, but eventually helped him to settle to watch a cartoon, Pingu. As he watched, he rolled a pen lid back and forth between his thumb and forefinger.

Later still, Jaimie and his mother had a brief conflict over an item she said he could not have. Jaimie said to his mother that he was very angry with her and that she was not to smile at him. She seemed to accept this and returned to the living room, and Jake. Jaimie then asked me to join him in his game. But soon it was time for me to leave.'

Reflections

In this observation, Jaimie is at pains to get to know Anne, showing her his room, selecting the matching game, and introducing her to his baby brother. But when his mother's attention turns to the baby, Jaimie competes for her attention, wanting her help with the game and asking for a plaster, his hurt finger representing rather a veiled guise for his hurt feelings and a parallel demand, which echo Jake's tears. When questioned, Jaimie claims mum did it (hurt his finger). Attempts to occupy the space that Jake now holds – in mother's arms – are met with tolerance, but his 'hugs' and kisses were too rough. Efforts to get Jaimie to be gentler led to his threatening to bite her, later openly voiced by his saying he was very angry with her. Watching Pingu and seeking solace with Anne are momentary distractions in an otherwise turbulent time for this young boy.

Second Observation

This observation took place two months later when Jaimie was 3 years 8 months and his baby brother, Jake, just over three months old.

'I arrived at the house at midday and Jaimie answered the door shouting, 'It's Anne!' I entered the house and said hello. Jenny was feeding baby Jake who was on her lap, feeding hungrily, his cheeks bright red. Jenny later said that both Jaimie and Jake had colds last week.

At this point, Jaimie was looking into a toy box, but was moving from one activity to another. Jenny helped him set up some Lego while continuing to feed the baby. As she fed Jake, she talked to me about the difficulty of finding the right childminder, in anticipation of her returning to work in four months. Simultaneously, Jaimie was running up and down the room becoming very excitable. He ran up to Jake and squeezed him in a way that upset him. Jenny tried to refocus Jaimie on the Lego. I felt uncomfortable and had to resist offering to hold the baby or to set up the Lego myself.

Jenny returned to her concern regarding the childminder, stating that it was preoccupying her and that this was stopping her from enjoying the rest of her maternity leave. I noted a serious look on Jake's face and Jamie continued to run up and down. He appeared unsettled and unable to concentrate on the Lego or the other game that his mother had set up for him.

Jaimie began shouting and again ran up to Jake and squeezed him in a 'hug' that made him cry. His mother tried to distract him again, but he started to throw his toys around. Jenny told Jaimie not to do this explaining that it was dangerous as it might hit someone, but he continued to stamp about the room. Jenny said firmly that he was not to do this, but Jaimie ran away to his room shouting that he was angry. He remained there a couple of minutes, shouting, but in a way that also sounded as if he were upset.

Jenny called to Jaimie to come back into the room. She put Jake in a baby seat on the floor. Jaimie returned from his room with a memory stick for the computer which he said he had found in his shoe. Jenny spoke to him about not taking things (he had previously taken her mobile phone and hid it in his room). He said he was sorry and for a time he was able to settle watching a cartoon on TV.

Later, he and his mother built a train track together, fitting the different pieces in the correct positions. He placed the train on the track. He placed two plastic grey-headed figures in one of the trains saying that they were grandma and granddad. He moved the trains around, saying to one of the trains at the back 'I don't want to be at the back' and moved it to the front. As the play continued, Jaimie knocked down the bridge and often the trains crashed or came off the track. At one point, he stopped the game and started to 'hug' Jake, but in a different, more companionable way.'

Reflections

During this observation, Jaimie was excitable, restless and unable to settle to playing with his Lego. But his mother was also preoccupied, worried about finding the right childminder and returning to work. As his mother talks to Anne about this, each time Jaimie appears to feel upset or anxious, he squeezes and upsets Jake, literally projecting his anxiety and upset into him. However, Anne also notes that Jake seems to have a serious expression and that both boys had colds the previous week. Anne too feels mother's discomfort and dilemma, at times describing wanting to either hold the baby or to help Jaimie with his Lego. How difficult it is to deal with the needs of two young children at the same time!

Mother's complaint that Jaimie is taking things seems to coincide with his taking the very things that take his mother away from him – her mobile phone and the memory stick for her computer – and perhaps also reflects *his* preoccupation with her thoughts about returning to work and leaving him. But his wish to make reparation, to return the stick and to say he is sorry is later played out when he and his mother build the train track together. However, the train doesn't have an easy ride and there are worries about being 'at the back.' How to be part of a family and to manage conflicting feelings is clearly a difficult task!

In these observations, there are also many parallels with the story of *Katie Morag and the Tiresome Ted*. Like Katie, in his play with the train, Jaimie places his grandparents in a key position. Like Katie, Jaimie's anger and upset about the birth of his little brother seems plain for all to see. Yet, Jaimie, also like Katie, struggles to manage these feelings and to re-establish a more loving relationship with his mother and Jake. But in the second observation, we see a different dynamic emerging. When Jenny talks to Anne about returning to work, at this point, the two boys are not in competition with each other, but here there is the potential for their having to bear a shared experience. They are literally 'in the same boat' in relation to their mother and their circumstances. Towards the end of this observation, Anne notes a different quality to Jaimie's hugging Jake. Here he does not seem intent on projecting his anxieties, but there are intimations of the beginning of a sense of their being siblings and comrades – part of another generation and separate from that of their parents. Here might we also see the beginning of Jaimie taking on another aspect of his developing identity – that of 'big brother' in relation to his baby brother.

Some Psychoanalytic Perspectives on the Birth of a Younger Sibling

In Freud's (1909) 'Little Hans' there is much rich evidence for the impact of a new baby's arrival. Hannah, Little Hans' younger sister, was born when he was three and a half years old (just the age that Jaimie was when Jake was born). Shortly after this, he developed a fever and was heard saying, *'But I don't want a baby sister.'* In Freud's case study, there was much evidence of his jealousy towards her, rivalry for his mother's care, death wishes against the baby and fears of a new pregnancy.

At the end of the second section of Freud's discussion, he emphasizes the impact the birth of his sister had on Hans. 'That event accentuated his relations to his parents and gave him some insoluble problems to think about; and later, as he watched the way in which the infant was looked after, the memory-traces of his own earliest experiences of pleasure were revived in him.' As Sherwin-White (2007: 8) succinctly summarises, 'The changes for Hans, losses – initial separation from his mother and privation with regard to the hitherto exclusive care from his parents – excitation of his emotional needs, the consequent stimulation of defensive phantasies and sexual action (masturbation), and the stirring of what was later to be called epistemophilia about the huge subject of where babies come from are richly delineated by Freud.'

It would be impossible to give justice to all that Freud has written about brothers and sisters and their complex relationships. Much has recently been written about sibling relationships by Coles (2003) and Mitchell (2003) and also in a special edition of the *Journal of Child Psychotherapy*, 33 (1), 2007. But Klein poignantly reminds us of the importance of sibling relationships and the longing for and meaning of having a sibling. In her paper 'On

Identification,' Klein (1955) states, 'Particularly youngest and only children often have a strong sense of guilt because they feel that their jealous and aggressive impulses have prevented their mother from giving birth to any more children. Such feelings are also bound up with fears of retaliation and persecution... The longing for friendly brothers and sisters is strongly influenced by such anxieties.'

In the story, Katie reconciles herself with her mother and her baby brother and achieves a new position as 'big sister.' It doesn't 'just happen,' neither does Katie (or Jaimie in the observation) 'just get over it.' It involves a process that cannot be overtly seen or observed, but can be surmised (as when Jaimie rolls the pen top between his thumb and fore finger). It is about something happening inside, in the child's inner world. What good literature does, and children's literature in particular, is capture these states of mind and to portray this through writing and illustrations in a ways that can capture our imagination and also facilitate the kinds of working through that are so necessary throughout our lives.

Sylvia Wilson

Children on the Edge: Insights from Literature and Psychoanalysis

IN THE NARRATIVES of literature the creation of believable characters brings to the reader a sense of emotional truth. In the narratives of psychotherapy the emergence of emotional truth has the potential to enrich the personalities of both the patient and the therapist. This concern with meaning through emotional truth is clearly part of what enables the dialogue between literature and psychoanalysis. It is also part of what the reading child will listen for and what the child in therapy will recover through.

In this paper I will draw on material from psychotherapy with an 8-year-old child who, through the story and ownership of his own narrative, brought me a new way of seeing his experience and those of many children like him. I shall link this to the work of Anne Fine, and her characters and narratives in *The Tulip Touch* and *Step by Wicked Step*, to consider the experience of children 'on the edge' – on the edge of society and family life and on the edge of what can be articulated or emotionally borne.

In *Step by Wicked Step*, the setting of a school trip in a castle felt to be haunted is the theatre for shared discovery. Five children, each of whom feels burdened with a unique and lonely experience, tell their stories of loss, relationship with step-parents, siblings and accommodation to change. The book holds together like a set of musical variations on a theme, each story and narrator distinctive and separate in detail of theme, pace and tonal quality, reflecting and conveying the range of emotional experience and atmosphere that reconstituted families can yield and provide. The setting, and the link to history in the Dickensian tale of Richard Clayton Harwick, the boy who previously lived in the castle, conveys the sense of cross-generational dilemmas and the idea that telling the stories is a means for the children of exorcising both present and future ghosts. The children are often the peace-keepers in the families, but they are also the eavesdroppers. The sense of secrecy, truth, lies, or what Wilfred Bion might call + / - K, is woven around like the spiders' webs, which wait to be broken only when the room in the castle tower is opened and history is revisited, opening it up to re-evaluation.

In Claudia's story, we are shown how the realisation of active agency in one's own life can be a turning-point, important to resolution of oedipal conflict. Over time, she frees herself from her mother's and her own rivalry with her step-mother for her father's affections. Her moral sense of the sheer rudeness of her father's friends towards her step-mother is a point of recognition of her own behaviour; and a point of choice. She enables for herself a hesitant, but meaningful start to forming a new relationship, and thus not cutting herself off from experience open to her.

Ralf, Pixie and Robbie all contend with complexities of multiple step-siblings and relationships. "Complexity, not woe" is how Ralf describes his dilemma. In Robbie's account of his sister Callie, it is also clear that the complexities are compounded by wishes and phantasy that separated parents will get back together again; and that difficult behaviour in the children can be reflections of these common phantasies and complex Oedipal struggles.

Colin is perhaps the saddest child, locked as he is in unresolved grief, frozen mourning and a world of absent and part objects. He clings desperately to his Dad's tobacco tin and their favourite song, skating poorly on the ice rink and through life, more encapsulated in sensory experience than alive in emotional experience, looking to disappear in search of his Dad.

Colin reminds us of the importance of mourning. He says of his Dad, "I never finished with him." Hope comes in the sense of being able to tell the whole story, which was until then a 'No story', perhaps what Wilfred Bion would call an "Empty thought". The process of telling the 'No story', and finding its contents, becomes the much needed whole experience and the 'autistic' object, the tobacco tin, is transformed into the transitional object of a small wooden cow, carved by Richard Clayton Harwick, given by the group to Colin. A child's capacity for tolerance of frustration and what might be reasonable to expect of any child arises again when Colin says, "It isn't very nice to have to keep waiting and hoping."

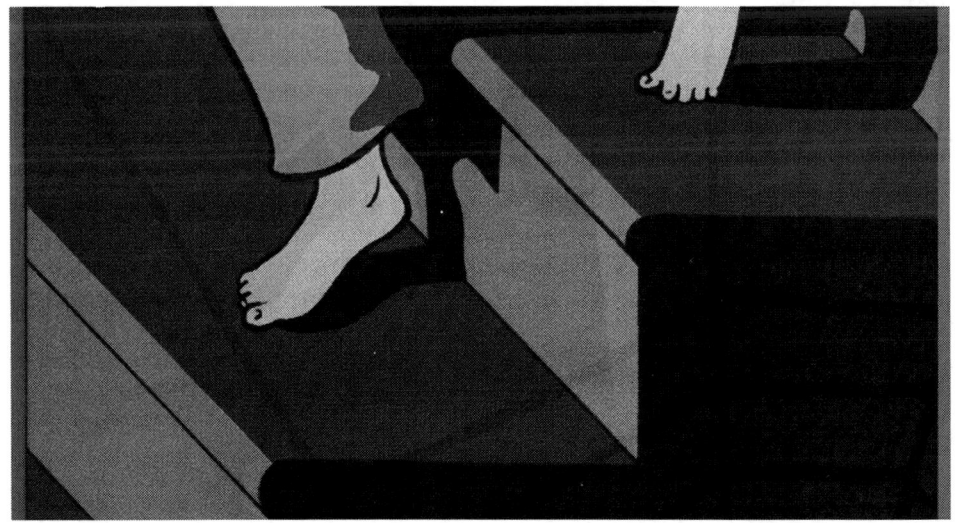

The Tulip Touch is a book which raises serious questions about how we become who we are. Tulip's story is revealed through Natalie, the fallible narrator, who both tells the story and is a party to the plot, humour, passionate excitement and dark obsession in the friendship.

Tulip, a volatile, neglected and abused girl, is from the start seen as 'on the edge' – on the edge of the field, where the girls first meet; on the edge of her social world at school; on the edge of reality in her phantasies and lies; and increasingly on the edge of speechless, fearful rage, which ultimately finds its expulsive and explosive expression in her violent act of arson. She destroys the Palace Hotel, which is Natalie's home and the closest thing Tulip has ever known to a caring environment.

Experience has placed Tulip on the edge, but in her self-portrait, painted at school and executed contemptuously, we glimpse what we often see in therapy with such youngsters, a sense of a self without edges, a devouring whirlpool of terrifying confusion.

In Natalie's story we see something different, a fragility which makes her vulnerable to becoming Tulip's coat holder and victim of cruelty; but a minimal environmental containment, which allows her to live, not on the edge, but just inside the perimeter of life, eventually able to find her way back to the centre of things. If neglect is present in Natalie's early adolescent world, so too is the space – both physical and emotional – to play, pretend and explore boundaries of the external and internal world. Her world is occupied by welcome and unwelcome guests. Boredom and rivalry, and their potential to invade family life, seem to be the source of Natalie's conflicts. What is not damaged by experience in Natalie is the capacity for emotional experience and reflection itself. While she says, "it is difficult to get sufficient attention in a busy hotel (unless you are a paying guest)", life has somehow empowered her to feel an active agency in her own life. She realises that even the quality of her relationship with her parents is not without her own responsibility. With the recognition of her own role in the relationship, insight and integrity stay intact, as does her healthy moral indignation that something more might have been done for Tulip and herself, if it had not been more comfortable for the adults not to see.

As child and adolescent psychotherapists, we know we cannot afford to be sentimental about the lives or destructive capacities of the young people we see. Anne Fine clearly knows that compassion is tough and avoids the dishonesty of sentimentality, challenging it constantly. Sentimentality as dulled and dishonest emotion, which barely grasps at meaning and ultimately sickens the mind, rather than strengthens it, is shown for what it is in Tulip's earlier, endless drawings of "children with huge forlorn eyes, copied from soppy greetings cards she has lifted from the shop beyond the bus stop." Such repetition of a single frozen image, in the clinical setting, often gives us a clue to the child's dilemma and state of mind.

In the narratives and character of Tulip, I feel we encounter the question of limits of what a young mind can tolerate when confronted by neglect, cruelty and the barren, weary despair of parents already broken by life themselves. Anne Fine captures what we see in the consulting room with children, when the consequence of relentless abuse is not simply the trauma of events in themselves, but a deeply insidious impingement on the very process, fabric and formation of mind and personality in the growing child. In the organising, evolutionary processes of childhood, states of mind so easily become traits of personality. If their origins are not understood, they can be seen as unavailable to change and only as part of the person's moral make-up, which they must be unequivocally responsible for and sometimes condemned to.

When Calum came into therapy at the age of 7 years he was in serious danger of obliterating his own capacity for thinking. His unarticulated mental distress was erupting into dangerous mindless violence and in danger of becoming a trait. His disappointment in the adults around him was becoming disappointment and contempt of all adults. Like many children we see in therapy, family life and education had broken down completely for him. He lived in a children's home and was excluded from school. He refused any idea of a foster family. He was passionately attached to his mother, vehemently defensive of her should anyone criticise her, but equally violently aggressive towards her. She was heavily addicted to drugs. He was necessarily omnipotently defended against his vulnerability. Like Colin, he was left endlessly waiting and hoping. Like Tulip, repeated traumatic experience was rapidly limiting his chances of recovery.

Early in our work together he brought me an image; and with it something of his experience of terrifying confusion and growing despair.

Session material

He began to paint a lively colourful scene of family, a house, people, a garden and a deep red and yellow warm sun filling the sky behind the house. I felt surprised and hopeful. But without a pause he mixed a large quantity of brown, black and blue paint into the water; and dropping the brush spread this with both hands over the image, the table and himself. It dripped from his fingers. My heart sank. Violence and sadness seemed to be leaking from him. I felt witness to an overwhelming, contaminating depression, which permeated everything in its reach, spoiling and obliterating the realities of an ordinary infants' disposition towards joy, warmth and the hope of relatedness.

He grasped the picture at its edges, as if to rip it up. I quickly commented to him that I thought he wanted me to understand something about his disappointments and the way he feels that good feelings between people and his own efforts get spoiled and messed up; and while he is worried I might mess things up here, he also wants me to know he can sometimes get himself into a mess. He paused and so I continued, saying, "although we now only have the memory of your bright sunny picture, perhaps understanding the messed up picture and your own feelings of getting messed up is important; and I think we should keep the picture to think more about it." He placed it on the couch. It remained in the room with us for many months.

In not totally destroying the picture, but in responding to my interpretation, he stayed engaged with the possibility of understanding something in therapy. But emotional understanding for a child, who feels himself to be in constant danger of spilling out, is hard won. We had months of relentless testing of boundaries in which mess was created, graffiti was smeared on the therapy room walls and dangerous and violent behaviour never seemed far away as he sought out the electric sockets, swung on the curtains or leapt up onto the windowsill, attacking my capacity to think as he did so. Interpretation, when I could find the words, often seemed to escalate his defensive omnipotence as he struggled, only to evacuate pain and thought. However outside the sessions things were improving and he had returned to education in a small unit. I began to realise that his activity kept me on my toes, and kept me, in his mind, as a lively if still troublesome adult. I was at least conscious.

Session Material

One day, as he stood dangerously on the window sill, reaching for the electric light, towering above me, I said, "It is as well someone here has her feet on the ground because if no one did, where would we be?"

The speed with which he jumped down surprised me, as did the sense of contact with him in this moment. For the first time I felt he had a sense of humour.

While the change was gradual, it did come, and just over a year into his therapy he had begun to explore the toys in his box and to feel sufficiently safe to play. He would also make jokes and enjoy teasing me in a less contemptuous way. But there was an increasing seriousness in him.

Session Material

He came into one session subdued and said he wanted to be quiet today. He took the toys from his box and lay sprawled out on the floor close to me with his head under my chair, as if perhaps he wanted protection for his thinking. He began to play with the small animals, some wild, and some domestic. He arranged them in their family groups, naming the parents, children and babies. He then gathered a small group of young lambs, pigs and tigers together and placed them at a distance from the main family groups. He looked up at me and said, "But what is going to happen to these?" Without waiting for a response from me, he placed a police car beside them and said, with a serious tone, "They are the 'left-over children' – they don't have families to look after them and we get into trouble. The police will have to go and round them up now."

The scene enacted became one which I knew to be vividly akin to events for him during that week, as he had absconded from the children's unit with some older boys. But what touched me and enabled me to talk a little with him about the events and his wish that people will come after him to keep him safe was his naming of 'the left-over children'. This was a creative contribution to our joint understanding of his narrative and the meaning of his emotional experience. It is a statement of social definition as much as a statement of personal history. This was how, through experience, he had come to perceive himself and others in the eyes of society. The narcissistic pain of being left out in some degree is to be negotiated and come to terms with by all of us, as we negotiate our Oedipal conflicts and the meaning of our social relationships, but to be 'left over' implies being superfluous and redundant to the needs of society.

Like many children we see in therapy today, this child's self-esteem was negligible and a terrifying abject despair permeated his sense of self when he came into therapy. Not only had he been subjected to the pain and chaotic experience of his parents' neglect and suffering, but being without family or education he had lost both a sense of internal containment and the essential scaffolding in which to develop a social existence. At the end of *The Tulip Touch* Natalie reflects,

> "There is no particular moment when someone goes to the bad. Each horrible thing that happens to them makes a difference .... But people aren't locked doors. You can get through to them if you want to."

Calum had not quite imprisoned himself behind the locked doors of complete mistrust. Despite his mother's problems, in his picture he was able to show me that although something was in danger of being obliterated, something good and hopeful had perhaps once been there. As he began to recover, he was able better to consider that his mother failed to look after him because of her problems and illness, not because he was of himself bad. He began to experience his sadness rather than evacuate it in violent and antisocial behaviour and, with this experience, to find complexity and some space for his struggle with conflicting feelings of love and hate.

The subjects and characters of children's books both express and to some degree define what society perceives as belonging to childhood and children's experience. Psychoanalytic psychotherapy is a process that can help children such as Calum to articulate their stories and so unburden themselves of unmanageable experience. But we need to grasp that the urgency and hope, in trying to help children in childhood, rests in the view of childhood, not as a waiting time for entrance into adulthood, constantly speeded up and rushed through, but as an essential passage in which processes of mental organisation are occurring; minds are developing; personalities are taking shape, and lived experience is making us who we are.

AUTHOR'S NOTE
To protect confidentiality, the name of the child referred to has been changed and every effort has been made to disguise his identity, but not in ways that change the meaning of the observation and clinical material.

REFERENCES

Anne Fine, *The Tulip Touch*. London: Hamish Hamilton, 1996.

Anne Fine, *Step By Wicked Step*. London: Hamish Hamilton, 1995.

W. Bion, *Learning from Experience*, London: Heinemann, 1962.

P. Coles, *The Importance of Sibling Relationships in Psychoanalysis*, London: Karnac, 2003.

S. Freud, 'Little Hans' *Standard Edition 10*, London: Hogarth Press, 1909.

P. Fonagy, M. Steele, G. Moran and A. Higgins,'The capacity for understanding mental states: the reflective self in parent and child and its significance for security of attachment', *Infant Mental Health Journal*,12: 201-218, 1991.

M. Hedderwick, *Katie Morag and the Tiresome Ted*, London: Random House, 1986.

M. Klein, 'On identification', In *Envy and Gratitude and Other Works*, London: Hogarth Press, 1955.

M. Klein, 'Love, guilt and reparation', in *Love, Guilt and Reparation*, London: Hogarth Press, 1937.

J. Mitchell, *Siblings: Sex and Violence*, Oxford: Blackwell / Polity, 2003.

M.E. Rustin and M. Rustin, *Narratives of Love and Loss: Studies in Modern Children's Fiction*, London: Karnac, 2001.

S. Sherwin-White, 'Freud on brothers and sisters: A neglected topic', *Journal of Child Psychotherapy*, 33 (1): 4-20, 2007.

Andrea Peterson

The Representation of Shell Shock in Michael Morpurgo's *Private Peaceful*

IN HIS POSTSCRIPT to *Private Peaceful*, Michael Morpurgo highlights the fact that during

> ...the First World War... over 290 soldiers of the British and Commonwealth armies were executed by firing squad.... Many of these men we now know were traumatised by shell shock (Morpurgo, 2004, p.187).

In this paper I will examine the representation of shell shock in *Private Peaceful*. Morpurgo's narrative is focalised through Thomas "Tommo" Peaceful as he waits for his brother, Charlie, to be executed. Tommo looks back over their lives, from their schooldays to the more recent events that led to Charlie's court-martial.

Morpurgo's Postscript suggests that when Charlie disobeys his Sergeant's orders to 'press home' an 'attack' (Morpurgo, 2004, p.171), he is suffering from shell shock. During the First World War, shell shock was a controversial term and its use was not encouraged. Many men who suffered from shell shock had never been in close proximity to an exploding shell; hence, the use of the term was officially banned in June 1917. General Routine Order No. 2384 informed all medical personnel that men who became 'non-effective' but were 'without any visible wound' were to be sent to 'the Special Hospital' (quoted in Macdonald, [1980] 1993, pp.236–237) without any diagnosis being made. Their papers were to show them as '"NYDN" (Not Yet Diagnosed, Nervous)', and '[i]n no circumstances whatever' was 'the expression "shellshock" [to] be used verbally or... recorded' (Macdonald, [1980] 1993, p.237). This directive regarding official terminology is highly significant. It indicates that it was officially recognised that many 'forms of mental disturbance [...] could not be attributed to isolated incidents or obvious causes', and that very few cases of 'nervousness' were actually 'the result of having been blown up or injured by an explosion' (Macdonald, [1980] 1993, p.235). Moreover, the use of the term 'nervous' rather than 'shellshock' pre-empts Edwin Ash's post-war position that war-induced nervousness was remarkably similar to civilian nervous breakdown. In his study, *The Problem of Nervous Breakdown* – published in 1919 - Ash argues that

> breakdown on the field of battle... is enormously favoured by certain predisposing conditions. So much so... that one is tempted to believe that a complete record of

> *the past life of each man who suffers from a war neurosis would certainly reveal the occurrence of one or other [predisposing factors]* (Ash, 1919, p.273).

Further, Ash explains that 'careful inquiry into the life history of sufferers from nervous disorders very often reveals the fact that from [their] earliest years there have been manifestations of instability' (Ash, 1919, p.240).

Although it is Charlie who is ultimately tried by court martial and executed – thereby suggesting he is one of the many shell shocked men Morpurgo refers to in his Postscript – it is Thomas who exhibits an hereditary predisposition to nervousness, thereby seemingly rendering the closure of Morpurgo's narrative problematic. I would suggest that the trauma of feeling responsible for his father's death causes Tommo to experience sustained 'nerve tension' (Ash, 1919, p.244) and that this, consequently, makes him, rather than Charlie, predisposed to war neurosis. A detailed analysis of the conduct of the two brothers would seem to support this notion.

Of the two brothers, it is Tommo who is the nervous child. Charlie always protects him – Charlie has 'done everything and knows everything. He's strong, too' (Morpurgo, 2004, p.8). Tommo is 'proud of him' and describes him as 'the bravest brother in the world' (Morpurgo, 2004, p.24).

Tommo is such a nervous child that he is frequently frozen by fear. In contrast to the passive or inactive Tommo, Charlie is held up as the epitome of masculine action. When Tommo tries to collect eggs, 'something [makes him] draw back, [makes him] hesitate', so he can't 'blow them… and lay them in cotton wool' in a tin 'like Charlie' (Morpurgo, 2004, p.9) does. At school, although there is 'a lot of fighting', Tommo confesses that he 'was never much good at it' (Morpurgo, 2004, p.22), and when he is provoked into fighting by the bullying Jimmy Parsons, Tommo doesn't 'manage to land a single punch' (Morpurgo, 2004, p.23). Instead, he 'curl[s] up in a ball like a hedgehog' until the attack 'finally stops' (Morpurgo, 2004, p.24). The reason Parsons stops kicking Tommo is that 'Charlie [is] grabbing him round the neck and pulling him to the ground' (Morpurgo, 2004, p.24). Charlie saves Tommo and is also punished for fighting by the Head Teacher, Mr Munnings – a pattern that is to be repeated during the War.

Much later, when the brothers go poaching, Charlie stands in the river fishing, whilst Tommo acts as lookout. Tommo falls asleep at his post and is caught by the Colonel's gamekeeper, Lambert. Charlie 'could have made a run for it and got clean away', but he wouldn't let Tommo take the blame for him and so they were both marched away '[a]t the point of a shotgun' (Morpurgo, 2004, p.49) in another scene that prefigures the crucial wartime events leading to Charlie's execution.

Throughout the narrative, Tommo's fragile psychological state is further evidenced by the nightmares he suffers. He says:

> *I used to have nightmares filled with... monster children, but whatever my nightmare it would always end the same way. I would be out in the woods with Father and the tree would be falling, and I'd wake up screaming* (Morpurgo, 2004, p.34).
>
> *I had my terrible secret, a secret I could scarcely ever put out of my mind. So in my guilt I kept more and more to myself* (Morpurgo, 2004, p.27).

This is the key to Tommo's trauma. The first time he is frozen by fear, Tommo finds himself responsible for the death of his father in a dramatic enactment of the Oedipal crisis. He says:

> *I looked up to see the great tree above me swaying.... Only slowly did I realise it was coming down... that I was going to die and there was nothing I could do about it. I stood and stared, mesmerised... my legs frozen under me, quite incapable of movement. I hear Father shouting: "Tommo! Tommo! Run, Tommo!" But I can't....*
>
> *I have inside me a secret so horrible, a secret I can never tell anyone.... Father needn't have died that morning in Ford's Cleave Wood. He was trying to save me. If only I had tried to save myself, if I had run, he would not now be lying dead in his coffin.... I have caused this. I have killed my own father'* (Morpurgo, 2004, pp.14 & 17).

Freud argues that 'the Oedipus complex reveals its importance as the central phenomenon... of early childhood' and that 'it is the experience of painful disappointments' (Freud, [1924] 1981, p.395). Further, he argues that

> [t]he first object of a boy's love is his mother.... The [father] is felt as a disturbing rival and not infrequently viewed with strong hostility.... [T]he child's wishes extend beyond... [his mother's] affection to all that we understand by sensual satisfaction.... We give the whole mental structure the name of 'Oedipus complex', after the familiar Greek legend.
> With the end of the early sexual period it should normally be given up, should radically disintegrate and become transformed.... (Freud, [1926] 1981, pp.32-33).

This transformation or dissolution is achieved when 'the child's ego turns away from the Oedipus complex', and 'object-cathexes are given up and replaced by identifications. The authority of the father... is introjected into the ego' (Freud, [1924] 1981, p.398). However, Freud cautions that if 'this is not effected radically enough... puberty brings about a revival of the [Oedipus] complex, which may have serious consequences' (Freud, [1926] 1981, p.33). Further, he explains that '[m]ental health very much depends on the super-ego's being normally developed.... And that is precisely what it is not in neurotics, whose Oedipus complex has not passed through the correct process of transformation' (Freud, [1926] 1981, p.42).

A Freudian analysis of Tommo's childhood development suggests that his initial Oedipal crisis was not resolved, thereby leaving him neurotic. Even when he has killed his father, who is perceived as his rival in Freudian terms,

Tommo fails to win his mother's affection and attention, as her time and energy are monopolised by her eldest son, Big Joe, who is brain-damaged having contracted meningitis as a baby. Tommo expresses his feelings of abandonment:

> Joe doesn't have to go to school.... He stays at home with Mother.... I wish I could be at home like him.... I don't want to go to school. I look back, over my shoulder, hoping for a reprieve, hoping that Mother will come running after me and take me home. But she doesn't come and she doesn't come (Morpurgo, 2004, p.8).

Consequently, Tommo's Oedipal complex is not effected and, therefore, it is not surprising that it is revived as he reaches puberty.

Charlie, who is three years older than Tommo, grows to replace their father and become the family patriarch:

> Charlie worked in the hunt kennels and in the stables.... [He] would come home late in the evenings as Father had before him, and he'd hang his coat up on Father's peg and put his boots outside in the porch where Father's boots had always been. He warmed his feet in the bottom oven when he came in out of the cold of a winter's day, just as Father had done. That was the first time in my life I was ever really jealous of Charlie. I wanted to put my feet in the oven, and to come home from proper work, to earn money like Charlie did (Morpurgo, 2004, pp.53-4).

Further, Tommo transfers his love for his mother onto a local girl, Molly. Molly initially becomes a substitute mother for Tommo as she is a little older than him. On his first day at school, she helps him to tie his shoelaces and this small act of kindness prompts him to declare: 'Suddenly I no longer want to run home. I want to stay here with Molly' (Morpurgo, 2004, p.13). She is gradually accepted into the Peaceful family as a surrogate 'sister' (Morpurgo, 2004, p.25) and daughter. However, as Charlie and Tommo reach puberty, they both begin to harbour feelings of sexual desire for her. As usual, Tommo is passive, whereas Charlie is active. Tommo confesses that '[l]ate one evening, sitting by the bridge... *Molly took my hand in hers and held it tight*.... I had never been so happy' (Morpurgo, 2004, p.41, my italics). In contrast to this rather innocent display of affection, instigated by Molly, Charlie 'take[s] off all his clothes' and together with Molly, runs 'shrieking and bare-bottomed into the water' (Morpurgo, 2004, p.44) of Okement Pool. Tommo's passivity is demonstrated further, as he explains that '[w]hen they called me in after them, I wouldn't do it, not in front of Molly. So I sat and sulked on the bank and watched them splashing and giggling' (Morpurgo, 2004, p.44).

This is, nevertheless, an early erotic experience for Tommo. He admits that this is 'the first time [he] ever saw a girl with no clothes on' (Morpurgo, 2004, p.44). His voyeuristic pleasure is heightened further as 'Molly got dressed afterwards behind a bush and told us not to watch. But we did' (Morpurgo,

2004, p.44). Freud writes that '[it] is usual for most normal people to linger to some extent over the intermediate sexual aim of a looking that has a sexual tinge to it' (Freud, 1981, p.300), particularly as a precursor to sexual intercourse. However, he warns that 'this pleasure in looking [scopophilia] becomes a perversion... if, instead of being preparatory to the normal sexual aim, it supplants it' (Freud, 1981, p.300).

Both Tommo and Charlie evidently continue to derive pleasure from watching Molly as they mature. She is described as having

> [h]er hair... cut shorter. The plaits were gone, and somehow that changed the whole look of her. She wasn't a girl any more. She had a different beauty now (Morpurgo, 2004, p.52).

However, Tommo notices that although 'she was as kind to [him] as she had always been', Molly was 'too protective, more like a little mother to [him]' (Morpurgo, 2004, p.54). It later becomes apparent that Molly has embarked upon a sexual relationship with Charlie. This suggests that for Charlie, his 'pleasure in looking' was indeed 'preparatory to the normal sexual aim'; whereas Tommo's desire cannot be satisfied in any other way. Again, he is passive. He can only look at Molly – he cannot become sexually active with her.

In an intertextual narrative reminiscent of L. P. Hartley's "coming of age" novel *The Go-Between* (1953), Tommo becomes the 'go-between postman' (Morpurgo, 2004, p.68) for Molly and Charlie. Like Leo in *The Go-Between*, Tommo naively assumes that he has won a special place in an older woman's affections because he carries letters for her. He seems not to understand the full extent of her relationship with Charlie and feels 'betrayed' when it is revealed that '[t]hey'd been meeting in secret' (Morpurgo, 2004, p.72). Their sexual exploits are hinted at when Molly's mother accuses Charlie of 'leading [her daughter] into the ways of wickedness and sin' (Morpurgo, 2004, p.73). But Tommo later finds them together in their meeting place – James Peaceful's 'old shack' (Morpurgo, 2004, p.75) – in tragic circumstances. Shortly afterwards, Molly is discovered to be pregnant and she and Charlie are married. This again emphasises Charlie's phallic superiority – his masculine activity and virility. In contrast, Tommo's status is eroded and his development arrested. As if he is their child, he tries to imagine and to interpret their sexual activity: 'In the next room slept the two people I most loved in all the world who, in finding each other, had deserted me.... I thought of them lying in each other's arms and wanted to hate them' (Morpurgo, 2004, p.92).

It would seem unlikely that Charlie, having demonstrated his successful psychosexual development so emphatically, would succumb to shell shock rather than his nervous and neurotic younger brother. Indeed, it is Tommo who initially exhibits symptoms of war neurosis, such as nightmares during which he '[cries] like a baby' (Morpurgo, 2004, p.139) and hallucinations which he describes as 'visions' where he 'relive[s] each and every horror' and 'see[s] a thousand silent screams' (Morpurgo, 2004, p.142).

In the trenches, Tommo is again characterised by passivity or inaction. During an attack he is 'overwhelmed by fear, numbed by it' (Morpurgo, 2004, p.124). When breaking into the German trenches he 'does nothing' and then a grenade blast 'throws [him] back against the trench wall' and he is 'stunned' (Morpurgo, 2004, p.130). When he is shelled, he notes that he '[tried] to run with the others, [tried] to keep up with them. But [his] legs [were] leaden and [would] not let [him] run' (Morpurgo, 2004, p.141). Later, when Charlie has been sent home with a "Blighty wound", Tommo is 'frozen with panic' (Morpurgo, 2004, p.153) during a gas attack. However, Tommo seems to be aware of his increasingly fragile mental state as he reveals that he keeps 'two letters', one from his mother and one from Charlie and Molly, and rereads them to fortify himself, to discover 'the strength [he] need[s] to stop [him]self from going *mad*' (Morpurgo, 2004, p.160, my italics). In this context, this reference to madness must surely be to shell shock.

When Charlie is well and returns to the Front, the brothers must finally go "over the top". During the attack, Tommo is seriously wounded by shell fire:

> [A]ll I can see is darkness.... It must be night and I am lying wounded somewhere in no-man's-land, looking up into the black of the sky. But then I try to move my head a little and the blackness begins to crumble and fall in on me, filling my mouth, my eyes, my ears. It is not the sky... but earth.... My legs cannot move, nor my arms.... How slowly I come to know and understand that I am buried, buried alive (Morpurgo, 2004, p.169).

Charlie digs him out and they take refuge in a shell hole in no-man's-land. Their Sergeant finds them there and orders them to 'press home the attack' (Morpurgo, 2004, p.171). Tommo whispers to Charlie 'I don't think I can make it. I don't think I can stand up' (Morpurgo, 2004, p.171), so consequently, when Sergeant Hanley gives the order to 'Go!' (Morpurgo, 2004, p.173), Charlie refuses as he doesn't want to leave his wounded brother alone. In this way, Charlie defies military authority.

At first, this might be considered a rational act, an humane decision to protect his brother as he always has done. But even by staying with him, Charlie cannot guarantee Tommo's survival as he has a serious head wound. As has already been mentioned, Morpurgo asserts that many of the men who were court-martialled and executed by firing squad 'were traumatised by shell shock' (Morpurgo, 2004, p.187). In this instance, Charlie chooses certain death by firing squad over possible death in an assault on enemy lines. This, then, could also be interpreted as a suicidal act, indicative of madness. Ironically, in this instance, Charlie chooses to be passive – to remain stationary in no-man's-land – in the knowledge that his death will also be passive. Instead of dying actively and heroically "in action", he will die passively in front of a firing squad, although he is keen to point out that he is not 'a coward' (Morpurgo, 2004, p.177).

Here, it is worth considering the case of the poet, Siegfried Sassoon. For his act of insubordination, publishing a letter of protest against the War, Sassoon was not executed, but was, instead, sent to be treated for shell shock. Sassoon wrote:

> *I am making this statement as an act of wilful defiance of military authority.... I am a soldier, convinced that I am acting on behalf of soldiers.... I have seen and endured the sufferings of the troops, and I can no longer be a party to prolong these sufferings for ends which I believe to be evil and unjust. I am... protesting against... the political errors and insincerities for which the fighting men are being sacrificed....* (Sassoon, quoted in Graves, 1981, p.225).

In *Goodbye to All That*, Robert Graves writes that such a protest would invoke a harsh 'penalty... namely to be court-martialled, cashiered, and imprisoned' (Graves, 1981, p.226). Graves campaigned for Sassoon to face a medical board rather than a court martial' hence he was sent to Craiglockhart Hospital, 'a convalescent home for neurasthenics' (Graves, 1981, p.228). Graves's account suggests that such protestations about the War would commonly be regarded both as cowardice and as madness. He writes:

> *I took the line that everyone was mad except ourselves and one or two others, and that no good could come of offering common sense to the insane.... They would accuse him of ratting, having cold feet, and letting the regiment down.... The army could... only read it as cowardice, or at best as a lapse from good form* (Graves, 1981, p.227).

Charlie Peaceful appears to count amongst the 'one of two others' who would have agreed with Graves and Sassoon, although it is necessary to note the differences in class and rank between Sassoon and the fictional Charlie Peaceful. Morpurgo writes:

> *Charlie [spoke] up, very quietly... "No point in going out there and getting ourselves killed for nothing, is there, Sergeant?... I'm just letting you know what I think.... [T]he thing is, Sergeant, even if I wanted to, I can't go with you because I'd have to leave Tommo behind.... I'm not leaving him.... [W]e'll make our way back later when it gets dark* (Morpurgo, 2004, p.172).

By directly disobeying an order, Charlie calls into question the whole ethos behind the War. The Sergeant tells him he will face 'a court martial' and then 'the firing squad' (Morpurgo, 2004, p.172). He even 'threaten[s] Charlie with his rifle', placing 'the bayonet' just 'inches from [his] nose' and saying 'I should shoot you right where you are and save the firing squad the trouble' (Morpurgo, 2004, pp.172-3). When he is later court-martialled, Charlie states:

> [Y]es, I did disobey the sergeant's order because the order was stupid, suicidal – we all knew it was…. They knew a dozen or more got wiped out in the attack, that no one even got as far as the German wire. They knew I was right, but it made no difference (Morpurgo, 2004, p.177).

If Sassoon's defiance of military authority and outspoken criticism of the War could be considered as evidence of shell shock, then so, perhaps, could Charlie's, even though he has shown no earlier signs of a predisposition to nervousness or mental instability.

Like their father, Charlie sacrifices himself to compensate for Tommo's passivity or inaction. Charlie, however, saves Tommo physically and mentally. To emphasise that this is a revival of his Oedipal crisis, Tommo 'dream[s] again [his] childhood nightmare', about his 'Father's finger pointing at [him]' (Morpurgo, 2004, p.174). This time, however, Tommo's Oedipal crisis is resolved. Before Charlie dies, he bequeaths his patriarchal role to Tommo by making him promise to take care of Molly and their baby. Charlie says, 'You'll make him a good father, like Father was to us' (Morpurgo, 2004, p.180), thereby encouraging him, in Freudian terms, to introject the authority of the father into his ego. Tommo will replace Charlie, his father-figure and rival, and become the patriarch of the Peaceful family, surrogate husband to Molly and father to her baby (however untenable this sort of substitution may be, as Molly's wishes are not taken into account).

Consequently, when Tommo 'goes further down the line' (Morpurgo, 2004, p.182) to fight in the Battle of the Somme, he is no longer passive and neurotic, but determined to 'survive' because he '[has] promises to keep' (Morpurgo, 2004, p.185). This sense of closure, I would argue, is indicative of the conclusions of Kate Agnew's survey of 'recent British children's novels about the First World War' (Agnew, 2001, p.55). She states:

> *Those novels for a younger audience published in recent years rarely seek to… promote the values espoused by First World War novels written earlier in the [twentieth] century…. Late twentieth-century children's novels present their protagonists… as ordinary people…. Above all they demonstrate the inner strength, resourcefulness and determination of ordinary people*
> (Agnew, 2001, pp.55-56).

Indeed, Tommo's narrative concludes positively as he finds his 'inner strength' and consciously states his 'determination' to survive and return home. However, the narratives written by the men and women who participated in the First World War do not share this optimistic, almost celebratory, attitude towards their service. In fact, those who survived tend to reiterate the myth of the lost generation (although this notion, like many literary accounts of the First World War, is largely concerned with middle-class men) and emphasise that those who returned were broken, physically and psychologically, by their experiences. For example, in her autobiography *Testament of Youth* (1933),

Vera Brittain remarks that 'though a few isolated persons may be better for having been in the War, the world as a whole will be worse; lacking first-rate ability and social order' (Brittain, 1979, p.472). However, in 1951, she went on to conclude retrospectively that 'the War took even the second best. It left nothing' (quoted in Berry and Bostridge, 1996, p.136).

Whilst Agnew goes on to suggest that it is 'unsurprising that children's fiction should... move towards a critical examination of the war itself coupled with a psychological examination of those who lived through it' (Agnew, 2001, p.57), I would argue that it is surprising that Morpurgo chose to tell his fictional narrative from the perspective of one of those 'few isolated persons' who benefited from their war service. If the purpose of contemporary children's fiction about the First World War is 'not to inculcate an active sense of patriotism in... young readers, but rather to educate them about the misery of war' (Agnew, 2001, p.57), then Tommo's personal triumph remains problematic as it suggests an ambivalent attitude to war and bereavement. Also, there remains much more to be said about class and gender differences within Morpurgo's deceptively simple text.

REFERENCES

K. Agnew, 'The First World War' in Kate Agnew and Geoff Fox, *Children at War: From the First World War to the Gulf*. London: Continuum, pp.55-83, 2001.

E. L. Ash, *The Problem of Nervous Breakdown*. London: Mills and Boon, 1919.

P. Berry and M. Bostridge, *Vera Brittain: A Life*. London: Pimlico, [1995] 1996.

V. Brittain, *Testament of Youth*. London: Fontana, [1933] 1979.

S. Freud, 'The Dissolution of the Oedipus Complex', reprinted in *The Essentials of Psycho-analysis: The definitive collection of Sigmund Freud's writing*. Ed Anna Freud. Harmondsworth: Penguin, pp.395-401, [1924] 1981.

S. Freud, 'The Question of Lay Analysis', reprinted in *The Essentials of Psycho-analysis: The definitive collection of Sigmund Freud's writing*. Ed Anna Freud. Harmondsworth: Penguin, pp.7-65, [1926] 1981.

R. Graves, *Goodbye to All That*. London: The Folio Society, [1929] 1981.

L. MacDonald, *The Roses of No Man's Land*. London: Penguin, [1980] 1993.

M. Morpurgo, *Private Peaceful*. London: Harper Collins Children's Books, [2003] 2004.

Jenny Plastow

Making the Man

IN GENERAL, BIOGRAPHERS do not dwell to any great extent on the importance of childhood reading. Unless recorded in a diary or some such, it is difficult to establish exactly what a child did read. Yet that reading may be of greater and more lasting importance than the activities of the ancestors in the lives of children. The social position of one's grandfather has an undoubted effect on one's upbringing -- but the events that really stand out to the reading child at the time, and those that shape irrevocably the mind and imagination, are books. The power of the interaction between a book and the mind of a receptive child is an event, nothing less; yet this is an encounter which is entirely private. It may never be discussed, and its consequences may find expression only – only? – in re-enactments, the playing of games influenced by the book, and by the adoption, perhaps temporarily, or perhaps with lasting significance, of the codes and pre-occupations of the author. This trying on of roles allows a child to experiment with ways of being. Reading is at its most significant in the lives of children from about the age of ten, when they begin to look for alternatives to the parental model. This significance persists through the teens and twenties. Many adults cease to be such voracious readers of fiction in their thirties; those who continue to read may become more discriminating and critically aware, especially those who read professionally. The need for entry into other worlds diminishes as one achieves some status in one's own; and an adult reading, particularly an adult who is also a writer, is often concerned more with analysing the writer's technique than with losing himself in an undiscovered world.

A reading child, of course, apprehends a book in a manner quite different from that of a reading adult. The child seizes onto the imaginative content of a book, de-contextualising it in ways that suit itself, using the parts that have most relevance at the time and possibly ignoring the rest – as I did myself, with a beloved book, *Little Women*. Bruno Bettelheim, in *The Uses of Enchantment*, suggests that the structure of fairy tales and the roles enacted by their characters reflect the psychological development of the individual. His argument is that the importance of nursery literature should not be overlooked, as familiarity with the stories provides a literary correlative and an objectivisation of the child's inner experience which allows that child to come to terms with what he or she feels. He suggests that the kind of obsessive interest which children may display for a time in a particular tale is an indication that the child is working psychologically with the elements represented within it. As Marie Louise von Franz argues, at different ages and stages of development, a person may find a tale relevant to psychological concerns; at such a time, figures from the fairytale or myth may appear in dreams.

Bettelheim contends that a boy or a girl, reading or hearing tales, will identify with characters of either gender; sometimes s/he will identify with an animal character, when that character's role holds meaning. But some nursery tales appear to be gender-specific; who could doubt that the three little pigs are boys, learning the lessons of becoming a man? They are really each a part of the whole self on the learning journey. First, the lesson is that you can't get away with making a shoddy house out of straw. That self fails and disappears, gobbled up by the Wolf. The house of sticks is a bit better, but still won't do. It is not till the self-pig realises that he is going to have to plan, and to really put his back into his house-building – a point beautifully illustrated in the Ladybird version – that he can use his skills to survive in the real world. Those skills may be more appropriate to a rural economy but the point is still valid. Have you ever wondered why the three Billy Goats Gruff go to all that trouble of crossing the rickety rackety bridge one by one? Why doesn't the big goat go first, and get rid of the troll? This is also a learning fable. While still small and weak, the little billy needs guile to survive; he negotiates and bargains with the troll just as a little boy wheedles his mother. The half-grown billy goat relies on the same skills. But once the billy is grown big and strong he doesn't need to negotiate. He can just bash the poor troll out of its home, and get his own way without speaking.

Bettelheim confines his analysis to nursery tales, but his hypothesis holds for children's reading at any stage of intense psychological growth – perhaps especially at puberty. For boys of nine or ten, the cusp between childhood and manhood has become visible. The end of childhood is in sight; the billy goat's horns are growing. Models are sought for the transition into the next phase, the journey into manhood. This is the stage at which boys are likely to become fascinated by the Greek myths, with their tales of heroes struggling to overcome monsters. The monsters in the Greek stories, in their antagonism to the emergent masculine power of the young man, are not nice safe big bullies like the Troll, who can be overcome by force. They are representatives of the feminine in their stated intention to confuse, emasculate and overwhelm, defeating the heroic project. The Medusa, Circe, the Sphinx, the Hydra, all represent the feminine in their fearsome, manipulative power. The growing boy needs to identify with the hero as part of the separation from the mother. Bettelheim's recent study has suggested that the horrible fate of Oedipus is a result of his having failed to kill the female monster – the Sphinx – that stands in his way. His compromise with it, by answering its riddle, does not effect a separation and Oedipus is fated to remain his mother's lover until he is freed from her by her death.

But it is not only mythic literature that is of significance in the establishment of gender roles. Kimberley Reynolds, in *Girls Only*, analyses the texts that were given to children to read from the middle of the nineteenth century onwards, in terms of their importance in establishing gender roles. Reynolds works with the theories of Mikhail Bakhtin, to consider the language of texts produced for children. In her view, the majority of books produced for girls to read encourage identification with, and acceptance of, adult authority figures. Often in the stories, girls are helped by adults to resolve difficulties. The essence of boys' fiction, she suggests, on the other hand, is the rejection of adult authority, especially in comics, and disrespect for institutions. Such fiction involves boy characters who solve problems on their own, that is, without the help of adults or females. Often they are temporarily removed from society, like Robinson Crusoe or Jim Hawkins, while they learn to overcome their fear and loneliness and rely on their own skills. This celebrates isolated effort as the road to success, tacitly rejecting a position in the community 'until spurs have been won'. The struggle of boyhood, by this account, is a lonely one.

In her analysis Reynolds suggests that boys' literature, rather than having a single 'voice' strictly subordinated to the writer's purpose, is polyphonic, including a variety of tones and dialects, and that it frequently comes within Bakhtin's definition of 'carnivalised literature'. This is especially true of comic-strip papers, which tend to be more popular with boys than with girls. In Selden's account of carnivalised literature, 'the festivities are collective and popular; hierarchies are turned on their heads, (fools become wise, kings become beggars); opposites are mingled (fact and fantasy, heaven and hell); the sacred is profaned. The "jolly relativity" of all things is proclaimed'. The carnival effect is as much present in comics as in the Menippean satire and Socratic dialogue Bakhtin himself refers to, perhaps because the origins of comics are also still close to 'the immediacy of oral dialogue, in which the discovery of truth is conceived as an unfolding exchange of views rather than as an authoritative monologue'. In other words, they speak the language and practical wisdom of ordinary people.

In a presentation entitled 'Travesty and Transgression', at the 1997 conference on 'Women, Drama and the First World War', Annabelle Meltzer considered the significance of theatrical presentations in the trenches in relation to soldiers' views of women. Meltzer emphasised that the Bakhtinian concept of carnival was of particular importance in the homosocial environment of the Front and in relation to the power-structures within which the men were living. She provided photographic and documentary evidence to support her assertion that British soldiers were drawing to a large extent on their boyhood reading of comics and school stories. The school stories of P.G. Wodehouse, the Greyfriars stories of Frank Richards (writer for *Magnet* and *Gem*) and all the comics, even to the present day, are not only carnivalised literature, but present images of boys engaged in the 'lonely struggle' of becoming men. In accordance with Bakhtin's theory, the serious and the carnivalised co-exist. Wodehouse's early school stories, for example *The Gold Bat*, though filled with 'japes' have story lines in which the young boy hero, not yet the cricket captain or an acclaimed leader, must struggle against injustice and investigate alone. The hero of *The Gold Bat*, for example, feels that 'all hands seemed turned against him'; he must struggle alone to clear his name; he has been accused of a crime he has not committed. The adventure stories of Rider

Haggard, G. A. Henty, Charles Kingsley, Rudyard Kipling, Captain Marryat and Robert Louis Stevenson reinforce those images of the lonely struggle which must be successfully completed in order to allow the boy to be accepted back into society with the raised status of manhood. Quite simply, they are a version of initiation rites.

Kimberley Reynolds' argument, in the first chapter of *Girls Only*, that images presented to girls were intended to limit change is convincing, but she refers to the fact that whilst girls often read boys' books, boys seldom read those intended for girls – especially in the last years of the nineteenth century. In this case, it would be boys, not girls, who are actually limited. Girls, whether overtly or subversively, have access to the whole canon, whereas boys interact with only those images which tended to promote the transmission of desirable qualities of masculinity. Thus boys, as readers of literature intended to inculcate a sense of masculinity, were, and are, likely to be heavily conditioned by this imbalance. Writers of children's literature are, now, redressing this balance to some extent, as we shall see, but it still holds sway. Books intended for girls have radically changed in the representation of femininity, but does that help boys?

That didactic literature for girls, closely related to the religious or moralistic tracts with which children's literature began, was intended to limit change and keeps girls girly, but the higher quality literature, which has gone on being read over many decades, offered images of tomboy behaviour and subversion of authority. This literature tended to be that produced by American women; Louisa Allcott's Jo March (*Little Women*, 1876) and Susan Coolidge's Katy Carr (*What Katy Did*, 1872), written in the period when women's issues were first widely discussed, have been prototypes for uncounted numbers of ambitious and unconventional women. Reynolds argues that even these conform in the end to adult conditions, and so they do; but are girls conditioned into this position in any worse case than boys? If the images of masculinity perpetrated by the boys' literature are isolated effort, misrule and subversion, without any final acceptance of the conditions of adult society, would boys be effectively prepared for what life in that society will bring? This is of course not what carnivalisation is about. The effect of misrule is to reinforce the conditions of adult society, which is why, to refer to comics of the second half of the twentieth century, Dennis the Menace and Roger the Dodger always finish up over Dad's knee. In boys' stories, the winning of spurs, and the integration into adult society in an accepted role, are essential features of successful adulthood.

While images of tomboy behaviour are present in books intended for girls, there are few images in boys' books, even today, of boys who can correspondingly get away with 'cissie' behaviour. Even the reading of books is a suspect activity in boys' stories of the twentieth century, which is a strange thing when one considers that the writers must perforce have themselves been readers as boys. Writers of that period were also, frequently, educated in the public school system; the carnivalisation of boys' stories, and the types of 'japes' the boys' characters play, thus extended the public school code to many boys who barely completed elementary school. If a book reader appears as a character in a school story, he is likely to be a victim, providing a moment of inattention while a 'jollier' character sneaks up behind him to empty a jar of jam on his head. All these writers promote images of masculinity which privilege the active boy and poke fun at the book reader. Wodehouse, in *The Gold Bat*, goes so far towards sanctioning reading as to describe a sixth-former taking a book and a rug into the hills to pass an afternoon, but the boy's action makes him a noted eccentric. When another character claims 'I want to read', his friend knows that this is merely a cover. The boy wants to be alone in order to perpetrate some secret plan. The role of 'reading' therefore is complicated, something that will separate a boy from his friends. Lynne Segal, in the context of the 1999 concerns about boyhood achievement at school, commented that 'boys don't want to be clever at school. To succeed at school is to be a girl'.

Boys' literature certainly has very few examples of central characters who succeed at school. Mac an Ghaill and Haywood, in an essay called 'Schooling Masculinities', illustrate the existence of a wide range of masculine hegemonies in a boys' school in Britain in the 1990s, but only a narrow range of such power structures is indicated in boys' school stories. Whereas Mac an Ghaill and Haywood were able to demonstrate that one of the most respected groups in the school was that of the academic boys, who eschewed, for example, sporty behaviour as beneath them, the school stories suggest no acceptance of 'swots', despite the fact that the writers themselves may well have been such swots. James Joyce, in *A Portrait of the Artist as a Young Man*, (begun as *Stephen Hero* in 1904 and serialised in *The Egoist* from February 1914 to September 1915, finally published in book form in 1916) breaks new ground in claiming legitimacy for a model of masculinity built around being a swot, and in the presentation of a masculine central character who was weak-eyed and fearful of sports and bullying. But *A Portrait of the Artist* is not likely ever to become part of the general canon of boyhood reading. For change to occur, it needs to happen not only within high culture, but also in texts that people are buying and reading; this is why the literature provided for children is of such importance. Children use it in the construction of a view of their society.

J. M. Barrie's *Peter Pan*, written as it was out of Barrie's unusual experience of caring for young boys without female intervention, is ground-breaking in its explicit recognition of boyhood fears and fantasies about the self, but it was also popular, and so might have met those criteria. Extant as a play in 1904, it was not published as a story, with its comic reflections on honour and the observance of form by its public-schoolboy villain, Jas. Hook, until 1911 – too late to be of any real use in challenging the stereotypical view of masculinity for the 1914 generation, who simply died for it. The similarity between the existential terrors which haunted the prototype of Peter Pan, George Llewelyn

Davis, which find expression, through Barrie, in the text, and George's recorded feelings as a young officer in the trenches - he was killed in 1915, aged twenty-three - are made explicit by Andrew Birkin in his *J. M. Barrie and the Lost Boys*. Peter Pan can be considered as an early incursion into children's literature of deconstructed male stereotypes, but in general its level of psychological insight was largely obscured for a contemporary readership by its popularity as a stage piece. The book's importance as a discussion of masculine behaviour was finally recognised as the nineteen-nineties discussion about masculinity began to develop; its characters and story-line were the basis for a cinematic sequel, *Hook*, which dealt with issues of fathering. A grown-up Peter, who has forgotten what it is to be boy and has somehow become American, has to revisit Neverland and recover his old skills in order to rescue his children, who have been kidnapped by the pirates. The film however does not refer to the fathering issues in the original play, in which the cowardly bully Jas. Hook is played by the actor who plays Mr. Darling. Mr Darling, like Hook, despite his talk of honour, is not above a few Billy Goat Gruff tricks himself, and he needs Mrs Darling to fix his stiff collar for him.

The position of the author in the old-fashioned boys' stories, especially in school stories, is interesting in terms of the discussion of the development of a discourse of masculinity. Despite the authorial tone, which is chatty, the author is not just invisible but actually transparent, so that the boy reader looks, as it were, through the text he is reading to the presented image without catching any glimpse of the author. The author himself is presenting representations of masculinity which do not represent him as an adult man and do not reflect his childhood experience and which, therefore, he should know to be inauthentic. What appears to be happening, however, is that the purveying of these images of boyhood is so automatic that the writer himself is not asking the question 'Is this what boyhood is like?' but continues to create images on a received model without questioning them. This parallels the fact already noted, that, while in the late nineteenth century there is in existence an 'authentic female voice', there is not a similarly authentic male voice. With the exception of the early Modernist writers in the nineteen-tens, Joyce and Ford in particular, this authentic voice comes into existence through the fiction and autobiographical writing of the nineteen-twenties, in the period following the war.

Joseph Bristow, in *Empire Boys*, suggests that the promotion of the qualities of active masculinity through boys' literature was no accident, but a deliberate policy on the part of the writers. He considers that, barely emerged from its period of origin as religious didacticism, much boys' literature of this period was specially written because, as the writer Charlotte M. Yonge decreed in the eighteen-eighties, 'true manhood needs, above all earthly qualities, to be impressed upon them.' One of the most important of the masculine virtues is silence. – and most religious – of these productions, and persist through the development of the genre. The importance of masculine silence is stressed again and again throughout the century, even when, becoming more secular, the literature has lost its most obvious association of manly silence with that of Christ under torture. This was the understanding of masculinity with which most young British soldiers went to war in 1914. Its values were thrown chaotically into question by the experience of the Western Front.

Most boys' stories end with a movement back into the accepted hierarchy, after the spurs have been won alone. But it is of no value to a boy to win his spurs unless there is someone to confer them. There is an analogy here with the process of a young child learning to walk; moving away from, and back to, the parent. If the parent is not there, on one of these returns, the child breaks down in panicky despair. Just so, for the model of achieving heroism to work, the existing order must be able to support it. There is a convention of referring to the combatants in that conflict as 'men', but many of them, both officers and troops, were only boys, some as young as fourteen. Very many of them had not yet achieved their status as adult males, and the psychological work of their adolescence had to be carried on under conditions which conspicuously failed to provide a structure within which this could be done. Not because of battle – adolescent males have historically achieved adulthood through battle – nor because of the risks, which as the boyhood reading testifies, are a test of mettle, but because the authority structure within which deeds of heroism could and should be recognised was crumbling and suspect. Every bad decision – and there were many – on the part of the generals, every order made only to be immediately superseded, made it more difficult for the boys to believe in the authority structure which would grant them their spurs.

Psychoanalytic analysis, applied to children's reading, suggests that the young man, in achieving adulthood, must overcome his father. As Freud so famously recognised, Oedipus slays his. The struggle between boys and their fathers is a familiar trope, both in literature and in family life. But what does this look like in the modern world? In a world where fathers may be attempting to behave like 'new men' and to be sensitive to, and close to, their sons, rather than playing the old role of Authority Figure which asks to be thrown down and overcome? If a father is being a 'new man' to his sons, who will the sons be able to fight? What does the Oedipal struggle look like, in Nick Hornby's world of *About a Boy?*

If we are looking for a new metaphorical working out of this question, we cannot do better than to look at Michael Morpurgo's *Kensuke's Kingdom*. Morpurgo himself, in speaking about how he came to write this book, mentions his love of *Robinson Crusoe* and *Treasure Island* - books which have built into their very structure the experience of isolation and separation from society, of being thrown on one's own, very limited, resources – that Kimberly Reynolds identifies as endemic to the masculine condition. These works are the lonely struggle of boyhood made into literature, the books that, at one time, formed part of every boy's experience. The matter of *Kensuke's Kingdom*, for those of you who have not read it, and still have that treat in store, is this. The young protagonist, Michael, aged eleven, an only child, suffers when both his parents lose their jobs in a Thatcher-era shut down of the local brick industry. The mother finds some other work but the father, unable to provide for his family, falls into a depression. Here we have a modern metaphor for the loss of the traditional masculine role. The father travels far and wide but is unable to find work (sounds Grimm!) and the stability of the family is damaged, with young Michael turning in on himself as he broods over his parents' problems. They are unable to keep up their family hobby of sailing.

His father, however, finds a completely new solution to his problem, and sinks all of his and his family's money into buying a yacht. He determines that they will sail round the world and see what fortune brings them – very Robert Louis Stevenson. After some resistance, the mother agrees. She is the best sailor, and becomes the skipper and the boss of the outfit; a further development of the metaphor of the shift in gender roles. Michael recovers to some extent a lost friendship, and takes with him on the trip a football which his best friend has had signed by other members of his football team, the Mudlarks. The family dog, Stella Artois, is also of the party. The early part of the voyage represents, in this psychoanalytically situated reading, the stable latency period of Michael's childhood. His parents are in harmony; the family overcome practical difficulties together; Michael enjoys the company of Stella Artois and has his signed ball representing internalisation of his friends. It looks as if this will last for ever. They are on the other side of the world, in the Pacific, leaving Australia, when things begin to shift.

The first frightening accident is that Stella Artois gets washed overboard. For a time, it appears as if she will be lost forever, and the family are having to come to terms with the possibility of their loss when she is suddenly found. But this tremor is followed by a storm, which makes Michael's mother so ill that she is not able to skipper the ship and the self-steering mechanism of the yacht is damaged. It is while his parents are resting below – leaving Michael, significantly, alone with the responsibility for the ship – that his precious ball rolls over the side. With a bark, Stella leaps after it – he has not put on her harness, nor his own, which is a ship rule – and both ball and dog vanish from his sight. In a moment of horror which could be from the Oddyssey, Michael makes a lone decision of personal responsibility, and leaps into the water to try to save Stella. Now he is really alone, really separated from his society; his sleeping parents do not even know what has happened. In seconds, he is separated from everything he has loved. Both dog and ball have completely vanished.

Michael loses consciousness.

When he regains it, he finds himself, like Robinson Crusoe, alone on an island. He has entered into his own lonely kingdom, and must find out how to manage it. To his enormous relief, Stella has also been saved, but they wander the island for the whole day in an unsuccessful search for water. At last, Stella discovers some – but it is in a bowl, and has evidently been laid out for her. There is also some, and some fish, for Michael, yet despite this evidence of a beneficial influence, he seems still to be alone.

His benefactor, when he does appear, does not provide Michael with much-longed for company. Instead, the elderly Japanese who provides the food appears only as a setter of boundaries; in a stick drawing of the island, he makes a line across the middle which Michael is not to cross. He shouts out words such as Damida! (forbidden) and is extremely angry when Michael, desperate to be re-united with his family, tries to light a fire as a beacon. He kicks it out, condemning Michael to solitude and desperate loneliness in a land governed by incomprehensible rules, though Stella Artois treacherously proves fond of Kensuke, the bringer of food. This heightens Michael's sense of powerlessness in an isolation governed by such an old-style father figure as his own father could never be.

Michael's increasing anger against the rules Kensuke formulates expresses itself in a defiant act. Despite Kensuke's Damida! Michael goes swimming in the bay, not realising that a recent storm has swept in hordes of dangerously stinging jellyfish. His defiance results in paralysis from the stings, and another period of unconsciousness, which, as it retreats, brings in the second phase of Kensuke's substitute fathering. He adopts aspects of the feminine as he nurses Michael after this near-death experience, and in his own reflection comes to realise that the insistence on obedience, when no explanation had been offered, was bound to result in rage and defiance and thus to endanger Michael's life. Michael has no choice but to trust him and a new mood of closeness is engendered by their both having shifted position.

Out of this, there grows a further bonding experience. As Michael recovers strength he begins to ask questions, and as he learns about Kensuke's experience – a doctor and an ex-sailor, who himself was bereft of comrades before he reached the island, he has been hiding on the island since he heard on the radio of his deserted ship about the bombing of his home city, Nagasaki. It his belief that all his family are dead, and he has no wish to return to a world in which everything he loves has been destroyed. Kensuke's, too, is a lonely struggle, and Kensuke has not succeeded in re-uniting himself with his society. He is angry and terrified when killers come to the island, shooting mother gibbons and snatching their babies, and threatening the orang-utans who are Kensuke's friends. In these talks, Michael comes increasingly to recognise that he has a role to play in relation to Kensuke. This diminishes his sense of powerlessness and gives him a sense of identity. He distresses Kensuke by throwing into the sea a message in a bottle, asking for rescue, but Kensuke manages to overcome himself and shares his change of thought with Michael. This is a real, worked-out relationship of love and respect. Michael is able to provide a listening for Kensuke's experience and though he cannot persuade him to rejoin society, he is able, after his own rescue from the island by his diligently searching parents – the father gave up hope but the mother did not - to contact Kensuke's son, with whom to some extent he has become identified. His bringing together of cultural understandings from opposite cultures is the foundation on which his own manhood will be built.

Like Jim Hawkins in *Treasure Island*, Michael leaves the island a man. He has endured. He has overcome his own terror and the challenges of isolation, and acted bravely in unexpected circumstances. He has achieved his own masculinity in reaction against, and in harmony with, a representative of an older-style masculinity, whose capacity to oppose and contain him has met his needs. He has learned how to have a relationship. He has understood that, though his own father has seemed diminished in his authority by the loss of job and having to take second place to his wife, the masculine role needs to encompass nurturing and weaknesses if it is to be entirely successful. When he is re-united with his parents he is able to transcend the experience of the family, and feel secure in his own identity. He has internalised aspects of Kensuke, who he has grown deeply to love.

One of the things that Michael Morpurgo offers the boy reader of *Kensuke's Kingdom* is a metaphor for the achievement of adult masculinity despite a role model which is damaged, inadequate or missing. David Almond does something similar in *Skellig*. It is a troubled time for masculinity, but we can see in the work of some of our foremost children's writers the signs that the challenges are being met, and the boys of our own generation are being offered images of a masculinity at once strong, thoughtful and capable of reflection and reparation. That was what we wanted, wasn't it?

REFERENCES

Bruno Bettelheim, *The Uses of Enchantment*. Harmondsworth: Penguin, 1982; first published 1976.

Andrew Birkin, *J.M. Barrie and the Lost Boys*, 1979, Macdonald Futura 1980.

Joseph Bristow, *Empire Boys*. Harper Collins Academic, 1991

Brad Buchanan, 'Samuel Beckett and 'The Death of Man'', paper delivered at *Representations of Masculinity in the Twentieth Century Conference on Men's Studies*, August 2000.

Marie Louise von Franz, *Interpretations of Fairy Tales*, New York, Spring Publications 1970.

Mac an Ghaill and Haywood, 'Schooling Masculinities', from *Understanding Masculinities*, Buckingham, Open University Press, 1996.

Annabelle Melzer, 'Travesty and Transgession; performing 'woman' on the Western Front 1914 – 1918' *Women, Drama and the First World War* Conference presentation, at Brunel University, Twickenham, 20th September 1997.

Kimberley Reynolds, *Girls Only*, Harvester 1990.

Lynne Segal, 'Reforming Masculinity?' paper delivered to the *Representations of Masculinity in the Twentieth Century Conference on Men's Studies*, August 2000.

Raman Selden, *A Reader's Guide to Contemporary Literary Theory*, Harvester Press 1985, 18

Pat Pinsent

The Theme of Facial Disfigurement in some Recent Books for Young Readers

THE HUMAN FACE serves both as a means of expressing emotion, voluntarily or involuntarily and as a virtually unique icon by which people can be recognised. It is perhaps scarcely surprising that my somewhat elderly *Dictionary of Quotations* lists more than 200 references in literature up to the 1950s, and I'm sure that today an internet search would yield many more. As someone with considerable difficulty in recognising faces (prosopagnosia), I have often discovered that people are more hurt if I do not remember their faces than they are by the failure of others to remember their names. Since so much of our identity is lodged with our faces, facial disfigurement can be more traumatic than other, more obviously disabling, conditions.

During the first week of July 2006, purely by chance, I read in sequence three children's books with protagonists who had suffered facial disfigurement: Vivien Alcock's *Travellers by Night* (1983), about a circus girl whose face has been badly scarred in a trapeze accident; Melvin Burgess's *Sara's Face* (2006), treating the very contemporary subject of face transplant; and Robert Cormier's *Heroes* (1998) about a soldier, most of whose face has been blown away by a grenade. This coincidence reminded me that only a month before this I had encountered, in Philip Reeve's quartet about 'Traction Cities', the character of Hester, who has been badly scarred in childhood. I then looked back at my notes on Benjamin Zephaniah's *Face* (1999), featuring a boy injured in an accident involving a stolen car, and started to think I should write a paper on the subject! In these books, both the causes of the trauma and the literary treatments are various but it is pertinent that all have appeared during the last twenty-five years, a period during which there has also been increasing publicity about the feasibility both of face transplants and of 'improving' the face one has been born with.

In this paper I propose to examine all these texts, looking firstly at how characters who suffer facial disfigurement are perceived by others, and secondly how this perception, together with the loss of their established facial image, can affect how the individuals concerned see themselves and, consequently, their sense of identity. Inevitably there is some overlap between these themes. With a theme as broad as this, and some lengthy texts, it is impossible to explore every relevant aspect in every book, so I shall not be looking specifically at the identity theme in the 'Traction Cities' quartet, whereas this subject is so important in *Sara's Face* that I shall only consider this complex text in that context. I shall explore both themes in the other three texts, from a variety of psychoanalytic perspectives, chosen in relation to their appropriateness to both book and theme.

The effect of facial appearance on how people are perceived

Inevitably, representations of faces in art, literature and photography have carried a good deal of symbolic 'baggage', notably in the traditional link (often deplored today) between facial beauty and goodness. Injury to a person's face, turning it into a form regarded by onlookers as ugly, inevitably has significant effects on how that person is regarded. It demands conscious effort for all of us not to import external appearance into our judgments about character – the result of having been exposed all our lives to the implicit ideology of fairytales such as 'Cinderella' or the many film versions of 'Frankenstein'. It is inevitable that this reaction also has an effect on the psychology of those involved. In much literature of the past, ostensibly unattractive heroes or heroines, such as Andersen's 'Ugly Duckling', generally improve their appearance and by the end of the book have developed the status of being attractive, whereas the truly evil dwarfs and witches remain ugly. However, in real life, those who are perceived as unattractive don't have the luxury of becoming more beautiful – unlike, for example, Mary Lennox in Frances Hodgson Burnett's *The Secret Garden*.

Monika Cavicchioli, in an unpublished Roehampton MA thesis, describes her own research which has led her to conclude that facial disfigurement provokes profound and complex emotions in observers as well as in those disfigured. She cites work by Hatfield-Specher describing how stereotypes are formed (1986): although most people feel that to do so is unfair, we have been conditioned to perceive attractive people as being desirable beings, and as a consequence almost inevitably treat people differently; those with good looks get better treatment, and the prophecy becomes self-fulfilling. The coping strategies of those disfigured may be withdrawal, aggression, or being excessively charming (Cavicchioli cites F.S. McGregor (1974)). Beatrice Wright (1960) claims that in our cognitive development we make a link between appearance and quality, so that people with facial disfigurement often have bad character traits associated with them, and Seymour (1998) describes how people frequently feel that external appearance relates directly to the essential nature of the person. The work of Ekman and Friesen (1975) suggests a possible reason for this association, given how important the face is as a channel of emotions, which are shown by signals which may be static, slow or rapid. The face broadcasts messages about the mood, attitudes and intelligence of the person concerned, and the type of face anyone has may affect our reception of these emotional messages. Sandra Gountas of La Trobe University, Melbourne, suggests in a private communication (2007) that being unable to feel confident about 'reading' different facial expressions in disfigured people may makes us wary at a deeper level.

It almost goes without saying that the majority of novelists writing in the last twenty-five years will have made an effort to avoid the kind of stereotypical responses so characteristic of fairytales and older literature. In most of the books I have been looking at, it is evident that the authors, while truthfully displaying the responses of other characters to those affected, also provide a corrective to the negative reactions, and even in some instances suggest an actual moral growth in those who are disfigured.

This is certainly the case in Vivien Alcock's *Travellers by Night*. The first time we see Belle's disfigurement is through the eyes of three young children, one of whom bursts into tears while another tactlessly suggests the similarity between Belle's scar and a worm. At this encounter Belle is both devastated and violent, but by the end of the book, as a result of her experience of saving from the knacker's yard an old and scarred elephant, with which she feels kinship, she has found a coping strategy. When her face is seen by another group of children, she takes on the role of a clown, describing herself as 'old Scarface'.

There is also some evidence in this book that the author has intuitively understood the way in which misinterpretation of emotions can be a factor in arousing hostility. We see Belle through Charlie's eyes, in a vivid description which simultaneously denies and affirms the effects of the scar:

> Her face still seemed cut in half, one side white, where it had been hidden from the sun, one brown. The scar had healed, its ugly livid colour gone. It ran from the hairline, missing her eye, right down to her chin. The left side of her mouth was pulled up a little, so that she appeared to be smiling, though her eyes were miserable. (p.74)

Charlie, who knows her well, is able to recognise the dissonance between the apparent smile and her real misery, but this would not be obvious to others; in fact her fright at the encounter with the children at the end makes her look 'arrogant'.

The protagonist, Francis, of Robert Cormier's *Heroes* has no face by which to display emotion, as we learn from the horrific description by him as narrator at the beginning of the novel:

> I have no face ... Oh, I have eyes because I can see and ear-drums because I can hear but no ears to speak of, just bits of dangling flesh ... If anything bothers me, it's my nose. Or, rather, the absence of my nose. My nostrils are like two small caves and they sometimes get blocked and I have to breathe through my mouth ... I have no eyebrows, but eyebrows are minor, really. I do have cheeks. Sort of. I mean, the skin that forms my cheeks was grafted from my thighs and has taken a long time to heal ... I wear a scarf that covers the lower part of my face ... I keep a bandage on the space where my nose used to be. The bandage reaches the back of my head and is kept in place with a safety pin ... So I am well covered up, face and body, although I don't know what I am going to do when summer comes and

> *the weather gets hot. ...*
> *Anyway this gives you an idea of what I look like when I walk down the street. People glance at me in surprise and look away quickly or cross the street when they see me coming.*
> *I don't blame them* (pp.1-3)

The visual nature of this passage means that almost inevitably the reader has already responded with a feeling of repulsion, triggered perhaps in particular by phrases such as 'bits of dangling flesh' and 'the absence of my nose', so in a way we are likely to be complicit in the avoidance behaviour of the passers by. Both his own perception and the responses of others clearly affect Francis's self-image, but as, during the course of the story, he gains more knowledge, he realises that he could be worse off. He has returned to his home town with the intention of killing Larry, previously his best friend and mentor, because he discovered that Larry had raped Francis's girl friend, Nicole. But Larry is now a psychological victim of war, more incapacitated even than Francis. Francis is able not only to reject his own destructive urges but also to cope with the fact that, despite her loving concern, Nicole cannot 'face' seeing him again; he sets off with the determination to live life positively.

In Benjamin Zephaniah's *Face*, the protagonist, a schoolboy, Martin, encounters some hostile perceptions of his badly burnt appearance. His friends all act 'as if they hardly knew me' (90); a girl at school dinner-time says 'You're putting me off my food' (135); some children hurl insults (*'Dog face'... 'If you look at him for long you'll go blind', 'Get away, bogey man'* (pp.176-7, italics in original), and his girl friend rejects him. Instrumental in Martin's developing ability to cope with the responses of others is his introspection about his own reactions to another boy, Anthony, 'with a face so disfigured that he [Martin] gasped with surprise ... he now realised how his friends must have felt when they first saw him' (pp.99-100).

By contrast, in Philip Reeve's four lengthy novels, Hester, though a very significant character, is only one of a large cast. Consequently the focus on her facial disfigurement is less intense, integral though it has been in the formation of her character. We first see her through the eyes of Tom, the man she goes on both to love and, because of her jealousy of his possible relationship with another woman, to betray:

> *She was no older than Tom, and she was hideous. A terrible scar ran down her face from forehead to jaw, making it look like a portrait that had been furiously crossed out.*
> *Her mouth was wrenched sideways in a permanent sneer, her nose was a smashed stump and her single eye stared at him out of the wreckage, as grey and chill as a winter sea.* (*Mortal Engines*, p.26)

We can see here the potential for misinterpretation of emotions that facial injury can occasion: the 'permanent sneer' of her mouth, which is also referred to later, and the 'grey and chill' of her 'single eye' – facial expressions that do not accurately portray her actual feelings. Other characters whom she meets in the course of the saga are similarly negative in their reactions to her: 'her face split in half by an old sword-blow that had robbed her of one eye and most of her nose and twisted her mouth into a snag-tooth sneer,' 'That girl! The ugly one!', 'Eugh! She's so ugly', 'a poor disfigured girl' (*Predator's Gold*, pp.9, 142, 147, 155). Even in the final volume the reader is not allowed to forget Hester's repulsive appearance; a youth, Fishcake, speaks of 'That face – enough to put you off your breakfast' (*A Darkling Plain*, p.491). We never see any evidence that Tom's attitude towards her is conditioned by her appearance but she seems to be constantly worried that he will discard her love and this leads her towards a possessive attitude towards him. It is tempting to conclude that she has internalised the negative responses of those around her and thus lacks self-esteem but on the whole she is not seen introspecting. What is emphasised is that Hester has an innate savagery and rather than this being attributed to her disfigurement, she herself seems to relate this quality to the fact that her father, who incidentally was responsible for her injury, himself betrayed his own city. The reader is perhaps consoled by Tom's final thoughts about Hester, which appreciate her positive qualities and even see her appearance in a different light: 'How lucky he was to be loved by someone so strong, and brave, and beautiful' (*A Darkling Plain*, p.518).

The books I have mentioned seem to suggest that in order to live positively after their disfigurement, the characters need to accept the likelihood of negative responses by others, and to admit that, confronted with seeing disfigured people, they themselves might have felt similarly repulsed. At the same time they need to adopt coping strategies, whether by humour or positive action; most important is to maintain a sense of self-worth, an aspect crucially linked with the treatment in these texts of the theme of identity.

Identity Loss and Disfigurement

An immense amount of work has been done by people from a range of disciplines on the subject of identity, so I can only briefly draw out some themes specific to the way in which loss of the established facial image, which they have perceived in the mirror since infancy, may affect the individuals concerned. While the theoretical material considered here has some relevance to all my texts, in order to avoid excessive length I have limited the focus; it has also been convenient at times to consider the texts out of chronological order.

Firstly, as hinted in the preceding paragraph, a brief mention of the work of the French psychoanalyst Jacques Lacan seems appropriate. He is perhaps most famous for his conjecture that a vital period of human development is 'the mirror stage', when the infant between six and eighteen months old, seeing 'its own reflection in the mirror, begins to conceive of itself as a unified being, separate from the rest of the world' (Barry 1995). I would like to suggest that because of the importance of the image formed at that stage to the infant's development, the loss of the accustomed image after some traumatic event may also have a considerable effect. A young person, past the stage of infancy, whose image has drastically been altered could be said to go through a kind of second mirror stage in which a new identity is forged. In practical terms this recalls what Wright (1960) has to say about the importance of the disfigurement needing to be integrated into the self.

The relevance of this suggestion is most apparent in relation to Zephaniah's novel *Face*, in which Martin, soon after he has discovered the extent of his facial injuries, demands a mirror, to the dismay of his carers. In a kind of way he is recreating his identity, beginning at the time when he has the courage to look at the mirror (pp.68 & 71). This sense of a new start occurs for instance when he arrives home from hospital:

> *Before going to sleep that night, Martin had a long hard look at himself in the mirror. It was different now. Looking like he did at home was somehow different from looking like he did in the Burns Unit. He was now in familiar surroundings with an unfamiliar face.* (p.110)

Martin is growing towards self-acceptance and recreation of his new identity, which appears to be more unified than his somewhat fragmented previous self-image. Zephaniah has portrayed Martin before the accident as, in effect, putting on a new 'face' for each new situation. Early in the novel, when he is challenged by the police, Martin puts on his 'reasonable' face, and then, when he is alone with his friends, he puts on his 'victorious' face (*Face*, pp.17 & 18). When he is first injured, his face is described as blackened and burnt (p.55) and inflexible with no feeling (p.58); as his face begins to heal he feels it as 'an unexplored wilderness with miniature mountains (p.80), but he gradually begins to gain more control over his facial muscles (p.95). By the end of the novel, the changes in his face image his growth. Martin's achievement in creating an integrated new identity is particularly signified in the final scene of the novel, when he is photographed with the gym team that he has been instrumental in inspiring:

> The whole team knew Martin didn't want his photo taken [but] 'The Echo wanted a picture of the team. The team didn't want to do it without you...' Martin looked at the photographer ... 'No problem,' he said ... Martin's smile was at the centre of every flash' (Face, p.206)

In a way Martin could be said to have lacked a true 'face' even before the accident and his acceptance of the image that will be exposed to a wider gaze in the local paper symbolises his ability to accept his new identity. Thus Martin's loss of his face and subsequent reformulation of his life could be said to have both a literal and a symbolic meaning.

The same kind of internal and external meaning seems to me to be true of all the texts I am discussing. In this context I recall what Margaret and Michael Rustin say of the works they discuss in *Narratives of Love and Loss*:

> States of loss have both external and internal meaning in these stories ... writers have found metaphoric ways of constructing a situation quite recognizable as a representation of a moment in social history, while nevertheless writing within a chosen convention adapted to what child readers can imaginatively respond to ... Just as central to our argument, however, are the meanings in the inner or mental world of the events represented in the stories. Many of the children or child-like central characters in these stories are shown to experience relationships and states of loss not only in external fact but in their imaginations, through symbolic representations of themselves or their loved objects... (1987: 249-50)

In each of the texts I am considering, the characters have sufficient external reasons for distress but while these remain 'real' to them, their disfigurement also works as a metonym of other aspects within their lives; as they recover, not their original 'beauty' but a way of living with their altered appearance, they also achieve a healing of the initial adverse situation. Their disfigured faces serve as images of their inner being, while their ability to accept their disfigurement signifies significant improvement in their actual situation.

In Alcock's *Travellers by Night*, Belle has not only lost her facial beauty, she is also losing her job at the circus because her self confidence and ability with heights have also vanished. She is faced with living with distant relatives while her parents are abroad, and hiding her scar behind either a golden mask or a lock of her hair – just as she herself is in hiding. At the same time the elephant, for which she has had a particular care, is condemned to death for being useless and scarred. By the end of the book, however, with her increased confidence, Belle has become widely popular, her relatives have become more friendly, and she anticipates working at a safari park. What is even more important is the way in which she has been able to joke about her new appearance; while initially she has hidden her scar and herself, by the end she has the confidence to avoid concealment and has also 'found' herself metaphorically. This recalls what Wright (1960) says about the need for disfigurement to be accepted and integrated into the identity.

The first person narrator of Cormier's *Heroes* initially conceals not only his disfigured face but also his identity, as he returns to a town where he would without his injury certainly have been recognised. This anonymity is at first useful to him, as he is seeking out his erstwhile friend, Larry. His destroyed face reflects how he feels that his life has been destroyed even before he was wounded; it also relates to his desire to annihilate his own identity, to the extent that his falling on the grenade to prevent it killing his comrades was equally motivated by a desire to extinguish his life from a world of betrayal. While at the end of the novel his face is no better, his resolution to 'face up to' life has returned, and he is at least looking into the possibility of further surgery to improve his appearance.

In Melvin Burgess's *Sara's Face*, the eponymous character could certainly be said to be suffering from a lack of sense of identity in her life well before she has a relatively minor facial injury; her distinctive burn could serve as a metonym of this absence. The major thrust of this complexly narrated novel however is concerned with the prospect that she will sustain the loss of her face and this aspect seems to lend itself to a different psychoanalytic perspective from those used so far, one dependent on the work of Jung. I have selected this as a framework for discussion here because of Jung's emphasis on the persona, or mask, 'a functional complex that comes into existence for reasons of adaptation or personal convenience, but is by no means identical with the individuality' (Jung, quoted by Stevens, 1990). Jung complements this concept with that of the shadow, which 'possesses qualities opposite to those manifested in the persona' (Stevens, 1990). A good deal of the story of *Sara's Face* depends on the concept of face as mask or persona. Additionally, there is a near identity of appearance between Sara's face and the original face of her idol, the pop personality Jonothan Heat (who has however ruined his face by incessant plastic surgery). The reader is therefore encouraged to think in terms of him as her 'shadow' side – a notion fostered to some extent in the novel by the dark and shadowy nature of the hidden and possibly haunted room where the operation is to be performed to give Sara's face to Jonothan, a room with which Sara is familiar even though she hides from herself the fact that she knows it (a good image of the unconscious!).

This text combines narration purporting to be from Burgess himself, 'a novelist doing a journalist's job' (p.2 – another 'persona'!), with video diaries of Sara's own words (but with the narrator's description of the action). The narrator also retails the occasionally conflicting versions of the 'truth' derived from other players in the story: Sara's ex-boyfriend, Mark; Bernadette, a nurse and counsellor; and the surgeon, Dr Kaye. The Introduction conveys to the reader the impression that the story is 'fact', particularly as it assumes, as common knowledge, that the characters described have already featured in the media. The Epilogue both reverses the immediately preceding Conclusion and provides Sara's own slant on the events, as expressed through the new persona she has adopted, 'Lucy Smith,' which she sees as being her true self at last.

Sara's sense of identity is shown to have always been insecure – she is described as 'incredibly elusive … it's as if she has done her best to extinguish her real self in favour of her own legend' (p.2). Early in the book, while still at school, she has frequently taken on new personae, incorporating role plays into her daily behaviour and different accents into her speech. The impression is created that in her quest for becoming a 'personality', she has lost out on becoming an individual – as Stevens says, 'should the compensatory relationship [with the shadow] break down, it can result in the shallow, brittle, conformist kind of personality which is "all persona"'(Stevens 1990). If indeed Sara has no 'shadow', this feature is amply provided by Heat, who having started by being Sara's ideal has become a horrific vision of what it is to have 'no face'; thus, perhaps, he could be described as 'all shadow':

> *Under the mask, the wreckage was terrible. The skin had peeled off, the blood supply dried up, the nervous system gone haywire. Flesh had begun to die and to grow and to bleed without order. The muscles detached themselves from the bone and cartilage and sagged inside his skin – 'like a bag of butcher's meat', as one ex-staff member put it.*
> *Masses of scar tissue began to form at an accelerated rate and within a few months, Heat began to look more like the elephant man than an international idol.* (p.30)

At the climax of the novel, Sara undergoes an operation which ostensibly is to remove her minor facial scar but which she, and we, know is really intended to remove her face and transplant it on to Jonothan. At this point the impression is given that this has been done:

> *The cameras snapped and rolled, and revealed to the world the now famous image of Sara's face, inert in a way no face ever should be. But it wasn't Sara who was wearing it – it was Heat himself.* (p.243)

This bears out the narrator's initial conviction, as expressed in the Introduction, about Sara's fate: 'madness or death, or the terrible nature of her injuries seem to be the most likely options' (p.2). But the Epilogue shows the narrator meeting Sara, with her replaced face revealing relatively little damage. Though it has become 'a kind of living mask' (p.248), it is one that Sara sees as expressing 'the real me' (p.260) – presumably at last an integration between the different parts of her individuality, incorporating her true shadow now that Jonothan, as we are told at the beginning of the novel, is in prison.

This complex novel is surely Burgess's comment on contemporary issues such as the cult of the beautiful which encourages 'celebrities' to undergo frequent facial surgery to the extent that their real selves, if such have ever existed, are totally submerged. That he shows a girl who has been an obsessive follower of a celebrity and lacks any true individuality coming out of this state to become a whole person – as a result of her face having been removed to let the unreal person out and then replaced to fit her new identity – could be described as a somewhat over-optimistic conclusion to a generally dark story.

Conclusion

In looking at these texts I have employed several different psychoanalytic perspectives, and I am sure that they would be open to a range of other interpretations. In particular it would be rewarding to look more closely from various viewpoints at the two most recent works, Burgess's *Sara's Face* and Philip Reeve's quartet. And from the point of view of the production of fiction for young readers, I am sure we have not seen the last of a surge of books treating the theme of facial appearance in original ways.

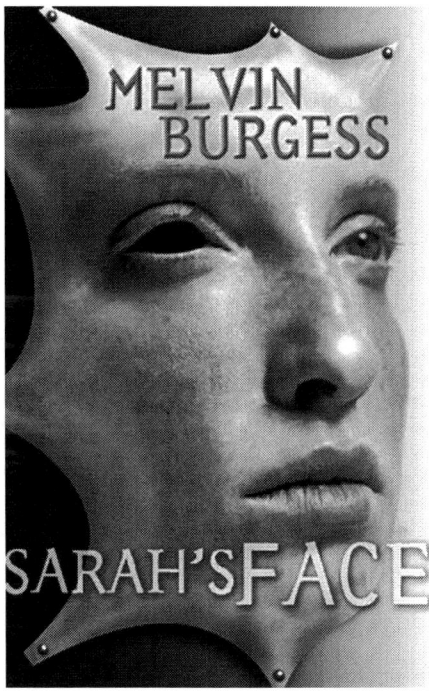

REFERENCES

Primary Texts

Vivien Alcock, *Travellers by Night*. London: Methuen, 1985; first published 1983.

Melvin Burgess, *Sara's Face*. London: Andersen, 2006.

Robert Cormier, *Heroes*. London: Penguin, 1999; first published 1998.

Philip Reeve, *Mortal Engines*. London: Scholastic, 2001.

Philip Reeve, *Predator's Gold*. London: Scholastic, 2003.

Philip Reeve, *Infernal Devices*. London: Scholastic, 2005.

Philip Reeve, *A Darkling Plain*. London: Scholastic, 2006.

Benjamin Zephaniah, *Face*. London: Bloomsbury,1999.

Secondary Texts

Peter Barry, *Beginning Theory: An Introduction to Literary and Cultural Theory*. Manchester: University Press, 1995.

Monika Cavicchioli, *Construing Facial Disfigurement*. Roehampton University, Unpublished MA dissertation, 1994.

Paul Ekman & Wallace Friesen, *Unmasking the Face: A Guide to Recognizing Emotions from Facial Clues*. Englewood Cliffs NJ: Prentice Hall, 1975.

Hatfield-Specher, *The importance of looks in everyday life*. Albany University NY, 1986

Lois Keith, *Take up thy Bed and Walk: Death, Disability and Cure in Classic Fiction for Girls*. London: The Women's Press, 2001.

Jacques Lacan, 'The mirror stage' in Eds Philip Rice & Patricia Waugh, *Modern Literary Theory: A Reader* (2nd editn.). London: Arnold, 1992.

Margaret & Michael Rustin, *Narratives of Love and Loss: Studies in Modern Children's Fiction*, London & New York: Verso, 1987.

Wendy Seymour, *Remaking the Body: Rehabilitation and Change*. London: Routledge, 1998.

Anthony Stevens, *On Jung*. London: Penguin, 1991; first published 1990.

Beatrice Wright, *Physical Disablity: A Psychological Approach*. New York & Evanston: Harper & Row, 1960.

Websites

www.lets-face-it.org.uk

www.changingfaces.org.uk

Jake Hope

Fairytale Heart: an exploration of memory, story and childhood through Philip Ridley's novels and plays

FROM A GIANT crocodile residing beneath the urban landscape of Lizard Street in his early novel *Krindlekrax* to a beast adhered from fragmented relics of Milo Kick's destructive piques in *Mighty Fizz Chilla*, Philip Ridley's body of fiction for children – whether drama or novels – offers a rich vein for psychoanalytic reading.

Whilst Ridley's children's fiction will be given consideration, it is his most recent adult play *Mercury Fur* (2005) that will provide structure to this paper, offering opportunities to explore some of the preoccupations of its author and the means by which they manifest themselves across his work.

Philip Ridley's fiction is characterised by its urban landscape. This is typically represented as being caught within the flux of regeneration, firmly in the throes of decay and disrupted rule.

Mercury Fur is set in a derelict flat in the East End of London. This flat forms a microcosm of the outside world and within the theatrical space of its simulated walls, we learn about a society where the civilising influences of society have degenerated so wholly that three days of bombing have been planned as a means to rid the chaos and disorder:

> *Open ya window, for fuck's sake. It's a shithole out there. Riots. No law. We need the fucking bombs and soldiers to bring some fucking order back. I'm all for it!*
> (Ridley, 2005)

This compares with the derelict flat in one of Ridley's plays for young people, *Moonfleece*:

> *The peeling wallpaper and decrepit furniture... indicate the place has not been 'officially lived in' for years.* (Ridley, 2004)

In this work, the flat represents a site whereby resistance is established against the destabilising influences exerted upon society by the political extremities of the far right.

In a similar vein, in another play for children, Ridley chooses a ruined house as the setting for Brokenville, one of his plays for children:

> *Signs of family life are scattered everywhere; framed photographs, toys, etc. Also, a bed, table, chairs. Everything damaged by some nameless catastrophe. In the moonlight this becomes a dreamscape of broken memory.* (Ridley, 2001)

The decayed urban landscapes are metonymic devices that draw out a past life and history. Explicit link is made between constructions of dreams and of memory. Within *Kasper in the Glitter*, (Ridley, 1995) the derelict environs beneath the arch of the railway bridge arch becomes the habitat for an emergent power hierarchy in which The Glitter – capitalised and assuming God-like omniscience – exerts control.

What function do the similarities amongst these settings pose? Structured around Ridley's writing is an autobiographical commentary that has been viewed as key to the gestation of his work. The published screenplay for *The Krays* (Ridley, 1997) includes an author interview in which Ridley details the importance of the East End of London to his writing and relates his own story involving Ronnie Kray. The settings can be viewed as unlocking a part of Ridley's construction of his own childhood, which he views as being central to his writing. Viewed figuratively, a landscape of urban decay creates a past that whilst being signalled by the text, suggests historic legacy and reference points beyond the text. This parallels initial childhood experience, where a history and understanding of one's environment is alien to the child and therefore assumes a dream-like and mythic quality upon which desires and neurosis can be projected and played out. In *Scribbleboy* this takes the guise and form of an epic quest whereby, under the tutelage of Ziggy Fuzz, Bailey Silk seeks the history and origins of various 'tags' carried out by a legendary Scribbleboy:

> If you look around the neighbourhood, you'll see lots of graffiti. Most of it is ugly and boring. But there are some pieces of graffiti that are not totally ugly and boring at all. That's because... they're not graffiti! They're Scribbles! (Ridley, 1997)

Memory and place seem to be explicitly linked for Ridley. Talking about his own childhood in the author's note to the play script of The Krays, he describes

> ...vivid memories of people clustered together, gossiping about violence and murder. I remember one particular night, lying in bed and listening to my Mum, Grandmother and Aunts discuss how the Krays had beaten someone unconscious. Then ran over his body in their car. 'They deliberately aimed of his head,' I remember someone saying. 'They crushed it!' This image of a crushed head haunted me for ages. (Ridley, 1997)

This is comparable to *Mercury Fur*. Violent childhood memories manifest themselves through a transgression of setting. Fictions are set amidst dystopian environs where choice and reaction become a microcosm of the fictional worlds referenced through the works. Civilised order is lost in these settings, necessitating a return to a base set of ethics and values whereby survival, and an understanding of one's personal situation, become crucial in the establishment of a power hierarchy and the ensuing power struggles that lead toward this end point. In *Brokenville* the resonance memory holds for characters is shown as power over others. Where memory fails, story succeeds in making sense of the landscape that surrounds them. The old woman in the play adopts the form and guise of the fairytale in making sense of the landscape around her.

> Old woman: There was once a land where everything was in ruins. Like this place. No one knew what had caused everything to be broken. But Broken it was. And this land was called...
> Satchel: Brokenville?
> Old woman: What - ? Oh, yes! Very good. Brokenville. Now we're getting somewhere. There was once a land called Brokenville. And, like all fairy-tale lands, it had a...
> Satchel: Castle!
> Old woman: Exactly! (at Child) You see the top of that wall? The jagged brick. That's just what the turret looked like... (Ridley, 2001)

Imbued with the power of story-telling, the old woman becomes the narrator. The universality of the common-language of fairy-tale, however, creates a democracy and memory of story that transforms the landscape that surrounds them. The shattered and fragmented relics of the world that surrounds them are adhered by the language of the story. The seemingly senseless can be made sense of through narrative placement.

In *Mercury Fur*, the actualisation of memory becomes a means whereby the horrors and atrocities of human history become merged and ill-defined. There is a blurring between acquired knowledge – implied through a sense of failed education – personal memory, and the fictitious. One of the two organisers of a party, Darren finds himself subject to the will of his brother Elliot; his notions of understanding of the past are so weakened that his present is now completely reliant upon his brother. Darren describes his own decidedly skewed version of history, more specifically, the assassination of President Kennedy, to Naz who, in Elliot's absence has entered the flat.

> *All I know is Kennedy won the war. I think he dropped a couple of atom bombs or something and turned all the Germans into Chinkies. He dumped the blonde tart for causing so much grief and started to go out with this dark-haired girl who lived in Camelot or something. And one day they decide to pay a visit to this place called Dallas...* (Ridley, 2005).

For boys like Zip and Newt of the Jingle family in *Zip's Apollo*, (Ridley, 2005) being dispossessed of the family home after the death of their father represents a trauma that gains the weight of significance of the grief and bereavement each of the family members feel. Zip, affectionately known as Bigbrov, becomes involved in understanding their position. This is drawn out through a dream-like sequence in which Apollo, a shopping-trolley, becomes a siphon for the boys' interest in space-travel and flight and forms a safe environment in which Zip is able to explore his memories and feelings regarding the forest where his father dies. He is then able to understand the letter left for him:

> *I'm enclosing a drawing of a place I visited when I was about your age. It was this place that got me interested in all the things that were to fill the rest of my life. In a way, my journey here to save the Ancient Oak started when I did this drawing. They were built – as far as anyone can tell – to celebrate the rising sun. Especially at solstice. Never forget the solstice, Zip. The longest and shortest day of the year. Remember?*
> *Celebrating the solstice is one of the oldest rituals known to mankind. I always think these stone structures look like doorways. Doorways to where? Who knows? Perhaps, one day, you'll find out Zip.* (Ridley, 2005)

A logocentric understanding of what the structure represents is avoided; instead it gains figurative meaning as a doorway of sorts. The doorway symbolises a transition between the known and the unknown – in this case life and death – and forms part of the way in which Zip becomes able to comprehend his father's death and the ramifications this has for him.

In the play, a blurring of history and sensationalist story is symptomatic of the repeated ingestion of mind-altering butterflies. In attempting to explain the initial occurrence of these insects, Darren's narrative is mythologised by failure of memory and lack of historical perspective.

> "There was a white butterfly. And... there was a sandstorm. One has something to do with the other but... Oh, fuck it, you'll have to ask Ell." (Ridley, 2005).

Darren's lack of comprehension means he has an inability to achieve coherence in his narrative; hence his eventual giving up. Darren's brother Elliot is cogent in the structuring of his recollections. He describes what he found amidst the sand on the night when the country was warned of a freak storm.

> A cocoon. A butterfly cocoon. I close the door. I keep hearing planes. I keep seeing sand and cocoons. But I don't see or hear any fucking storm. (Ridley, 2005)

The official story for the arrival of this sand was that it blew in on a storm. Nature and technology are juxtaposed. This juxtaposition is a development in Ridley's recent work that can be traced through his latest two children's novels *Mighty Fizz Chilla* (2002), in which urban anxiety is displaced amongst a backdrop of cathartic storytelling in Cornwall, and in *Zip's Apollo* where the fairytale forest setting results in heightened understanding of familial socio-politics.

The storm in *Mercury Fur* is constructed as nature, but is used as obfuscation for a political agenda for social control (whether internal from our government or external as a means of biological warfare). The butterflies themselves represent the culmination of combined beauty and barbarism, both in their physical bodies with their manifold colours and patterns, and in the effects they have when ingested. The associated loss of conscious restraint over our thoughts and desires returns individuals to a primeval state where control is disrupted. They are also a reference point for chaos theory, which suggests that the lone movement of a butterfly wing can have the resultant effect downstream of a hurricane. In *Mighty Fizz Chilla*, the natural is represented through many means, but culminates most interestingly in the 'Mighty Fizz Chilla' itself, a mythical beast. Captain Jellicoe attempts to describe the beast to Milo.

> The pattern on the skin – well, that's a bit like a tiger.
> A tiger it is laddy. A tiger's body! And, as I lie, day after day, I get glimpses of all these things. Sometimes a tentacle and horn. Sometime a shark head and horn. Sometimes a tiger body, tentacle and horn. But, no matter how long I watch, I never see the complete creature. Or how the various bits of its body are connected. (Ridley, 2002)

Bestial representation of fears, uncertainty and neurosis manifests itself as a constant theme across Ridley's children's work, whether through the *Mighty Fizz Chilla*, described above, where the natural and the manufactured are placed in balance as form for the creature is gained from the glass ornaments Milo smashes, in the crocodile that exists beneath Lizard Street in *Krindlekrax*, against which Ruskin Splinter must battle, the eels in *Dakota of the White Flats,* or the rat that kills Timothy in *Mercedes Ice* (1989).

In trying to rationalise the hallucinogenic effects the butterflies cause, Darren displays a rare clarity of vision. 'It only works if you've got a memory of an assassination in ya somewhere.' He later explains 'It can be from telly. Or old photos. Just look at as much of it as ya can before ya take one and – Bingo!' Images are presented as being indelible, affecting the sub-conscious, but not necessarily the conscious – as is shown by the lack of historical perspective. Television and photographs provide a simulated reality devoid from the necessities of responsibility; they are viewed but do not have to be 'assimilated' on moral levels and are thus representative of the disorganisation, chaos and disintegration of rules that characterise the play. The concpt of objects unlocking memory is key to the emotional drive of Ridley's work. Poppy Picklesticks and Rocky Nylon in *Vinegar Street* achieve this through their music, the potency of which has a transformative affect upon the landscape around them through empowering the influences of nature."

History in *Mercury Fur* is structured in so fragmented a manner that political motivations are lost to a series of visual representations of the past. Interconnections between these are lost, with the result that that context is saturated entirely by the visual nature of the images themselves. This compares with Ridley's children's work, in which characters, such as Bailey Silk in *Scribbleboy* (1997) seek an understanding of their own past as a means for engaging with their present. The difference is that, in *Mercury Fur*, that resolution is despairing – not without hope for the constructed 'others' outside the play, but entirely hopeless for the characters in the play. Such nihilism would ultimately impress further upon children the very confusions from which Ridley endeavours to tease out meaning in his work for younger audiences.

The image, whether barbaric – as in the instance of the atom bombs – or beautiful as intended by the archetypal ideal female, 'the blonde tart', Marilyn Monroe, becomes the whole. Narrative framing becomes a means only for the loose tying of these discursive images. What does this commentary on education – or its failure of application – say about contemporary childhood?

Commentary on and around the play by theatre critics has seemed reticent in the consideration of the implications for childhood. Ironically, the play itself falls prey to the very non-politicisation that leads to the incongruous nature of historical discourse presented within it. By consequence, the force of impact of the drama is lost through failure to engage with the notions of childhood that are presented. A brief discussion of criticism arising from the work highlights the lithe and slippery notions of contextualised understanding that seems to have been gleaned from the play's performance.

Philip Fisher, in a review for the *British Theatre Guide*, is nothing short of effusive about the play, but the interpretive space of Fisher's review slips between a series of uneasy comparisons. The review does not define *Mercury Fur* within the terms of the play's own discourse, but rather through a series of references that apparently give likeness toward or else sweepingly assume the dramatic impetus of the play. Ridley's play is described as 'pure Sarah Kane dystopia', it is recognised that 'William Golding's *Lord of the Flies* might also have been an influence'. Theatrical space is a 'Tracy Emin ante-room'. One of the characters, the party guest, is described as sounding 'Eric Idle' and as wanting 'to mix Rambo and Michael Jackson fantasies'. Peculiarly, this name-dropping from the popular conscience of the media lends Fisher's review and its inability to negotiate with the text of Ridley's play an image-heavy, though context-starved, base similar to that portrayed within the play itself.

Similarly effusive is Roger Malone's review for *The Stage*. This assures readers of being 'hijacked by thundering theatre, a black subject shimmering with jagged dialogue', but does little in exploring the nature of this subject or the repercussions of such jagged dialogue. Instead, Malone chooses for the most part to focus upon the performances of the actors... Shane Zaza is 'intuitive', Fraser Ayres, 'chilling'. Though the focus here is altered, the conclusion remains similar to Fisher's above. 'Images from Ridley's unsettling vision lodge uncomfortably and provocatively in the brain far longer than would some diluted alternative.' The nature of these 'images', however, and any context or negotiation of concerns raised through the play tend to be submerged by more specific visual elements. This appears to be standard through most of the criticism.

Paul Taylor in *The Independent* focuses for a large portion of his review on those who chose 'to leave prematurely during the interval-less two-hour piece.' Taylor claims, 'it is a play that offers more shocks than enlightenment and that never persuades me we are living on the brink of linguistic decay, civic breakdown and nightmare apocalypse' (Taylor, 2005)

Charles Spencer seems happier to assess the play alongside Ridley's previous work than to negotiate its component parts in his article for *The Independent*, making the extraordinary claim that

> ...his past form as a writer, and by the evidence of this play in particular, persuade me that he is actually turned on by his own sick fantasies and is offering no more than cheap thrills. And as is so often the case in sensationalist art, graphic cruelty is accompanied by a creepy, and in this case homoerotic, sentimentality. (Spencer, 2005)

Spencer is biting in his criticism, further stating

> Mercury Fur *is a poisonous piece, and I was particularly concerned that a 13-year-old child actor has to endure the revoltingly racist, four-letter dialogue while being treated like an object and tortured with a lighted cigarette on stage.* (Spencer, 2005)

Michael Billington in *The Guardian* describes an 'instant distrust of the play' that 'springs less from its violence than from its reactionary despair and assumption that we are all going to hell in a handcart.' (Billington, 2005).

A discrepancy exists between the reviewers of the theatrical publications – who admire the sense of drama and pace in the work – and the theatre critics in newspapers, who express unease about the ethics of the play. It is notable that Spencer, after implying an awareness of his past writing – negating any mention of his body of children's work, novels or plays – claims he is persuaded Ridley is sexually aroused by his subject matter. This seems peculiar, given that love and sex are depicted in two distinct areas. Ridley hypothesises that when sex is not an adjunct to love, it becomes barbaric. To suggest otherwise fails to negotiate with the elements of story – and most specifically the acts by which it is attempted that love succeeds.

Attraction between Darren and Naz, a customer of Elliot who operates as a butterfly-pusher, is portrayed as ejaculatory when Darren puts his hand to Naz's chest, the latter comments: 'Cut me neck right now, me blood'll spurt right across the room, I reckon.' Though the language is violent, the understanding of human emotion, of the heart as the symbolic centre of human attraction remains. In spite of the circumstances of the dystopian society, physical attraction as the first stages of love still remains.

This sense of attraction manifests itself through a desire for protection and survival. 'I was just thinking. What if there's any trouble? Here. While you're gone. Shouldn't I have something to... ya know... protect me and Naz?' The volatile nature of the atmosphere outside the flat, and the fear of its intrusion into the space of the flat is highlighted here. Weaponry is not constructed as a means for destruction but as a way of leveraging security and personal protection.

Like kinship derived from sexual attraction, familial bonds still live and remain in these most extreme and polarised of settings. Love continues to manifest itself even if its mechanisms are those of intolerance, hatred and violence towards one another. Papa Spinx – whose name itself indicates paternity – is a gangster baron, but one with a sense of protection of his own 'pride'. Talking of the 'Party Guest' he explains:

> He's paying with contacts. Where to go. Where to be safe. What to say. I'm trying to save us here. All of us! That why we've got to go ahead with this. (Ridley, 2005)

Papa Spinx strives for salvation of himself and his own in a godless society – it is not the act, but rather the price that must be paid for personal protection that comes under moral scrutiny. This is a direct reflection of the type of solvent that is sought in *Meteorite Spoon* (1994) by Filly and Fergal, to secure their parents' conjugal future in Honeymoonia, a setting that transports their parents in time and place to their honeymoon and to the emotional truths both felt at that point.

Attraction and appeal is mirrored by the beauty of language that Ridley achieves. This contrast between the barbaric and the beautiful is a constant theme throughout Ridley's body of work, whether this be in debut novel, *Crocodilia* (1988) where an anus is described in painful terms as swollen, but is tormented with jewels, or in *Dakota of the White Flats* (1989) in which Lassiter Peach, a reclusive author, bound by his own hatred, keeps a jewel encrusted turtle. Fairytale-esque language of beauty and opulence is incongruent with the graphic violence described within the drama. Here Naz articulates the effects of ingesting one species of butterfly:

> You get all the happy, floaty stuff of the blue. But ya still punch someone's face in. You do it all slow and graceful. Like ya gliding. Everything sparkles and shines. The face you're caving in sort of explodes like... what's that thing old people used to keep all their earrings and rings and stuff in. (Ridley, 2005)

Language is not constant. Ridley utilises a form of parapraxis whereby certain words are mistaken or omitted; in this instance, it is 'jewellery box'. Other examples in the play include the linguistic slippage of 'sister' which it becomes possible to define only as a female 'brother' – a fact that reflects the types of horror that Naz witnessed arbitrated against his own sister:

> Can hear Stace crying but I can't see her. The crying is real close. It seems to be coming from this big smashed fruit. It's all red inside and very juicy. It's got an eye. It's Stace! The gang has stomped on her head. One of her arms is gone. The gang drags her away and pull off her knickers. She's pissing herself. (Ridley, 2005)

What makes these descriptions more disturbing is that they are perpetrated against children and that they necessarily leave a footprint that has an impact upon the individual into early adulthood. Inability to achieve a sense of resolution or even of base rationalisation means that memories become suppressed and merely accepted as the everyday; a direct contrast to Zip Jingle's encounters with his father's letter, shown above.

Expressing incredulity at his brother's attempted deception as to the precise quantity of butterfly that was ingested, Elliot claims 'I've seen gang-raped toddlers act with more alacrity.' The statement is structured as an empirical truth, indicating the nature of the dystopian society that is presented as being simultaneously both within and outside the parameters of the text. Over-exposure has led to an evolved – or degenerated – form of language in which violence and atrocities are signifiers in linguistic terms but no longer have the moral impact of having been signified. The power of the play lies in the discrepancy between what the audience are provoked and stimulated to think and feel in relation to the violated child and the lack of conscience on the part of its subjects. The party that surrounds the child and of which he forms an integral part in *Mercury Fur* is in direct opposition to the protection and shelter that is afforded to the 'Child' in *Brokenville*, in which characters endeavour to placate him, using story-telling as a palliative device.

Hypothesising about the exact nature the 'party' will take, Darren interrogates his brother, desperate to find an identity which he is able to assume:

> *Was it gonna be a murder thing, Ell? We're detectives. Someone's been shot. A child's been gang raped and chopped up. Or chopped up and gang raped.*
> (Ridley, 2005)

Other people's fantasies, however, 'perverted', are manifested as normality. This lends the play a visceral quality. The role-play is reliant upon past experience, whether direct or circuitous, of violence and sexual transgression.

Childhood is presented as being the means by which the needs, functions and fantasies of individuals and/or society are best able to be met. Talking about the 'Party Piece', a ten-year-old boy, Elliot states: 'He's supposed to be lean'. In an attempt to divest himself of any need for responsibility, Elliot later describes how 'Darren has been feeding him…'. The responsibility and care that, it is implied, are needed to raise a healthy child, are absent. This idea of size and well-being is subverted still further when Lola states 'I wanna measure his waist.' Are the clothes being posited here as being made to fit the child, or is the child being made to 'fit the clothing' that is provided and passed down to him from the adult world? The idea of adults 'dressing' children is one in which function and fantasy meet. There is a power dialectic between appearance, perception and sub-conscious desires which mirrors Max's experiences in *ZinderZunder* (1998) when his talent for dancing is realised, although here the entertaining quality of that talent becomes all encompassing. The 'Party Guest' and his fantasies, which he wishes to actualise upon the 'Party piece', constitute a post-modern meta-theatrical element of the play when he assumes the guise of the Vietnamese militia. Affecting the role wholesale, the 'Party Guest' describes how a 'Judas' is in the entertainment corps dressed as Elvis Presley. He states:

> I'm gonna stick that meat hook in him and I'm gonna twist it and – (At Spinx) You won't film my face, will you? (Ridley, 2005)

From the phallic nature of the meat hook, this is a sexual metaphor but one, because of its pointed nature, that is a 'perversion' of normal sexual practice. That the act is to be filmed distances it from reality and context. Aware of his own role the 'Party Guest' is keen that his face should not be filmed so that anonymity can be preserved.

Childhood as being a time of powerlessness is demonstrable through Darren, who is brain-damaged following an altercation with his father involving a hammer on the head. Explaining the background to this, in a typically fragmented manner but with an unusual sense of comprehension Darren explains the motivation:

> It wasn't hate! It was the opposite of hate. They hit me 'cos they loved me. Okay? They loved me so much they wanted to save me from… from bad things. That sort of love don't exist anymore. It's prehistoric. I'm lucky, me. I've experienced it. I've got that inside me head and no one can ever take it away from me. (Ridley, 2005)

In this passage, love is presented as a cumulative formation of memories and feelings and emotions necessary to rationalise one's own past and reach some form of resolve. Children by turn are presented as sub-alterns, those whom power affects but are themselves devoid of power. Paternalistic power is taken to its extreme as the father exerts power over life and death. The semiotics of the hammer sign-post industrialism and represent a movement away from communist ideals whereby the agricultural and the industrial are place in alliance with one another. Totalitarian industry is present as being consumptive.

It is this process of consumption and the final act of being consumed that truly differentiates and distinguishes Ridley's fiction for adults and children. Critical response to *Mercury Fur* is wildly at variance with that of Ridley's often celebrated children's writing. This is epitomised most clearly by Dina Rabinovitch's selection of Ridley as 'Author of the Month' for the Guardian in April 2005. Rabinovitch states:

> His stories have a futuristic edge, psychology masked by flashing lights, emotions for the techy generation. So, in Zip's Apollo, the newest Ridley, shopping trolleys can read human minds, although, like newborn babes, the trolleys have to make

sense of the emotions around them. Meeting Ridley in person, you get the strong sense from him too of feelings that are still being worked out. (Rabinovitch, 2005)

Both grapple with emotionally complex subjects, but in adult work it is possible that their effects are so wide-reaching that they are mentally and – in the munitions-heavy climax to *Mercury Fur* – physically consumed entirely by the suppressed events and desires from childhood which have found no resolve. Whether children's fiction could ever be equal to such extreme nihilism is doubtful. In appraising the body of Ridley's work in readiness for the performances of his latest work *Leaves of Glass* (2007) Soho Theatre's publicity states that Ridley always describes his work as 'being primarily about love. Albeit a love that has to be glimpsed through broken glass'. In children's fiction, the glass remains transparent with the love and affection clearly visible behind it. In his adult work, opacity is a facet of the complexity which the audiences and readers are challenged to implement for themselves through their own individual interpretation.

REFERENCES

Michael Billington (3 March, 2005) 'Mercury Fur', *The Guardian*.

Philip Fisher (2005), 'Mercury Fur', *British Theatre Guide*.
<http://www.painesploughthestage.co.uk/reviews/review.php/6673> [viewed 01 April, 2007]

Roger Malone (2005), 'Mercury Fur', *The Stage*.
<http://www.painesploughthestage.co.uk/reviews/review.php/6673> [viewed 01 April, 2007]

Dina Rabinovitch (27 April, 2005) 'Author of the month: Philip Ridley', *The Guardian*.

Philip Ridley, *Crocodilia*. London: Penguin, 1988.

Philip Ridley, *Dakota of the White Flats*. London: Puffin, 1989.

Philip Ridley, *Mercedes Ice*. London: Puffin, 1989.

Philip Ridley, *Krindlekrax*. London: Puffin, 1992.

Philip Ridley, *Kasper in the Glitter*. London: Puffin, 1995.

Philip Ridley, *Meteorite Spoon*. London: Puffin, 1994.

Philip Ridley, *The Krays*. London: Methuen, 1997.

Philip Ridley, *Scribbleboy*. London: Puffin, 1997.

Philip Ridley, *ZinderZunder*. London: Puffin, 1998.

Philip Ridley, *Vinegar Street* London: Puffin, 2000.

Philip Ridley, *Brokenville*. London: Faber and Faber, 2001.

Philip Ridley, *Mighty Fizz Chilla*. London: Puffin, 2002.

Philip Ridley, 'Moonfleece', *Connections 2004*. London: Faber and Faber, 2004.

Philip Ridley, *Mercury Fur*. London: Methuen, 2005.

Philip Ridley, *Zip's Apollo*. London: Puffin, 2005.

Philip Ridley, *Leaves of Glass*. London: Methuen, 2007.

Soho Theatre (2007), Love songs for extinct creatures: the poetry of Philip Ridley.
<http://www.sohotheatre.com/pl1315.html> [viewed 01 April, 2007]

Charles Spencer (5 March, 2005) 'Mercury Fur and Breathing Corpses', *The Telegraph*.

Paul Taylor (9 March, 2005) 'Mercury Fur', *The Independent*.

Conference 2007 Photographs

Nick Midgley

The courage to be afraid: Fearful Encounters in the work of Neil Gaiman and Dave McKean

An earlier draft of this paper was presented at a conference on 'Fear and Fiction' organised by the Yale Child Study Centre and the Anna Freud Centre in New York in December 2006, and one section of it was included in the Psychoanalytic Study of the Child, Volume 61, as part of their report on that conference. Thanks to the publishers and editors of that journal for permission to use some of that material in the present chapter.
Nick Midgley, Anna Freud Centre, London

A brief word of introduction

NEIL GAIMAN – a British writer living in the US – has only recently become well-known as an author of books for children, but the range of work that he has produced over the last 20 years has a huge international following. Having established himself as the author of the extraordinary graphic novel, *The Sandman*, a fantasy/mythological tale which runs to over 2,000 pages and has sold over a million copies, Gaiman has gone on to write several best-selling novels, both for adults and for children, as well as plays, songs and a number of film-scripts. He has worked with many illustrators, but most noticeably with Dave McKean, whose distinctive style has come to be closely associated with Gaiman's work. Together, they have collaborated in different ways on three works for children that I will be discussing here – a picture-book for younger children, *The Wolves in the Walls*; a novel for slightly older readers (8-13 year olds), *Coraline*; and a film aimed more at a teenage audience, *MirrorMask*. The books are both written by Neil Gaiman and illustrated by McKean; and the film is directed and designed by McKean with a script by Gaiman. Each of these works, although written for young people of different ages, can broadly be described as works of fantasy, horror and/or supernatural mystery. In the words of one review, Gaiman's work is like 'Alice in Wonderland crossed with Stephen King', suggesting the odd mix of humour and horror that is so characteristic of these works.

In what follows, I want to look at these three works in order to think about the role of fear in the emotional development of children and young people. In what way can 'frightening fiction' play a role in such development? Do such works manipulate children's emotions and cause them harm, as some critics assert? Or can such works play a part in fostering emotional development? For the purposes of this chapter, emotional development is not understood as a straightforward, chronological set of 'stages', each with their own distinct challenges; but rather as a spiral, circling around certain core themes, which take on different contours and textures at different periods of our lives. What these themes are from a psychoanalytic point of view, and how they are revisited at different stages in childhood, is beautifully described in Margot Waddell's book, *Inside Lives. Psychoanalysis and the Growth of the Personality* (Rev edition, 2002), and I will draw upon this work in what follows.

Children and fear

It is perhaps helpful, however, to begin by saying something more generally about fear and childhood, and the way in which stories may (or may not) engage with this most primitive and powerful emotion.

Anyone who has lived or worked with children will know how central fear is to their lives. The child who lies awake in bed at night, terrified of the shadow cast on the wall by the moonlight coming from behind the curtains; the child at the door of the classroom, screaming as the parent tries to say goodbye and leave; or the child in the consulting room, scared that if they come to trust this person – the therapist – they will either be rejected or abandoned, or worse...

How should we – as parents, teachers, authors, therapists – respond to such situations? The historian, Joanne Bourke (2005), has written about the different ways in which child care manuals written in Britain and the US over the last hundred years have encouraged parents to deal with their children's fears. At the start of the twentieth century a whole series of books, with titles such as *'How to Keep your Child from Fear'* (1908) or *'Faith or Fear in Child Training'* (1934), encouraged parents to protect their children from being scared. In reaction to the hellfire and brimstone threats of damnation that were so much a part of nineteenth century British education, or the stories of the bogeyman used to enforce a paralysing obedience in the 'naughty' child, the 'modern'

approach to child-rearing emphasised protection and kindness. Such an attitude continued in the post-war years, with manuals such as Dr Spock's *Common Sense Book of Baby and Child Care* (1946), which encouraged affection and understanding as the cure for childhood fears, and warned against making a child scared unnecessarily. In his hugely influential book, Spock wrote:

> Fears are commoner in children who have been made tense from battles over such matters as feeding and toilet training, children whose imaginations have been over-stimulated by frightening stories or too many warnings...(quoted by Bourke, p.101)

As a child psychotherapist, I certainly know all too well the detrimental impact that fear, violence and threats can have on children's development. But in that phrase, where Spock warns us about children whose minds might be 'over-stimulated by frightening stories', there is something that makes me hesitate to quite go along with what is being suggested. I'll try and explain why.

Child psychoanalysis began, almost exactly one hundred years ago, with a little boy who was frightened that a horse would bite him. Throughout his life Freud was fascinated to try and understand from whence these anxieties and fears, that can have such devastating effects on our lives, derive, and what the strange attraction of terror is for us as human beings. In his 1919 essay on *The Uncanny*, Freud investigates one such emotion that 'arouses dread and horror', but which is more specifically, as the German word 'un-heimlich' (un-homely) indicates, 'that class of the frightening which leads us back to what is known of old and long familiar' (pp.339/40).

Through a detailed reading of Hoffman's disturbing tale of *The Sandman* (a work that clearly inspired Gaiman's own work of that name), Freud identifies some of the key features used by Hoffman to create a sense of the uncanny – a deliberate uncertainty about whether a particular figure is human or non-

human; a blurring of the distinction between fantasy and reality; playing on the fear of being damaged in the eyes; and a use of the theme of 'doubles' and 'doubling'. All of these themes, suggests Freud, have infantile roots, relating back to our earliest oedipal desires and the fears and anxieties that accompany such desires.

Freud's work makes clear the way in which confronting the terrifying and the horrific is an important aspect of emotional development. Tales of horror pose a threat to the delicate web of repressions and disavowals that forms our identity, but also allow us to re-engage with the deeper, repressed levels of our existence and our desires; just as psychoanalysis takes us on a difficult, un-settling journey within ourselves in order to re-vitalize and expand our sense of who we are as individuals.

And that brings us back to those 'frightening stories' that Spock warned us not to tell our children, and to those frightening tales presented to us by Gaiman and McKean...

The Wolves in the Walls

From the moment we pick up a copy of *The Wolves in the Walls*, we are already in no doubt that issues of identity and terror are at stake. The front cover shows us a young girl, defiantly looking out towards us, the reader/viewer, while her hand is turned towards a piece of paper on which is drawn a crude picture of a monster, its mouth open and its sharp teeth showing. Most disconcerting of all, however, are the tears in the paper where the eyes should be. From behind the torn paper, staring out at us with as much intensity as the girl herself, are two blood-red eyes. The title above this picture leaves us in no doubt, that these are the dangerous eyes of the wolves in the walls, watching us, waiting...

This theme, so common in tales of supernatural horror, of a house that is gradually invaded by dark and dangerous forces, surely builds on those common fears that almost all young children have: a fear of the dark, of creatures under the bed, of the shadows that are waiting to jump out and gobble us up. But why are such fears so common in early childhood? And why do these animals with ferocious, biting teeth – the wolves, the rats – play such a central part in these fears? It is not coincidental that two of Freud's best known case histories are built around the infantile fear of just such animals – *the Wolf Man*, with his petrifying dream of the wolves in the trees, and the *Rat Man*, with his dread of the anus-penetrating rat-torture that he hears about from a fellow army officer. Wolves, especially, appear to have a profound role to play in the archaic fears that each of us carry with us, straddling both fantasy (Little Red Riding Hood, the myth of the werewolf) and reality.
For Freud, of course, these terror-inducing animals can be traced back to infantile oedipal aggression and subsequent fears of castration, coloured, no doubt, by more primitive oral and anal impulses. Klein emphasises the

cannibalistic aspect, and the way in which the infant's own oral-sadistic fantasies of penetrating and devouring the inside of the mother's body result in equally terrifying fantasies of retaliation. Ernest Jones, in his classic study of the nightmare (1931), noted that wolves, in particular, have all kinds of powerful resonances in the mind, associated with insatiable appetite, with swift and dangerous movement in the light, a lust for blood – not to mention their open display of sexuality and unbridled passions.

Such are some of the connotations that we may bring with us when we read the title, *The Wolves in the Walls*. Then we open the book, and read on. Gaiman's book has at its centre a child, Lucy, who in some way has 'lost' her parents – a father preoccupied with his tuba-playing, a mother with her jam-making – too busy to really pay attention to their daughter or the fears that she is bringing them; or else ready to dismiss them with grown-up rationalisations.

Gaiman has said in interviews that this book was based on a nightmare that his young daughter had, in which wolves came out of the walls and took over the house. In one such interview (2006a), Gaiman explained how he began telling stories to his daughter about this nightmare scenario 'to make it funnier and easier for her'; but the story he tells by no means avoids the full terror of the situation. (And Dave McKean's wonderfully disturbing images play their part here too). I remember the chill that ran down my spine when I first read how Lucy's mother (and then her father and brother), calmly assure her that the noise she is hearing couldn't be wolves: "'Anyway, you know what they say about the wolves', said her father. 'If the wolves come out of the walls, then it's all over'. 'Who says that?', asked Lucy. 'People. Everybody. You know', said her father, and he went back to practicing his tuba."

True to psychoanalysis (and to the whole genre of horror movies), that which is most terrifying is that which can't be seen or even be identified – described by various psychoanalysts with evocative phrases such as 'psychotic' or 'unthinkable' anxiety, 'nameless dread'. This is the fear that *The Wolves in the Walls* evokes, and for a moment any parent considering whether to buy this book for their child (as I remember thinking myself) would be forgiven if they recalled Dr Spock's warning about over-stimulating children's minds with frightening stories, and put this book back on the shelf... after all, rather than insisting that everything will be alright, that there is really nothing to fear, the adult characters all calmly confirm our very worst fear: that if the wolves are to escape, 'then it is all over' – the un-nameable dread will be realised. And, what is worse, the wolves do emerge from the walls and the family are forced to flee for their lives. Surely this is too much for a young child's imagination to bear?

But then I read on. Lucy's courage in returning to the house which has been over-taken by the wolves to rescue her toy pig is the start of a process by which these creatures of terror become nothing more than a pale, infantile imitation of the family they have replaced: eating popcorn while they watch

TV, sliding down banisters and wearing socks on their tails. 'Overcoming fears is in itself therapeutic', writes the cultural critic, Marina Warner, 'and humour relaxes the grip of bogeys, real or fantastic' (1998, p.329). Inspired by Lucy's courage, the family decide to return to the house, and hide in the walls. When they begin to emerge, the wolves flee in terror, for the wolves all know the old saying: 'When the people come out of the walls... then it's all over!'.

Does this ending simply maintain the 'paranoid-schizoid' splitting, but with the human child now in the all-powerful position? Or does the humour of the book move us beyond such rigid defences, allowing us to play with emotions that might otherwise seem un-manageable? And should children's books be dealing with such 'dark' parts of the personality to begin with?

Gaiman himself has spoken passionately about his hostility to a definition of entertainment which meant 'something you can put a five year old in front of for two hours and come back safe in the knowledge that the child won't have been exposed to any "ideas"'. So too, he rejects stories made for children that suggests that 'the world is an incredibly safe, warm and comforting place and everything is lovely' (2006a). Children know all too well that this is not the case, both by looking inside – at their own powerful feelings of love and hate – and by looking outside at the world we live in. When un-palatable reality is denied, as psychoanalysis has shown, it will either return to haunt us in a more deadly form, or else such denial will be maintained at the cost of rigid, inflexible defences that cripple any emotional development. When it is confronted, it has the ability to lead to emotional development. But to be confronted, such fears need to be explored and elaborated. As Gaiman put it, very beautifully, in a recent talk:

The *Wolves in the Walls* began as an irritant, a nightmare my four year old daughter had about evil Wolves that took over our house ... I stole it from my daughter and I made it up and I carried it back from dreams, an irritant wrapped all in layers of wolfish pearl. (2006b, p.11)

Coraline

If we now turn to a book written by Gaiman for a slightly older audience, we will see that many of the same themes are explored, but they are articulated for a child at a slightly different stage in their emotional development. Whereas *The Wolves in the Walls* is probably written to be read aloud by a parent to their child, and speaks to the infantile fear of the dark, of the terrifying creatures that lurk in the shadows just outside our sight, *Coraline* is for a slightly older age group (the book cover suggests eight years and over) and is a more complex and disturbing tale, dealing with fears and anxieties related to a later stage of emotional development, in which the wish and need for separation from the parents exists alongside an on-going need to maintain the parents as loving and protective.

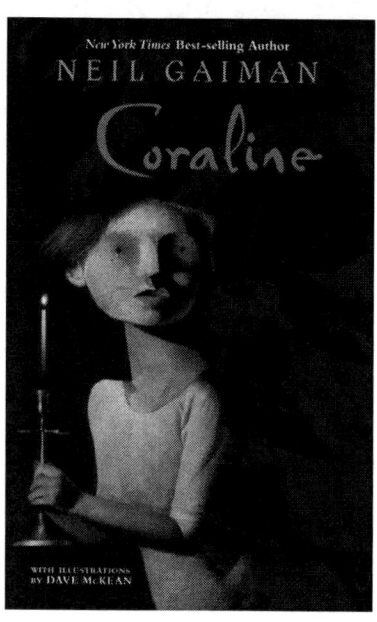 

This stage in early development has been described by psychoanalysts, perhaps rather unhelpfully, as the 'latency' stage, following Freud's view that this is a period in which the turbulent passions of the infantile Oedipus Complex have passed while the renewed tumult of puberty and adolescence has yet to emerge. In fact, this period of 'middle childhood' (as the developmental psychologists prefer to call it) clearly involves its own re-working of underlying fears and anxieties, especially as the child moves away from home and the family, towards a wider world, including school, friends and teachers. If there is, therefore, a certain degree of detachment from the external parents, this can only be achieved if they can be successfully installed internally, both in their loving and encouraging capacity (what has sometimes been called the 'ego-ideal') as well as their moral and prohibitive aspect (the 'superego' as it is traditionally represented). As Waddell puts it, 'the child is starting to experience a sense of having an internal world of his own ... Psychically he has the opportunity to shift to a situation in which he is less totally dependent on the external figure towards whom he has been directing such intense feelings, and more securely related to internal figures' (p.89). But the pull towards such autonomy depends on successfully negotiating the powerful pull – and the terrifying threat – of more regressive wishes.

Which leads us neatly into considering Gaiman's novel. Like many of the classic works of children's fiction, Coraline begins with the main character – again a young girl, like Lucy, but slightly older now – moving to a new house during a summer holiday and, with her parents emotionally somewhat absent and unavailable, having to find her own way of keeping herself occupied over a long summer holiday until her new school begins.

But the book also begins with familiar tropes from the horror genre too: strange noises that can't be explained; ominous warnings that tell Coraline that she is in danger, that something terrible is about to befall her. When our young heroine finds a door that leads into a parallel house, she inevitably walks through it, and finds herself in a terrifying mirror household (quite literally, both home and not-home - un-heimlich), in which she meets the 'other mother', who is, by contrast to Coraline's 'real' mother, attentive and prepared to give Coraline all that she wants (including all her favourite foods), in return for one thing: that she gives up her real home, and agrees to stay in this parallel universe. The offer certainly seems an attractive one. The only indication that something is not right comes when the other mother turns and shows Coraline her face: where her eyes should be, there are buttons – 'big and black and shiny'.

What makes the story so uncanny, in Freud's sense of the word, is the way in which the parallel world so closely mirrors Coraline's 'real' world, so that we are hardly aware of it being different. Yet something is not quite right. It is this sense of being both familiar and un-familiar, of being on the borderland between the human and non-human, which makes the other mother such an 'uncanny' figure, one whose true danger is sensed immediately, yet in a way that can scarcely be articulated. The other mother offers Coraline everything. If Coraline will only stay she will be indulged in every way (the way she speaks makes one sense that the other mother is hungry for Coraline, her teeth are just slightly too long, her look too ravenous); and the other mother asks only one thing in return: Coraline's eyes. When Coraline refuses, the other mother prevents her from going back, and holds Coraline's real parents as prisoners. It is up to Coraline to try and find a way to defeat the other mother, rescue her

parents and return home – but to do so, she must face some terrifying encounters that come straight from our deepest fears.

I will not describe all the horrors and dangers that Coraline faces – and overcomes – on her quest to try and rescue her parents and escape the clutches of the 'other mother'. But what comes across clearly from the way the story is told is that it is Coraline's own developing identity that is at stake in this story. At the start of the tale, everyone she meets gets Coraline's name wrong (they all think she is called 'Caroline', and don't notice when she tries to correct them); her identity is not yet clearly defined; she is dependent and emotionally attached to her real parents (when she is bored she goes and asks them what she should do) yet also resentful and angry at them (they fob her off with suggestions which mean she won't disturb them working). In contrast, the other mother can be seen as an idealised object, one who offers total attention and gratification. But she is an anti-developmental object, who offers this gratification at the expense of individual identity (the eyes) and emotional growth. The other mother's love is a wholly devouring or narcissistic love, that needs Coraline for her own sake, in the way a spider needs a fly.

I have to say that I almost believe there should be a warning on the cover of this book – Coraline is a toxic work that takes the child reader (or the child within the adult reader) into very primitive, psychotic parts of the personality. This is a dangerous place to go; yet such a journey, if successful, is of great emotional importance, and the story shows us what courage – what hard work – is needed to achieve such a developmental task. As G.K. Chesterton says, in a wonderful quotation that Gaiman places at the front of the book:

> *Fairy tales are more than true: not because they tell us that dragons exist, but because they tell us that dragons can be beaten.*

This sense of being able to overcome fear is embodied in the character of Coraline herself. From the start of the book, Coraline shows herself as a protagonist who enjoys a challenge. When her parents have been kidnapped by the other mother, and only Coraline can save them, her fear does not cripple her, and she begins a journey towards re-instating her parental internal objects, whom in fantasy she is somehow responsible for destroying. At the end of the story, she is able to reject the powerful appeal of this other mother. It is her 'own mother, her real, wonderful, maddening, infuriating, glorious mother' (p. 155), with all her faults, that Coraline manages to rescue and reaffirm at the end of the book, so overcoming the persecutory split between idealisation and denigration.

MirrorMask

The Wolves in the Walls and *Coraline* are both books written for younger children, and engage with fears that can be seen to relate quite specifically to

the developmental tasks of those periods of childhood. *MirrorMask*, however, is a film made primarily for a teenage audience, for whom horror and fantasy are popular genres; genres, moreover, in which anxieties about emerging sexuality and bodily changes, which are so much part of the adolescent process, are often at the forefront.

Made on a small budget, and drawing heavily on the visual style of Dave McKean's drawings for its design, we are once again in a realm of dream and nightmare, where an exploration of fear and emotional development is played out in the realm of fantasy and the imagination. In many ways, *MirrorMask* can be seen as a re-working of the story of *Coraline*, only now in the developmental context of puberty and adolescence: the main character in this film, Helena, a teenage girl on the cusp of sexual maturity, lives with her parents in their travelling circus, where she performs a juggling act with her father. But Helena resents this life, and begins the film angry with her parents and wanting to escape from her 'childish' dependence on them. In the heat of an argument, she wishes her mother was dead, only to see her collapse soon afterwards during the middle of a performance, and be rushed to hospital with a life-threatening illness, which requires immediate surgery.

This is, in Freud's terms, an 'uncanny' turn of events, one which both appears to confirm the infantile 'omnipotence of thought' that the rational mind has abandoned; and which touches on a repressed, infantile complex – that of Oedipus and the wish to get rid of the rival same-sex parent. Terrified at the idea that her anger might actually have been responsible for her mother's collapse, Helena makes manic attempts at reparation, drawing card after card to place at her mother's bedside, all wishing her to get well soon.

On the night when her mother must undergo life or death surgery, Helena herself goes on a dream journey into a parallel universe, while her place in the 'real' world is taken by a doppelganger, the 'other Helena'. In this dream-space, Helena must rescue the White Queen, who has been put into a charmed sleep (like her mother in hospital), and overcome the Black Queen (a terrifying re-incarnation of the 'other mother' from Coraline), both in order to save her (internal) mother's life and to re-gain her own place in the real world that has been usurped by the 'other Helena'.

As child analysts and psychotherapists – not to mention many parents – are aware, early adolescence can be thought of as a period of adjustment to a rapidly-changing body, brought on by the changes of puberty, as well as a revisiting of earlier infantile phantasies and anxieties. In Margot Waddell's terms, the 'psychic agenda' for the adolescent is a demanding one:

> ... the negotiation of the relationship between adult and infantile structures; the transition from life in the family to life in the world; the finding and establishing of an identity, especially in sexual terms; in short, the capacity to manage separation, loss, choice, independence, and perhaps disillusionment (p.140)

During this often turbulent period of life, old conflicts are re-worked, and the renewed anxieties about sexual and aggressive wishes can result in extremes of behaviour, with renewed hostility to parental figures combined with infantile-like dependence and an increased use of splitting and acting out to manage feelings that feel almost too powerful to contemplate. In Klein's terms, this can be understood as a re-working of the earlier gains of the depressive position in the face of renewed paranoid-schizoid splitting, a 're-engagement with the sense of guilt and responsibility for damage done, with fears of loss, with gratitude and sensitivity to others' (Waddell, p.148).

At the start of *MirrorMask*, Helena presents with a typical latency-style disgust about sexuality (she sees two people kissing on the back seat of a bus and looks suitably horrified); and she is very much her father's little girl, joining him in the circus ring to take part in their juggling act. When mother collapses and fails to appear in the ring to snatch back her husband, one could understand this as an imagined oedipal victory for Helena, who thereby gets rid of her mother and claims her father as her own. But it is an oedipal victory that is both the fulfilment of an infantile wish and a terrible fear – a fear that wishes can become reality, and that her murderous thoughts can actually destroy.

The doppelganger theme, which recalls Freud's writings on *The Uncanny*, illustrates well the splits that are so intrinsic to the adolescent phase. The anti-Helena, the version of herself that takes Helena's place in the 'real' world, rejects entirely any infantile dependency and transforms into the typical rebellious teenager – she dresses as a punk, smokes cigarettes, argues violently with her father, gets drunk and brings 'disreputable' boys back to her room. This is one form of adolescent development (or possibly anti-development) where action takes the place of thought, and identity is maintained by extreme forms of projection and splitting.

Meanwhile, in the dream-world, Helena falls prey to the other 'anti-developmental' solution to the adolescent dilemma: she is taken captive by the Black Queen, who like the 'other mother' in Coraline, promises her pretty frocks and dolls to play with and as much ice-cream as she would like to eat. Temporarily under the Black Queen's spell, Helena becomes polite and child-like once again, but at the price of losing her own personality, her own emerging adolescent identity. (Again, it is her eyes that register this captivity, which become empty and black, almost like the button-eyes of the other mother in Coraline).

This time, however, it is not simply Helena's own ingenuity that saves her – it is her relationship with a young man, appropriately named Valentine, whom she has met on her journey. When Helena is held captive by the Black Queen, Valentine helps to rescue her. It is when he invites Helena to juggle, as she used to do with her father, that she begins to revive from her 'deadened' state of mind. Together they manage to return Helena to her own world, where Helena confronts the anti-Helena for the first time. With the help of the MirrorMask, the faces of the two girls merge into one, 'like two beads of mercury slipping into each other' (Gaiman and McKean, 2005, p.300). At that moment, Helena's father arrives, with the news that her mother's operation has been a success, and that she is going to survive.

We can see how the ending of this film brings together many of the themes related to adolescence and emotional development that have already been presented. Helena overcomes the split between the two aspects of herself (dependent child and sexual adult) and the two aspects of her maternal imago, so that a more stable identity and a depressive concern for the feelings and wishes of others can emerge (Waddell, p. 147). The Black Queen is not destroyed, but rather a balance is re-established between the two sides of the mother-imago. This happens partly through forming a trusting relationship with a young man of her own generation. Both physically and in personality Valentine bears a certain similarity to her own father, suggesting the way in which oedipal love is transformed into age-appropriate sexuality.

But the change which Helena undergoes also reflects a more mature identification with her own mother. Significantly, the words she speaks to the anti-Helena when she confronts her for the final time ('Real life? You couldn't handle real life') are the same words that her mother spoke to her in the argument at the start of the film which led to her mother collapsing. Helena, it seems, has been able to re-discover a more positive identification with her mother, which allows her own personality to develop into that of a young, sexual adult with a partner of her own.

Conclusion

As I hope this discussion of the works of Gaiman and McKean has shown, emotional development cannot truly take place unless those deep fears – about loss, about abandonment, about our own destructive potential – can be reworked at each stage of our lives, continually confronted and engaged with. Simply closing our eyes to such fears does not aid development. But if we are to be able to face unpalatable reality, without being defeated by it, then it is essential that we do not have to do so alone. Stories are one way in which we no longer feel alone.

Lois Lowry, the American novelist for children, once spoke of the importance of books for children that talk not only of the 'bright streets', but also the 'dark paths' of loss, suffering and fear, 'so that real children with their own journeys to make will have fellow travellers' (2001, p.1). In the increasingly frightening world in which our children live, it is understandable that there is a temptation to try and 'protect' them from fear, to preserve their 'innocence' and to try and keep the horrors away. But those fears exist, and children are in need of guides – whether teachers, therapists or creative writers – to help create safe 'containers' for those fears to be explored and given words.

Such work takes courage on the part of us adults too. Wilfred Bion, an analyst known for his exploration of some of the darkest parts of the personality, once said that 'in a psychoanalytic treatment, there should always be two people who are frightened' (Bion, 1990). If stories are to help contain our 'unthinkable anxieties', to give structure to help overcome fear and gain the courage needed for emotional development, we need authors – and therapists, parents and teachers – able to face such fears in themselves, without turning away from these primitive anxieties. It is with good reason that the British children's author, Philip Pullman, once said:

At the best-selling end, adult literature is about childish things: *does my bum look big in this? Will Arsenal win the cup?* But children's literature is about grown-up things. *Where did we come from? Where do we go?* (quoted by Brennan, 2001, p.94).

For their courage in asking such grown-up – and frightening – questions, we have reason to be thankful to Neil Gaiman and Dave McKean, as well as all the other children's authors who help us on our journey through life.

REFERENCES

W. Bion, *Brazilian Lectures*. London: Karnac, 1990.

J. Bourke, *Fear. A Cultural History.* London: Virago, 2005.

G. Brennan, 'The game called Death: Frightening fictions by David Almond, Philip Gross and Lesley Howarth', in Reynolds, Brennan and McCarron (Eds.) *Frightening Fiction*. London: Continuum Books, 2001.

S. Freud, *The Uncanny*. Volume 17 of the Standard Edition of *the Compete Works of Sigmund Freud*, London: Hogarth Press, 1919/1958.

N. Gaiman, *The Sandman*. Comic book, 75 monthly issues. New York: DC Comics/Vertigo, 1989 - 1996. Collected in *The Sandman*, New York: Harper Collins, 1996.

N. Gaiman, *Coraline*. London: Bloomsbury, 2002.

N. Gaiman, *The Wolves in the Walls*. London: Bloomsbury, 2004.

N. Gaiman, 'About the book'. Interview with Neil Gaiman in the theatre programme for the National Theatre of Scotland's production of *The Wolves in the Walls*, 2006a.

N. Gaiman, 'Remarks'. Unpublished lecture at the Yale University/Anna Freud Centre Conference, October 2006b.

N. Gaiman and D. McKean, *MirrorMask. The Illustrated Film Script*. London: Headline Books, 2005.

E. Jones, *On the Nightmare*. London: Hogarth Press, 1931.

L. Lowry, 'Bright streets and dark paths'. Unpublished lecture at Brown University, March 2001.

M. Waddell, *Inside Lives. Psychoanalysis and the Growth of the Personality*. London: Karnac, 2002.

M. Warner, *No go the Bogeyman: Scaring, lulling and making mock*. London: Chatto and Windus, 1998

KEYNOTE
Margaret Rustin and Michael Rustin

The Regeneration of Doctor Who

Introduction

IN THIS ARTICLE, we shall be looking at the new series of *Dr Who*, currently in its third run on BBC Television since its revival in 2005. Our approach, which follows our earlier work on children's fiction and on drama, is in part psychoanalytic and in part sociological. From a psychoanalytic point of view, we are interested in the states of mind and feeling evoked in the dramatic action of the episodes, and the ways in which these provide imaginative spaces for the audience – especially children and adolescents – to explore aspects of their own development. From a more sociological point of view, we will suggest ways in which the show reflects aspects of the society in which it is set, including the ways in which it takes advantage of the opportunities of time and space travel to encourage its viewers to become aware of other 'possible worlds', different from their own. We shall focus on two episodes in particular, to demonstrate how much the production team has achieved in its regeneration of Dr Who.

Background to the Series

Dr Who was successfully revived in 2005, after a gap of sixteen years; what had been expected to be its final series ended in 1989. The show ran from 1963, with a succession of actors playing the Doctor, among them William Hartnell, Patrick Troughton, Jon Pertwee, Tom Baker and four after this – and taking the roles of his companions (there were twenty seven of these before Billie Piper's Rose, twenty of whom were female.) By the time it was taken off, *Dr Who* had become something of a parody of its former self, with its low-budget sets and poor special effects no competition for new genres of cinematic science fiction.

The new *Dr Who* is now into its third annual run, its second Doctor (in David Tennant) and now its second companion, in Freema Agyeman as Martha Jones, respectively following Christopher Ecclestone's and Billie Piper's great successes in these roles. The third series in 2007 continued to do well, both in terms of size of audience (over eight million for the first new episode of Series 3) and critical approval. What we want to explore here is how this has been accomplished, and what differentiates the 'new' Doctor Who of 2005 – 2007, from earlier versions.

There are many elements, of course, and we will first mention some of the more obvious. One of these relates to 'production values'. Partly because it has been assigned a large budget to these shows, and partly because of technical progress in special effects, computer graphics etc., since the previous series, Dr Who can do some visually impressive stuff – buildings exploding, fleets of spaceships, large-scale panics in the street – and competes with cinematic Sci Fi as well as any television productions have ever done. Another element relates to the narrative ambitions of the writers and producers of the show. The leading role of writers in these productions, particularly of Russell T. Davies, the designated Head Writer, is important in this. Davies has said that the setting of every episode is to be different. So, exploiting the possibilities for travel in both time and space that the traditional storyline of the series allows, we have been going from Victorian Cardiff and Scotland, to the moment of the formation of the earth in space, to political goings-on in Wales and London, to the France of Louis XV's court and Mme de Pompadour, to London at the height of the Blitz in 1941. The programme has been brilliant at times in capturing the styles and qualities of these moments and locations (this is an educationally-responsible purpose, in the best BBC tradition). A third dimension to note is the self-conscious location of *Dr Who* by its writers and production team in its own tradition as a series. The basic story-line of *Dr Who* has remained unchanged from the beginning. The Doctor is a Time Lord roaming space and time in the Tardis (his spaceship, unusually disguised as an old-fashioned Police Box), with a companion usually collected on one of his visits to contemporary Earth. His mission is to defeat various terrifying threats to humanity and life, these being embodied in various kinds of alien creatures or robots often commanded by megalomiacs,

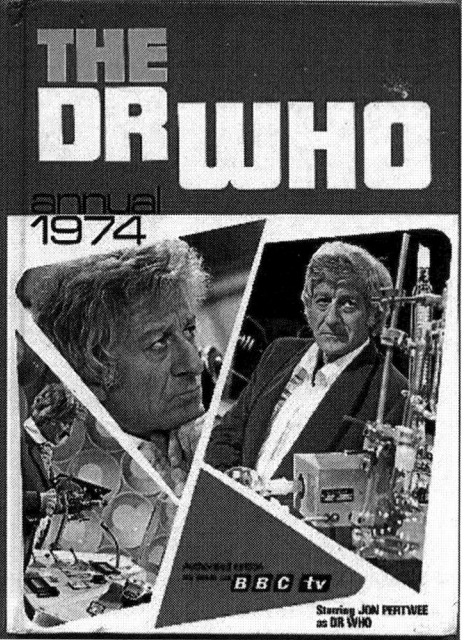

dominated by their will to destroy or enslave. The most famous, over forty years, have been the Daleks, with their mechanical-voiced battle-cry "exterminate, exterminate", known at one time by more-or-less every child in Britain. This galactic enemy has taken many different forms, Cybermen among them. The new series has retained these constant features of the show, and has succeeded in giving them a new life. We shall explore the ways in which this element of continuity has been an imaginative resource for the *Dr Who* team.

It is worth adding at this point that an important aspect of the *Dr Who* series is that it has always aimed to interest an audience of both children and adults. For a show broadcast early on a Saturday evening, this audience was conceived as children watching together with their parents, or more often perhaps their dads. This format creates a particular discipline for the show – it has had to be sufficiently confined, in language, emotion and violence, to be understandable to, and not too disturbing for, children, while being able simultaneously to engage its adult viewers' interest and feeling. The best fiction for children, even stories for the very young like those of Beatrix Potter, has always done this, but the necessary focus on achieving a targeted size and mix of audience make it a more immediate requirement for television and indeed cinema production. But the necessity to work on more than one 'level' of comprehension, to fill a space which children and grown-ups can (in part) share, makes valuable, indeed inspiring, demands on the show's producers.

'Regeneration' happens to the Doctor within the show, literally, as the physical regeneration of himself. This has allowed his part to be taken by a succession of new actors, and thus has made possible considerable variations in the role. He is said to be immortal, or virtually so, thanks to this capacity to be reborn in a new body. This fact, and the narrative option for the replacement also of one companion by another, has given the series writers an advantage over the creators of equally iconic hero figures in fiction, such as Sherlock Holmes and Dr Watson, or Hercule Poirot, who have only one life which must be lived in only one body, although their impersonation by different actors in screen versions has allowed scope for exploring various aspects of style and character. It has thus been possible for the Doctor to retain and develop his place in the imagination of writers, production teams and audiences for forty years. Russell T. Davies has said, in one of his more expansive moments, that *Dr Who* will continue for ever. This narrative possibility, built as it were into the 'genome' of *Dr Who*, has allowed the newest 'regeneration' of this television series to have had an exceptional quality.

Narratives of Love and Loss

We have been concerned in our writing about children's fiction (Rustin and Rustin 1989/2001 and 2002) with the primary experiences of relatedness and feeling which we believe writers of fiction explore for their readers. In our view, the real persons we encounter from the beginning of our experience as infants become figures in our imagination, or what psychoanalysts call the internal world. We build up an internalised picture of the world of our primary relationships – initially with parental figures and siblings, real and imagined, later extended to others we encounter – which then become templates by which we anticipate and give meaning to our later experiences of persons. Attachment theorists, following John Bowlby, refer to these templates as 'internal working models'; psychoanalysts have preferred the term 'inner worlds'. Our internal images of those we are emotionally close to are invested with strong feelings of both love and hate in the psychoanalytic view, the balance of these emotions depending on the extent to which our needs for care and understanding (sometimes described as 'containment') are attended to in our early lives, but also on our innate dispositions. In our development we cope with the feelings and anxieties inseparable from life by means of psychic defences, prominent among which, in Freud's account, is repression, and in Melanie Klein's later idea, *splitting*, the attribution of the good and bad to different 'objects', including different parts of ourselves.

Fiction allows us to explore in imagination our perception and understanding of these states of mind. This exploration, and the sense of order and meaning it creates, gives us pleasure. Small children enjoy thinking about even the frightening aspects of their experience, when they are safely lodged in the symbolic form of stories or pictures – the monsters of Maurice Sendak's *Where the Wild Things Are*, or the Mr McGregor of *Peter Rabbit* who will eat a baby rabbit who disobediently comes into his garden, if he can only catch him. Stories, and in present times of course films and television shows, allow us to explore many aspects of the world in our imagination. Early on, these are often spaces just a little outside our usual safe boundaries. But later on, they become the worlds of the adults around us – the world of an earlier generation in Philippa Pearce's *Tom's Midnight Garden*, for example, or the battling grown-up worlds of divided parents in Philip Pullman's *His Dark Materials* trilogy. And the experiences of other children like us, as we explore their world through their imagined adventures, as in so many stories for children from *The Chronicles of Narnia* to *Harry Potter*. In stories for smaller children a world of intense experiences of life and death can be seen in the lives of imaginary animals with human attributes, such as in E.B. White's stories, *Charlotte's Web*, *Stuart Little*, and *The Trumpet of the Swan*.

From one point of view, *Dr Who* is an adventure of this kind. The Doctor, in the earlier series, was a grown-up, a basically kind and somewhat avuncular person in most of his personations, who took an innocent younger companion on adventures in his special vehicle, and on these adventures protected her and everyone else from danger. Incidentally, the Tardis is similar to a pretend-space in a child's game, an ordinary sort of box from the outside, but where inside anything can happen – 'it's bigger on the inside' in many respects. The 'sonic screwdriver' which can fix so many problems is another device close to those of children's pretend-games. The story offered strange and exciting monsters, big battles, elements of futuristic science and technology which were magical in their incomprehensibility, and quite a lot of conversation between the innocent young person and the Doctor, with changing elements – kindness, condescension, instruction, telling-off, arbitrariness, attention and neglect – which young viewers no doubt recognised from their experiences of grown-ups in family and school. Indeed Tom Baker, in his longest-serving representation of the Doctor, most resembled with his immensely long scarf an eccentric but benign science teacher, conducting very exotic school trips to the outer reaches of the universe.

The New Dr Who

One of the achievements of the new *Dr Who* is the way it has given new depth to this basic and consistent story-line of the whole series. The multi-generational history and tradition of the show may be a reason for this accomplishment. In *Dr Who Confidential*, the interesting 'making of Dr Who' films which accompany the series on the minority BBC3, and in contributions to the published Shooting Scripts volume for the 2005 series, several writers referred to their own memories of watching Dr Who when they were themselves children. Here, then, are stories and characters of which the production teams have already had an intense experience in their own childhood, now being reinvented by them in their creative adult lives for new audiences of children. There was a tender moment in the first *Dr Who Confidential* of the 2007 series in which a child who had been frightened by the show at its preview, and needed to be taken out, was shown now asleep in his mother's arms, focusing our attention on the primary audience of children that the programme-makers have in mind.

What might it be like to be the Doctor?; what might it be like to be his companion?; and what feelings of children might be capable of being explored in this show? These are questions the writers and production team of the new series have explored with considerable intensity. We are going to discuss two episodes in particular, from this point of view, one from each of the first two series, but before we do this, there are some thoughts about how the 'narrative design' of *Dr Who* has made this a possibility.

Meeting Martha Jones (who is to become his new companion) for the first time, in Episode One of Series 3, the Doctor tells her, to her bemusement, that he has no other name, he is just The Doctor ("You will have to earn it for me," says Martha the medical student). This refusal of a name goes with the periodic bodily regeneration of the Doctor, in its symbolic function. The Doctor without a name thus becomes the bearer of qualities which have to be imputed to him or attributed to him. He is, as it were, an internal object, especially for the writers and producers who have to give him particularity as a person and an agent. The Doctor-figure is made to be 'filled out' with different qualities, by virtue of not being 'tied down' to a particular body, time, or place. Several of the Westerns starring Clint Eastwood, not least *The Man with No Name*, have similarly exploited the projective possibilities – for encouragement to phantasy and the imagination – of namelessness and non-belonging. The man with no name can become what others need him to be.

Not only were members of the production team growing to adulthood between the years of the earlier *Dr Who* series, and the making of the new, but British society and its sensibilities were also changing. One such area of change, important to the new series, lies in the sphere of emotional and sexual awareness. The earlier versions of the Doctor were for the most part stereotypically males of a certain cerebral, witty, and emotionally-cut off kind. Their female companions ranged between 'dolly birds' (for the dads in the viewing audience) and, in reaction to this, and probably to emerging feminist sensibilities, more feisty and adventurous young women. But what they did not have was much emotional understanding; either of themselves, or the Doctor, or their relationship with him. It was as if, given underlying assumptions about the propriety of relationships between a man in *loco parentis* and a younger woman, in the context of school or family, the incest taboo forbade any further imaginative exploration.

But partly thanks to television itself, whose soaps and serials have been exploring in the intervening years many kinds of emotional relationship, much more is now dramatically possible. Whereas earlier the Doctor's self-sufficiency and capacity to live without emotional ties seemed a positive resource for him (he was a jokey version of many earlier English adventure heroes) the programme-makers have now chosen to explore his underlying loneliness, and elaborate what this might mean as a source of pain to him. While Rose had little formal education, she was, as Russell Davies has pointed out, emotionally highly intelligent. Both her relationships, with her partially-abandoned boy-friend Mickey Smith and with her new friend the Doctor, involve a continuing conversation between these different partners about what each is thinking and feeling.

Psychologically, the earlier *Dr Who* represented a rather pure culture of what Melanie Klein described as the paranoid-schizoid position, in which all good was located 'on our side', and all evil was projected 'out there'. This is a state of mind and feeling which is commonly explored and enjoyed in popular fiction, in many different genres. Developmentally, it seems aligned especially to the latency stage (between infancy and adolescence), especially in boys, during which the softer and more complex emotions tend to be repressed, and psychic defences are sought in groups (boys together); solidarities which are reinforced by various kinds of symbolic conflict, in games and sports. In its fictional representations, aesthetic (playful) pleasure is gained from the various ingenious forms which the monsters can take, the use of wit, daring and intelligence to defeat them, the fascinations of the science-magic, the tension and its relief as doom comes near and is averted. There was protection for the mostly younger viewers of *Dr Who* in the fact that the adventurer hero was ultimately an invulnerable adult, who could never die. The transferences evoked by the Doctor seem to have some similarities in this respect to those evoked by

Sherlock Holmes. But while Oedipal anxieties are contained in such fictions by identifications with a fatherly figure, alternative identifications can also be enjoyed, for example with the ultra-thick-skinned Daleks and Cybermen (related in their psychic functions to model action men, perhaps, and to robotic killers in computer games). And other varieties of reptilian monster may represent objects of phantasy, which are felt to have been damaged by the self's internal aggression and which may now seek their retribution (we are suggesting here reasons for children's fascination with such monsters).

But while in the new series, the basic storyline has been retained (it would not be *Dr Who* otherwise) there has been a considerable development as the series has gone on from this 'paranoid-schizoid' baseline to the more complex states of mind known as the 'depressive position'. That is to say, towards recognition that the apparently different objects towards which we may feel love and hate may in fact be the same objects, and that some of the feelings of badness and hatred that we project on to others may belong in reality in ourselves. In the more 'depressive' mode, we may become capable to tolerating a measure of unhappiness and mental pain, without immediately having to get rid of it into someone or something else.

For example, in the Daleks episode in Series One, the last-surviving Dalek (as it was then believed to be) is no longer one of many invulnerable death-dealing robots. Instead, he is a single individual being tortured by a sadistic scientist-collector, and arouses Rose's compassion. His metal shell opens up, revealing a soft inner part that had only once been revealed in a previous series. The Dalek turns out to be not wholly the opposite of the Doctor, but similar to him, in respect of having lived with the knowledge of the destruction of his entire kind. When the Doctor rages righteously about the Dalek's monstrous evilness, and is about to kill him, Rose points out that it is the Doctor who is now pointing a gun, while the Dalek is helpless. The division between good and evil is no longer as absolute or straightforward as it had always seemed to be.

When the former companion Sarah Jane Smith (from many years before, in an earlier series, played then and now by Elisabeth Sladen) returned in Episode 5, *Family Reunion*, of Series 2, we learn how hurt she was by the Doctor's having left her, as she says, without even saying goodbye. In a sisterly way, she warns Rose of the risks of becoming attached to this self-absorbed Doctor who, unlike humans, seems to make no lasting emotional bonds. Rose sees that the Doctor has had other companions before her, and feels jealousy. When Rose chooses to go on her adventures in the Tardis, we see how painful it is for Mickey to be left behind, and, even when he is allowed to come along, how difficult it is for him to feel that he is fully respected. There is a subtle exploration in Mickey's relationship with Rose and the Doctor of the dynamics of multi-ethnic life in contemporary Britain in the dignified struggle for full recognition by Mickey, who is black. When Martha Jones becomes the new companion, these aspects are further explored, since Martha is also black. The series catches hold of the fact that black women have in general been more successful educationally and professionally than black men in contemporary Britain. When the 'Christopher Ecclestone' Doctor is 'regenerated' into the David Tennant Doctor, Rose is initially plunged into mourning, rejecting the Doctor in his new incarnation. Again this is no magic transition, not a manic death and rebirth, but an experience of emotional loss and recovery. In other words, in its new series, *Dr Who* is able to explore a much more complex emotional register than before.

The 'audience in the mind' of the producers and writers of the new series seems to be less confined to simple kinds of splitting between friends and enemies, good and evil, male and female, and is able to explore a more complex emotional universe. Perhaps the informing perception is that 'age grades' among children and young people in contemporary society are less fixed than they used to be. Thus children are less protected from, but also more aware of, emotional and sexual tensions in themselves and those around them. And perhaps adolescents and adults are more in touch with the child-like parts of themselves than it earlier felt safe for them to admit. In any case it seems to us that the new series represents a more multi-faceted representation of life and its possibilities than the earlier series.

A changed political context may also have its place in this change in register between the old and new series. Paranoid-schizoid states mapped well on to the era in which *Dr Who* was first created, that of the Cold War and the still-fresh memory of the anti-fascist wars. But in the post-Cold War period things are less clear-cut, and there is more awareness that such states of mind may not be fully justified by their objects.

The Empty Child, and *The Doctor Dances*

This double episode from the first series, with Christopher Ecclestone and Billie Piper in the principal roles, dominated by the image of the little boy whose face is fused with a gas mask made, we learnt, an iconic impact on some of its young viewers. Groups of small boys intoned repeatedly, with an accurate inflexion, his repeated question, 'Are you my Mummy?' for weeks after the episode was screened (something different from the ubiquitous 'exterminate, exterminate!'). Something of extraordinary resonance was condensed in this image which can help to explain the emotional power of this story, set in the 1941 Blitz of London.

Perhaps one should begin with the somewhat mythical place the Blitz has in British social history and folklore. Many of its elements are referred to in the episode – the bombshelters at the bottom of the garden, the evacuation of the children to the countryside, the absence of much variety of food and the function of the black market in keeping some people well-fed despite rationing, the air-raid sirens dominating everyday life, Glenn Miller's dance band to cheer up the troops and the beleaguered populace, the dark streets and the blackout, Big Ben as the symbol of the determination to survive, the selfless commitment of medical teams, and so on. The Doctor and Rose both comment aloud on the heroic significance of this moment of Britain's history. But these conventional reference points are undercut to enable different stories to emerge. The ambulance space-ship that Captain Jack Harkness (who is first seen as an American volunteer officer with the RAF – this is before the United States entered the war) – did not bring help but catastrophe. Evacuation to the countryside could be, not to a place of safety, but to an unprotected exposure to abuse by strange adults. A hospital could turn out to be the source of contamination, not recovery. Life in the cellars might enable gangs of lost children to survive their confusion, hunger, and sense of abandonment. The American servicemen coming to Europe might be bringing more than we bargained for.

There are some obvious literary roots – the young woman who feeds and guards the children's safety is called Nancy, bringing to mind the Nancy of Dickens' *Oliver Twist* who represented maternal tenderness to the boys recruited by the dangerous Fagin. The "lost boys" of *Peter Pan* cared for by Wendy might be another source, since the Nancy of the episode dispenses rules of good behaviour very much like Wendy bringing up her motherless brood (incidentally Nancy in her precocious, sad, self-possession is beautifully played by Florence Hoath). Nancy reminds one of children who find themselves having to take the role of parents – parentified children as they are sometimes called. The pain of childhood evacuees is a much-explored theme, most memorably in Nina Bawden's masterpiece, *Carrie's War* (1973). The strangeness of wartime life for civilians has also been a theme of important recent adult fiction such as Sarah Walters' *Nightwatch* (2003) which explored the freedom offered by the unusual circumstances of war to some marginal characters. In this episode, Nancy's incredible boldness in facing down the greedy black marketeer she is stealing from to feed the children seems to be of this sort. People become other than their normal selves in wartime, and of course *Dr Who* is a continuing exploration of people turning out to be different from what might have expected, since his companions are both located in the ordinary 21st century world of today, and share his adventures in time and space. The importance of the unexpected is central to the image at the beginning when Rose begins to climb up a rope with the intention of reaching the child she has heard and seen on the roof of a house. Instead she finds herself hanging in space, caught in the beam of a searchlight, as she is in fact climbing a cable attached to a barrage balloon which has broken free of its moorings. Terror and excitement mount. Grown-up viewers may find themselves recalling Ian McEwan's novel *Enduring Love* (1998) which begins with the tragedy of someone pulled to their death by holding on to the rope of a rising balloon. As her strength gives way she is rescued by the magic of 21st century technology and swept up into Harkness's invisible space ship parked up against Big Ben, and we move into a dream sequence of sipping champagne and dancing to Glenn Miller's *Moonlight Serenade* on a deck next to the huge clockface.

This recreation of war-time London as the back-drop to the story of the boy searching for his mother is quite brilliant, since it allows the story to investigate the implicit parallels between what is happening to the character of the Doctor, and what is going on in the social world he is exploring. He starts to become much more human as he embarks on the task of restoring the humanity of the gas-mask child. His perceptiveness, which is not usually orientated towards psychological meaning but towards technical superiority over his monster-enemies, is a vital link. At several points, we see the Doctor struggling to understand what is going on, bearing the uncertainty of not knowing until the truth becomes clear to him. He comes to realise that the child's question is not, as might at first appear, the cry of a lost child believing that any and every person might be mother, but can be heard in a more specific way. It is a question to Nancy that Jamie needs to ask – is she his lost mother, or the big sister she said she was? Nancy is distressed to hear this question, which seems to follow her everywhere. This insight is linked to the Doctor's realisation that Nancy's self-imposed task of feeding the lost children on the streets is a sublimation of her desire to care for someone she has lost. In other words, he sees the two people who need to be linked up, mother and child, and the catastrophic consequences of the broken link when they are separated. The boy's identity can only be recovered when he is recognised by his mother – this is an idea explored in its infantile origin by Winnicott in the mirror-function of mother's gaze, and written about by many psychoanalysts interested in the roots of identity in the mother-baby relationship. Of course it is rather fascinating to keep in mind that the study of evacuated children had such an impact on John Bowlby that it led him in the direction of attachment theory. Both Bowlby and Winnicott in different ways contributed to elements of post-war reconstruction and the shaping of the welfare state. Child psychotherapy, and interventions in parent/child mental health, both preventive and therapeutic, developed from awareness of the vital function of early relationships and the necessity to provide support to sustain them.

The regeneration of Britain at the end of the war in the form of the making of the welfare state is suggested by the scenes of Albion hospital, hardly a casually-chosen name. Here the heroic Dr Constantine has stayed on duty as all the patients and staff become contaminated by the transformation let loose by the nanogene technology unwittingly unleashed by Jack Harkness. The humans have all turned into gas-mask lookalikes, with only one mind between them, since they are now in effect clones of the traumatised child (we learn later that the nanogenes are programmed to repair whatever bodies they find, but have taken as their genetic prototype the traumatised boy with a gas-mask). They are zombies, Nancy fears, as she explains that the most terrifying thing about the little boy following her everywhere is that he is 'empty', there seems to be nothing behind the mask. The Doctor learns to see otherwise – it is not emptiness that has taken over but a traumatised moment which can only be healed by a truthful answer to Jamie's question. The disconnected telephones which ring repeatedly to echo the child's unanswered question reveal that that the connection must be remade and then the cycle can be interrupted. The child left out in the cold must be let in.

This brings us to another important element in the story which is the contrast between truth and lies. The glamorous Captain Jack gradually reveals himself as an irresponsible con-man who has covered up the ghastly consequences of his casual theft of the ambulance spaceship with ignorant and ill-based assurances. Nancy has to be helped to tell the truth by the Doctor's belief that she can do so. This reclaiming of her maternal identity, which will give her son back his, follows on a memorable sequence in which the Doctor is depicted as a stern father. We might suggest that this is another kind of truth being asserted. Usually, he holds to his free Time Lord position, much too unpredictable and imaginative ever to sound like a paternal authority. But here, faced with the end of the world for humankind (now let loose, the nanogenes will infect everyone alive) he stands his ground and uses not magic but ordinary fatherly authority to prevent disaster. "Go to your room," he tells the gas-masked Jamie very loud and clear, and Jamie obeys. The Doctor has set aside his penchant for the more romantic, and demonstrated the necessary place of fathers in the human world, which helps Nancy to become mother to Jamie, her son. "Trust me, and tell him," he says in a later scene. As the Doctor has grasped, "There isn't a little boy who wouldn't tear the world apart to save his mummy, and this little boy can."

The heavenly moment of regeneration of all the gas-masked people is possible when truth wins. Nancy insists to Captain Jack that the gas-masked boy has a name. "Not the child, Jamie', she says. Trusting the Doctor, Nancy says to Jamie, "I am your Mummy. I will always be your Mummy.' She embraces Jamie, whom earlier she was afraid to touch, and the nanogenes put things right, restoring Jamie to his humanity. The gas mask can now be taken off, and a rather delightful and seemingly relieved little boy emerges from it. This was voted by viewers deservedly to be one of the 'Top Television Moments' of 2005. The episode gave dramatic representation to one of society's most sacred bonds, that of mother and child.

"Everybody lives, Rose, just this once, everybody lives," is the Doctor's joyful summary (reminding us that everyone has not always lived in his adventures) followed by the charming joke as he plans to leave the London of 1941 to its future, "Don't forget the welfare state." In the final scenes aboard the Tardis, the Doctor is at first in an elated state at this triumph – "I am on fire", he tells Rose – until he is brought down to earth by Rose's question, "What about Jack? Why did he say goodbye?" We return to Jack, about to die bravely in his spaceship, having it seems sacrificed himself to atone for having put the world at risk. But the Doctor comes to his rescue in the Tardis, and now, with a good conscience, he at last remembers how to dance and – the soundtrack is now Glenn Miller's *'In the Mood'* – he can fairly claim Rose as his partner. They have together averted 'volcano day' through an internal volcanic development in which the core of the Doctor's being is being reshaped.

In this episode there is a remarkable bringing together of a personal drama, of the separation of a child from his young mother and their restoration to each other, and the realisation of a historical moment, of which this is made to seem emblematic. The threatened Nazi conquest becomes an equivalent of deathly threats from other worlds which normally feature in *Dr Who*. For once, the extra-terrestial danger in this episode has a contingent origin – it is a plague that threatens, not a conscious enemy, though to be sure the nanogenes have been programmed to repair their patients to become deadly soldiers. The idea that death and destruction could come from new plagues, spread by carelessness or delinquency, has a contemporary resonance too. As we have pointed out above, John Bowlby's and Melanie Klein's ideas of attachment and loss, and of reparation, were discovered in the context of work with children affected by war, and the restitution of family and other social ties was a major theme of post-war reconstruction. In the ending of this double episode, the Doctor is celebrating not only his triumph within the personal narrative, but also a key moment in British social history.

The Girl in the Fireplace

The themes of the 'Madame de Pompadour' episode draw on some preoccupations and imaginative devices familiar in children's literature. We have the 'magic doors' allowing entry into other worlds and other times, a trope recently and brilliantly exploited in Philip Pullman's *His Dark Materials* but also embedded in other twentieth century writing for children, for example in the wardrobe access to C.S. Lewis's *Chronicles of Narnia*, and in Philippa Pearce's description (in *Tom's Midnight Garden*) of Tom's access to the midnight garden where he meets Hattie in an earlier generation. (It is as a 'kind of magic door' that the Doctor explains the fireplace to Reinette, while Rose indicates by her inflection of voice that she is beyond such childish things). The magnificent clockwork figures in eighteenth-century garb also echo Pullman's interest in the phenomena of clockwork. And of course, the extraordinary power of the clock as symbol, which begins perhaps with Cinderella and the midnight chimes. The clockwork men have other resonances too – they are symbols of eighteenth-century scientific rationalism, put to perverse use. It is a technology familiar to children, and the Doctor is thrilled by it, in this beautifully crafted form. The clock as marker of the boundaries, between day and night and one world and another, is particularly apt for the imaginative life of children, for whom 'bedtime' marks both the exclusion from the adult world and the entry into the world of dreams, when all the magical transitions and explorations can take place. The dream focus is explicit, since the clockwork intruders, which have powers similar to those of other extra-terrestial aliens of the series, are identified as the monsters in Reinette's childhood nightmares, believed to lie under her bed. She is protected by her good angel in the guise of the Doctor, to whom she can call 'I need you' in expectation of his arrival. This episode gains a particular imaginative freedom from the way in which the story leaves itself open to interpretation as its heroine's childhood dream, an unusual alternative framing of a *Dr Who* adventure. This story, a historical romance, with a little girl who grows up into a beautiful woman, a hero who rescues her on a white horse, and the sad death of the heroine, must have been made with the girls in its audience specially in mind.

The notion of the imaginary child who serves as companion, a feature of many children's lives often explored in children's literature, is also suggested. These imaginary friends are important to lonely children in particular, but their existence is usually episodic or relatively brief (perhaps a later and elaborated version of the transitional object first described by Donald Winnicott and most often taking the form of a soft toy). Reinette ('Queenie', the name given to Jeanne-Antoinette Poisson, later Mme de Pompadour, by her friends) remarks that she has the unusual experience of a life-long imaginary friend, although clinical work in child psychotherapy demonstrates that she may not have been as unusual in this as she believed. She grows older, but the Doctor (only Reinette seems to have learned that he is *Dr Who*) stays ever the same, and he reappears at moments of crisis when the nightmares of childhood threatens to revisit or overwhelm her – he is the one who can assuage her terror. Conversations between Reinette and the Doctor make it clear they are aware they inhabit a world outside the realm of reason or the everyday. 'You never want to listen to reason,' he tells her with a grin.

What brings Reinette and the Doctor into such intimate involvement with each other? Their imaginations are entwined, but as in an intense pretend game between children. They show a profound conviction, as long as the game lasts, of the reality and serious import of what is happening. To that one must add that their relationship is also like that of lovers. As they look into each others' eyes and 'walk among the memories of another living soul' as Reinette puts it, we are in a world where the ordinary boundaries of an individual mind are porous, and the two can know each other's thoughts and feelings through direct acquaintance, going beyond the intuitions on which human beings ordinarily have to depend in understanding the mind of another person.

But it is their shared experience of loneliness which is at the heart of the link between them. Reinette, aware of her own loneliness as a child, can recognise that same experience in the Doctor, the lonely boy who has been making out as best he can and who, this new series shows us, can develop beyond omnipotent self-sufficiency into a man who can love others. Her recognition of this in him is a transformative moment, picking up on the vulnerability he has already revealed to Rose when, for example, she has observed his moments of intense jealousy. This sense of being understood at depth belongs in its first embodiment in the mother-child relationship – the child getting to know himself through being mirrored in mother's eyes in Winnicott's theory, and through the containment of projective identification as described in Klein's and Bion's work. Observers of infants watch this process unfolding in ordinary development – the identity of the infant taking shape through his sense of being given a place in mother's mind. Bowlby's 'secure base' starts off in exactly the same sequence of interactions, though it is differently described in his theory of attachment.

The safety Reinette seeks is fundamentally within her inner world, though in accordance with the conventions of *Dr Who*, the nightmares burst through into the waking world. So Reinette's nightmare clockwork figures appear as liveried court servants at Versailles, deferential but also sinister, to puncture the charmed reality of Louis XV's court. What is of special interest is Madame de Pompadour's understanding that the angels and demons belong together ("It's worth having the monsters to have one's angel," she says. "Tell me about it." Rose replies, recognising a fellow-sufferer.) We could reframe this as Reinette's insight (she is an exceptionally intelligent and 'feelingful' person, beautifully played by Sophia Myles) into the inescapable elements of psychic reality. The ideal is complemented by the persecutory – good and bad must each find their place in the mind of the growing child and access to both is the hallmark of the potentially integrated self. Another aspect of this is that internal and external reality have to meet up in a continually dynamic interaction if the individual's relationship to the world is to be a rich one. Without our dreams and our capacity for imagination we are at risk of losing our essential humanity, and becoming one-dimensional like the clockwork monsters. What the clockwork monsters want from Mme de Pompadour, when she is 'complete' (that is, thirty-seven years old) is her brain, needed to repair their spaceship. Her nightmare is thus that there are malevolent designs on the aspect of her for which she is most renowned, and most likely to be envied. (The spectre of the knives which might cut off her head also anticipates the image of the guillotine to come.)

One of the things Reinette and the Doctor discuss is their different relationships to time. He is the Time Lord who can pop in and out of worlds and historical time at will, like the gods of myth as well as the heroes of sci-fi. She, by contrast, as a mortal, has to travel on 'the slow path', living within the rhythm of birth, growth, ageing and death. Her early death makes this explicitly stark, and the portrayal of what the 'slow path' means for her is exquisite. It means a relationship to memory, the capacity to miss and long for what is absent, to mourn what is lost and to savour the present. Reinette's letter from her deathbed left for the Doctor, and given to him by her lover Louis XV, expresses her mourning for her lost youth and health. She revisits the loneliness of her childhood as she prepares to die, but is no longer prey to monstrous fears, because she can commune with the good figures of her internal world, especially the Doctor by whom she feels loved. His absence, even when she longs for him to come and see her for the last time, is not unbearable because she remains aware of their mutual love, and can write her letter to him in the belief that he will read it.

The conversation between Dr Who and Louis XV is deeply moving. The two men have shared affection and admiration for this woman. The Doctor sees the departing coach carrying her body back to Paris, and is able to pause from his usual restless movement through time and to experience her leaving him, very much the opposite of his usual mode in which he is the disappearing figure, always leaving others. The king speaks of the tragedy of her early death and says 'She always worked too hard.' This is a fitting epitaph since we have seen and heard of her working hard at sustaining the glory of Versailles – gardens, music, dancing, glamour and so on – but also at the inner work of being in touch with herself at depth, including her great fears. This has involved her in facing the reality of not possessing either the king or the Doctor, each of whom has other aspects of their lives which they must live, and yet also of being able to appreciate intensely what their love for her has made possible. We see that her creative work, earlier marvelled at by the Doctor, has been her way of coping with what, for all her advantages, she has had to renounce in her life. The image we are left with is that of the two men able to bear the limits of what they have had with her, each knowing of her importance for the other without feeling overwhelmed by destructive jealousy. When the Doctor returns to the Tardis, both Rose and Mickey are able to bear their different jealousies too, in their compassion for the Doctor's loss. There is often a subtle restraint in the way that intense moments of feeling are performed in the series.

The emotional intensity of this episode springs from Reinette's awareness that the Doctor has risked giving up his own Time-Lord freedom to defend her from the clockwork men. He did not let 'reason' (his knowledge that there would be no way back for him) over-rule his commitment to her but was prepared to accept being trapped in her time. His way through to her on the white horse, found wandering in the parallel world of the deserted space ship, reminds us we are in the imaginative world of the child-Reinette. The way back to the space-ship, appearing as if by magic, the revolving fireplace of her old bedroom, which she has had reconstructed at Versailles, completes the picture. The Doctor has been willing to give up his Time Lord freedom for her, she discovers, and her gift of love is to restore it to him. But her decision to lead him back to the fireplace, and return to his own world, is also her own recognition of the difference between imagination and reality, and the awareness of loss which this can entail. The sadness of the ending of this episode invites its audience to share in an experience of mourning, not for the only time in this new series.

In unconscious fantasy, as Freud described in *The Interpretation of Dreams*, the rules of linear time do not hold. This is the realm explored in the adventures of Dr Who and Madame de Pompadour, but the brilliant achievement is the simultaneous engagement with the ordinary human relationship to time. Reinette does stick with the slow path and does not fly off to the stars with him. He faces the meaning of the finite time of human relationships. In this sense, the regeneration of Doctor Who is a very specific one. He is not simply carrying on as before, when his super-intelligence was paramount, but is developing in emotional complexity and acquiring an inner life. The notion of being a lord of time is being modified by the humility required to encounter something he cannot omnipotently control, and to share awareness of limitation with humankind. The dance between the two of them ('there comes a time when every lonely little boy must learn to dance,' she tells him) which he at first resists but then accedes to, is a moment which marks out his opening up to all this. As we have seen, the theme of dancing and its mutuality was also explored in his relationship with Rose.

The opposite view of humans is the one the clockwork monsters hold – they are searching for 'parts', to mend their spaceship, and have no conception of the value of a whole person and of a completed human life. The profound humanism of the ethic of the series lies in just this contrast.

It is remarkable to see the profound developmental themes of children's fiction, which has relevance and appeal for adult readers too, embodied so beautifully in a popular television series. In these two episodes the production team (we should mention in particular Steven Moffat, who was the writer of both) have achieved work which we think comparable to that of the finest writing for children.

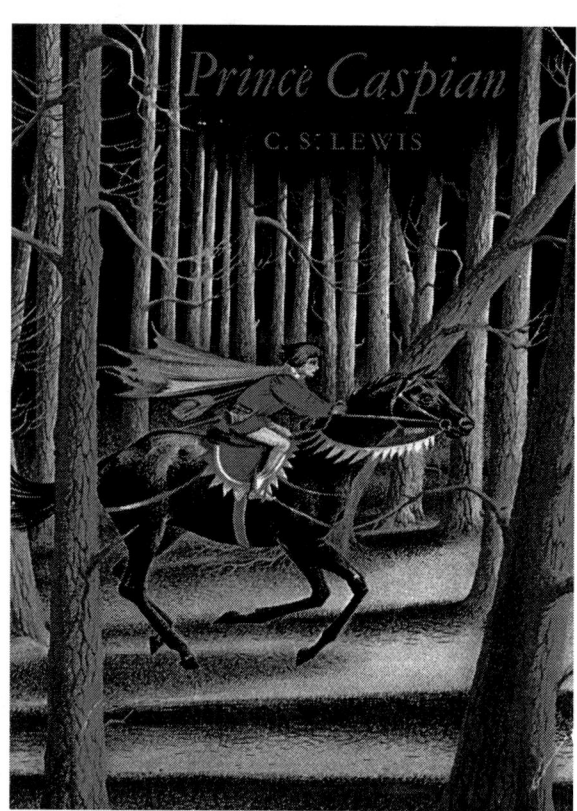

The three series of *Dr Who* are available on DVD from BBC Publications.

John Bowlby, *Attachment & Loss, Vols 1-3*. Pimlico, 1998.

C.S. Lewis, *The Chronicles of Narnia*. Harper Trophy, 1950-1956.

Sigmund Freud, *The Interpretation of Dreams*. Hogarth Press, 1900

Melanie Klein, 'Notes on Some Schizoid Mechanisms', in *the Selected Melanie Klein*, ed. J. Mitchell. Penguin, 1986.

Melanie Klein, 'Love, Guilt and Reparation", in *Love Guilt and Reparation and Other Works 1921-1945*. Free Press, 1984.

Philippa Pearce, *Tom's Midnight Garden*. Puffin, 1958.

Philip Pullman, *Clockwork, or All Wound Up*. Corgi Yearling, 1996.

Philip Pullman, *His Dark Materials*.
    Northern Lights, Scholastic 1995:
    in USA as *The Golden Compass*, Knopf, 1997
    The Subtle Knife, Scholastic, 1997: USA Knopf, 1997
    The Amber Spyglass, Scholastic/David Fickling Books, 2000:
    USA Knopf, 2000.

M.E. Rustin and M. Rustin, *Narratives of Love and Loss: Studies in Modern Children's Fiction*, London: Karnac, 1989/2001.

M.E. Rustin and M. Rustin, *Mirror to Nature: Drama, Psychoanalysis and Society*, London: Karnac, 2002.

D.W. Winnicott, *The Child the Family and the Outside World*. Penguin, 1969.

Peter Bramwell

Pagan Themes: The Green Man

THE GREEN MAN in literature may be traced back to the winter death and rebirth of the Green Knight in *Sir Gawain and the Green Knight*, and Jack of the Green is a traditional figure in pageant and mumming. Only in 1939 was the term Green Man controversially applied to the foliate heads found in churches (Simpson and Roud, 2000). The Green Man began to appear in children's literature in the 1960s, and in the last decade he has approached the pre-eminence that the god Pan had in fiction a century ago. Herne was a contender for a while, but his defining characteristic of hunting and his specific association with Windsor, however they were evaded or redefined, limited his appeal. By contrast, the Green Man is a blank slate on which current concerns can be inscribed, notably the desire to get in touch with the rhythm of nature and to act against ecological degradation.

Here I have selected one Green Man picture book and two novels to examine - Bel Mooney and Helen Cann (1997) *The Green Man*, Geraldine McCaughrean (1999) *The Stones are Hatching*, and Susan Cooper (2002) *Green Boy*. They present different models of childhood. The picture book makes use of the Green Man as a paradigm of maturation into social and environmental responsibility but its worthy didacticism can provoke resistant readings. The two novels question developmental quest narratives and uphold childness. Thus a central concern of this analysis is constructions of childhood in relation to the Green Man: how much agency child characters have; and to what extent they are allowed to be children. The Green Man has the potential to become a patriarchal and monotheistic figure, against the spirit of modern Paganism; but it is notable that in these three texts at least, the Green Man is balanced by the feminine.

In Bel Mooney and Helen Cann's *The Green Man*, the Green Man inspires the greening of a grey urban environment, an event which is anticipated by Cann's cover illustration. The top half of the picture, the 'given' information, depicts in grey, blue and white a city skyline of tower blocks and a dome which looks like St Paul's, making the city specifically London. The 'new' information in the bottom half of the picture shows the Green Man against a green background, facing the viewer with eyes and mouth wide open. His hair consists of green leaves and red berries, and his eyebrows, moustache and jacket are also made of leaves. One leaf is placed on his forehead like a 'third eye', and vines curl on his cheeks like tattoos. From his smiling or laughing

mouth, tendrils emerge. His brown hands are like wood, grained and knotted, and from them, leaves, flowers, berries and insects float upwards. This indicates that he is on the rise, in the ascendant, as do other upward vectors: his foliate hair breaks through the straight bottom line of the semicircle framing the title and this semicircle obscures much of the cityscape, its curved top edge again suggesting upward movement. Amongst the buildings are trees and a couple of the tower blocks have green growth climbing up them; leaves hang down in the top corners. The title page echoes the optimism of the cover. Against a plain white, unframed background, the semicircle is repeated but wreathed with a profusion of flora. The floating leaves, flowers, berries and insects are repeated as a rising diagonal.

Mooney's verbal text opens bleakly: it is winter, and through the window Luke sees 'the world all grey'. The words 'grey' and 'greyish' are used five times in the first two paragraphs. Window boxes are empty, the flowers indoors are plastic. The illustration on the left shows Luke looking at a view of the angular squares and oblongs of flat-roofed tower blocks with only a small patch of mottled grey sky showing. Picking up on Luke's Dad's newspaper mentioned in the verbal text, the frame of the window consists of a collage of squares of newspaper with fragments of company shares listings. There are several signals of change for the better to come: Luke's form interrupts the rigid, dark grey double border; he faces right, looking forward; the layers of his brown hair resemble dry leaves or wood shavings; the patch on his blue jeans is green with a swirling brown pattern.

Luke repeatedly encounters the Green Man in unexpected places, though his mother is dismissive. The Green Man's face appears in the lichen on a tree trunk, looking fierce. A supermarket cabbage blinks at Luke and in the picture the Green Man's eyes are downcast and his mouth sealed by a barcode sticker. In the car returning from the supermarket, Luke begins to notice how ugly his urban environment is. His stance in the illustration echoes the Green Man on the cover: face on (despite the side-view of the car), hands upraised. His hands are shaded like knotted wood and he wears a green jacket. Luke sees the Green Man again, friendly and talking, in a bush by the path to the flat, and then 'in the swirling brown grain' of the sideboard indoors.

Luke dreams of the Green Man breaking through the concrete pavement – like the tree on which Luke first saw the Green Man's face. The picture shows the Green Man's size: though sitting, his head intrudes into the frame, his foot is planted outside of it and his sleeve looks like a patchwork of fields. Luke is barely taller than his knee, but Luke has more agency in the picture than in the words. These say that the Green Man holds out a hand and commands 'Come with me.' In the picture, Luke puts his hands to the Green Man's thumb and wrist to help him up. While the verbal text rationally relegates the Green Man to a dream, there are no visual cues (as there could be) to indicate unreality.

The next day Luke once more spots the Green Man's face in the peeling green paint on an old shed. An old woman sees the Green Man too; she is dressed 'with all the colours of the rainbow' and introduces herself as Lily. 'Her hand was as rough as bark', and in the picture it has the wooden texture that the Green Man and Luke's hands have displayed before. The grey tendrils of Lily's hair echo the green tendrils hanging from the picture frame.

Lily is a wise old woman who mediates the Green Man to Luke. Lily tells Luke that the Green Man helps her grow fruit and vegetables on her allotment, but that he is fierce because he has been forgotten and ignored, though he 'will never go away'. The old woman claims 'He's the oldest spirit in the world [...] he's all growing things in one, and everything grows because of him.' When Luke sees the allotment, he feels 'something spring up inside him, as if a green shoot was growing there,' and Lily explains that the Green Man has chosen him to help him. In the illustration, Lily authoritatively looks down on Luke and points her finger at him, positioning him as subjected.

A running visual footnote is a line of pots, jars and cans with flowers growing in them. At the moment when Luke moves from reaction to action, these flowers reach full bloom. The hard work does him good: 'His hands were dirty, and his back ached a bit – but he felt very happy.' Luke's Mum and Dad join him and Lily in planting and nurturing seeds, while people in the ground-floor flats look on, happy or astonished. Generations, family and community are brought together by the Green Man – or by Lily's understanding of him.

Finally, Luke plants seeds in his window box and they wondrously flower over night. He hears the Green Man telling him, 'you can make things different!' The fringe of ivy around the window is 'just like the hair of the Green Man', and the last picture very precisely reflects the cover illustration. The border is the same design and the blue and grey bricks echo the buildings. Surrounded by flowers and insects, Luke has the same face-on, hands-raised pose as the Green Man; the fingers are splayed identically. Luke has been inspired by the Green Man and, through acting to improve his environment, has become him.

Mooney's 'Author's Note' is consistent with the main text in emphasising the Green Man's ambivalent character, 'as soft as rain on crops, as hard as winter [...] friendly, but fierce.' Mooney creates a mythology and antiquity for the Green Man: 'when churches were built, country people believed in the Green Man – a belief older than the Christian faith. So the priests let them carve him all over the place – just to be sure, you see.' But the 'country people' would not have been likely to make the connection between foliate heads and the name 'Green Man' that Lady Raglan first mooted in 1939 (Simpson and Roud, 2000). Other interpretations than Mooney's accommodating syncretism are possible: foliate heads in ecclesiastical settings could indicate the subjection of Pagan to Christian, or represent preaching the living word.

The importance of Mooney and Cann's *The Green Man* is in introducing the Green Man to a contemporary, urban setting, though in a rather schematic and idealised way. The inner city is not necessarily as grim and ungreen as Mooney, for the sake of contrast, makes out and the harmonising of generations and families in a common cause is very optimistic. Lily could be seen as the Jungian grandmother archetype and as the Crone aspect of the Triple Goddess, balancing the Green Man and interpreting and mediating him to Luke. While Luke is arguably empowered by becoming the Green Man at the end, along the way, as we have seen, there are tensions between words and pictures as to how much power the boy has in relation to the Green Man and the old woman.

Geraldine McCaughrean (1999) *The Stones are Hatching*

In *The Stones are Hatching*, Geraldine McCaughrean follows folklorists in associating the Green Man with mumming, rather than ecclesiastical foliate heads. Eleven-year-old Phelim Green is hailed as 'Jack o'Green' by a house spirit who warns 'Every moment the stones are hatching, the Worm is waking.' The Stoor Worm (from the northern Scottish folk tale – see, for example, Jarvie 1992) has been woken by the guns of the Great War and it is Phelim's quest to defeat the Worm and her 'hatchlings', the catalogue of mythical creatures the Worm is bringing to life. Phelim is aided, indeed propelled along, by the mumming figures of a Fool (Mad Sweeney), a Maiden (Alexia) and a Horse (Obby Oss).

As one might expect from Geraldine McCaughrean, not only is the style beautifully textured but also the characterisation is complicated and psychologically convincing. Quest narrative is interrogated through Phelim's extremes of resistance and euphoria and by the moral ambiguity of the outcome. *The Stones are Hatching* presents the Old Ways as harsh, but rues their passing, whilst satirising artificial revivals.

Mad Sweeney of the Trees is the Fool who addresses Phelim as 'Green Man' and whose wisdom leads him. Sweeney has been traumatised by war and knows that it is war, not himself, that is mad. But Phelim believes that Sweeney and the others all want something from him and he resists: 'I'm a boy, not a man. And I'm not Jacko Green. I'm Phelim Green, and I'm not going to fight any Worm.' Only when he encounters the faeries of Hy Brasil does he adopt the name and role of 'Jack o'Green'.

These faeries have 'no diaphanous tiny wings, no minute bluebell hat[s]' and they do not grant wishes; rather they relish and take advantage of the bloodshed of human wars. Phelim initially admires Murdo, Alexia's Uncle, despite Murdo's slurs: he claims that Alexia is 'a filthy Devil-worshipping, pin-sticking, curse-making witch'; that the Oss is a hatchling; and that 'They're never taking you to the Worm to kill it. They are taking you there to feed it, son' (there is a similar flawed assumption in Susan Cooper's *Green Boy*, discussed below). Even though Murdo turns out to be untrustworthy and obsessively greedy for fairy gold, the seeds of doubt have been sown.

Fleeing from the faeries, Murdo is shot and Phelim vainly appeals to Alexia to use magic. The moment of change for Phelim rings psychologically true because the trigger seems random and trivial: one of Murdo's shoes banging sets off a memory of his bullying sister and his absent father. He becomes resolute and authoritative and calls himself Jack o'Green. He simultaneously gives Murdo a sea burial and defeats the faeries and then pledges to stop the Worm waking. 'The others stared at him, this altered, confident Green Man of theirs.'

However, confidence turns into drunken arrogance in the ersatz pagan revival of 'burning the bush'. His companions have to save him: first the Oss and then, at the cost of her life, Alexia. Even after death she helps, her bones providing a Witch's Ladder for Phelim to climb the Worm. When Sweeney boils up her bones in an oil-drum cauldron, she is reborn. Thus Phelim, as the Green Man, depends on the feminine Alexia for his survival and it is she, rather than he, who takes the Corn King's death and resurrection role.

Phelim completes the quest but is 'repelled by what he [is] doing [...] the kill-or-be-killed pettishness of it all.' He feels not triumphant, but compromised: 'In fighting her, he could only become what she was: malevolent, destructive.' As Nietzsche observed in *Beyond Good and Evil*, 'Whoever fights monsters should see to it that in the process he does not become a monster. And when you look long into the abyss, the abyss also looks into you' (words revealingly quoted in *Snicket* 2004). David Wyatt's cover illustration of *The Stones are Hatching* suggests the same ambiguity by placing the Green Man and the Maiden among the hatching stones, their supposed foes. The moral complexity is maintained when Phelim lies about removing a ruby from a swallow in order to take away Sweeney's fear: the lie is an act of goodness.

The greatest challenge for Phelim is not the flawed heroic quest in the outside world, but asserting himself at home against his bullying sister Prudence. He has realised that 'He was the Stoor Worm in her landscape', and he returns not in triumph, but to feel 'the old helplessness come slurrying down on him, pinning him to the spot, pressing his shoulders into a stoop, oppressing his heart into speechlessness.' The root of Prudence's resentment is Phelim's resemblance to his father, a storyteller who refused to enlist for war, whom Prudence had committed to an asylum.

Phelim summons water-horse to take Prudence away but he is 'left with the same kind of emptiness as after killing the Worm'. But at last he is no longer pressed into maturing but is allowed to be a boy. Phelim has struggled with the role of Jack o'Green because, it is hinted (and spelled out at the end of the extended US edition), he has been mistaken for his father. Out of the shadow of his sister and father, with Aisling ('dreamer'; formerly Alexia, 'helper') for a companion, Phelim can be not a Green Man but a Green Boy. The Old Ways and magic are commented on by Sweeney, Alexia and, most of all, the Obby Oss in *The Stones are Hatching*. The opening sentences of the novel express Phelim's view of magic – that, if it exists, it is not conjuring tricks, nor is it supernatural but it is the wonder of nature: 'Sometimes, when the winter air turned into a puff of smoke in his mouth, or hail reclinkered the garden path, he suspected there was magic at work.' When Phelim claims that people have progressed beyond belief in fairies and the like, the Oss asserts the Pagan cyclic view of time:

> So why do Monday come round to Monday, and May to May and zummer to zummer and dawn to dawn? Generation to generation? Janner, lad! How do a man look at the great wheel of Time and zee a straight line? (McCaughrean, 1999).

The Oss is the most straightforward character; he 'had changed least of all and found no need to change. [He was] one of the last survivors of the Old World, still loved, still prized, still welcome.' He survives; but, along with Sweeney and Alexia, he regrets the thinning of the old beliefs, even though these beliefs are presented as entailing sacrificial tributes and bribes. When Phelim cuts down the last sheaf of a field of wheat, the harvesters think he should pay in blood:

> They had fallen back on the bloody ways of their ancestors. [...] The hot excitement gripping their bowels made them feel more vital and alive, convincing them still further that Old Magic was at work (McCaughrean, 1999).

Though the tone is sceptical about their belief, the assumption that 'the bloody ways of their ancestors' is historical fact is reinforced by the Oss asking 'So, Green Jack. Do you still like the Old Ways?' Saturating the Old Ways with blood could be argued to be a Christian smear on Paganism, whereas blood sacrifice is central to the Judaeo-Christian tradition: 'without shedding of blood is no remission' (Hebrews 9:22). Modern pagans would emphasise the celebratory over the placatory.

McCaughrean's only use of the word 'paganism' is satirical: 'a splendid day's paganism.' The day is organised by the librarian Mr Basil Pringle and is based on rootless book-learning; he is even 'unable, without his reference books, to give a correct name to the Obby Oss.' Although there is an anti-war strand to the book and Phelim's father refuses to join up, Mr Pringle is belittled for being excused service through ill health. The festivities are fabricated, their leader improbable:

> Mr Pringle had re-invented Old Ways which had never even been practised in Storridge. [...] Mr Pringle had taken on a virility and authority no one had ever suspected in him. And the very transformation of Mr Pringle from rabbit to magician seemed in itself part of his Magic (McCaughrean, 1999).

The satire continues: 'Not since the opening night of the Storridge Players' *Charley's Aunt* had he felt such a surge of adrenaline.'

There is a carnivalesque feel to choirboys dressing in bishops' mitres and the procession through Storridge, though the latter might be seen as resembling a Worm... Indeed, the 'frenzied, terrified joy' turns bad; when the villagers decorate Phelim, a very emotive comparison is drawn: 'They made him as anonymous as a Ku Klux Klansman.' Phelim's participation, intoxicated by attention and drink, is what leads to Alexia's death. Mr Pringle is the unmitigated hate-figure of the book; Phelim brings himself to kill the Worm's soul-mouse in vengeance for Alexia, imagining the mouse is Mr Pringle.

Pagan readers may react to Mr Pringle's travesty of paganism as some Christians do to Philip Pullman's satirical version of the church in *His Dark Materials* – as not resembling their own faith but still representing a possible danger that they would equally condemn.

Susan Cooper (2002) *Green Boy*

Green Boy is narrated by Trey Peel, whose sex is never specified. Trey's environment in the Bahamas is threatened by an ecologically disastrous tourist development. At the suspended moment between tides, Trey and Trey's younger brother Lou access another world. Whether Pangaia is a parallel, future, or past (lost civilisation) world is deliberately left unclear but what is clear is that Pangaia's over-development writes large the ecological warning.

Trey observes that in Pangaia, 'Everywhere we had been, the land was paved or concreted and built-over, jammed with people. The air was hazy and the water was brown, and no stars shone.' The only green is the Wilderness, but this harbours fearsome mutants from genetic engineering and cloning. There is an Orwellian tinge to Cooper's dystopia: people do not talk but are constantly exposed to television pictures of war.

An underground movement is fighting a 'Greenwar'. As Bryn, one of the ecowarriors, explains:

> *Pangaia is a planet, but it is also an organism. This whole world. It's made up of everything on it, in it, around it, but it is also a single mind, and its mind is called Gaia.*
> *It is a mystery. It will save itself from destruction; it always has. It will save itself from the human race by its own methods - and it plans to use us. We are its agents* (Cooper, 2002).

Most of this conforms to the Gaia hypothesis of James Lovelock (1979) – with the important exception of Gaia's election of human agents. As we shall see, this is not the only mistake Bryn makes about Gaia.

Trey's seven-year-old brother Lou cannot speak and has seizures, but has an exceptional sensitivity to animals. In Pangaia, he is 'strange and special';

according to underground member Annie, 'he is magical, he is predestined. We have been waiting for him. Only he can save this world, only now and only here.'

A number of the rebels have Celtic names – Math, Bryn, Gwen – and Lou is homophonic with Lugh, the Celtic God of light. Annie thinks that the boy Lou has come to fulfil an ancient prophecy from Gaia which predicts that the god Lugh will save Pangaia at his feast of Lughnasa, August 1st (one of the pagan festivals of the Wheel of the Year). A quest through an chthonic labyrinth (a symbol of the Goddess) leads to an encounter with Gaia, 'a woman with kind eyes and a strong mouth' who speaks 'like the voice of the whole earth.'

Just as in *The Stones are Hatching*, Murdo suggests that Phelim will be fed to the Worm, so in *Green Boy*, Bryn expects Gaia to demand sacrifice. He is wrong. She rejects heroism and sacrifice: 'You mistake me always. You dream of monsters, who will kill your heroes. No! No monsters are needed. I ask not for sacrifice, but for renewal.' There is no blood shed when the Green Man is called up, but red flowers flow out of his mouth, along the streets and into the sea. Cooper's Green Man is huge, unstoppable, and full of laughter. Like Mooney and Cann's Green Man, he erupts into and transforms an urban landscape: 'sharp green sprouts came breaking up out of stone and concrete and brick, bursting up, cracking the paved ways.'

Cooper's Green Man only has life and power through the wisdom and direction of Gaia, and she places children at the centre: 'the weaver of his rebirth [...] is a child. [...] Children weave story.' Children's tag games and chants summon the Green Man, and Trey perceives that

> We all have these rhymes and games that we learn from other kids when we're small, and the younger ones learn them from us, and so on. But when we grow up, we forget them. Only the little ones keep carrying them, only the little ones know them (Cooper, 2002).

Like McCaughrean, Cooper rejects the model of childhood as a developmental stage to be got through, which is the drive of the quest narrative these authors interrogate. Trey's thoughts affirm Peter Hollindale's model of childhood as a distinct culture, 'an autonomous part of life, [...] its passage [...] entailing some losses' (Hollindale, 1997).

In Trey's Bahamian home, a hurricane puts paid to the development of the tourist resort. Trey interprets the hurricane as an echo of the Green Man:

> In Pangaia he had destroyed the works of humans and reclaimed the land for Nature. Here, Nature wars erupting to claim land and sea for itself. Himself. Herself. Herself seemed the most right, somehow. Maybe Nature was just another name for Gaia (Cooper, 2002).

The Green Man does not appear directly in the primary world; the focus is all the more on the earth Goddess, Gaia. Trey expresses the pantheistic belief that Nature (with a capital 'N') can be equated with divinity but privileges Gaia: Trey thinks 'Maybe Nature was just another name for Gaia' – not 'Maybe Gaia was just another name for Nature.'

Cooper's Green Man is one whose rebirth is a single, apocalyptic event to redress ecological crisis yet his resurrection is tied to the repeating seasonal festival of Lughnasa, and the flow of red flowers suggests feminine cyclic renewal. In pagan theology, the Green Man is often regarded as Great Mother Goddess's son and consort, dependent upon her for his rebirth (Crowley, 1996). This dependency is rarely depicted in fiction but *Green Boy* shows it. *Green Boy* is just as distinctive in making children's imaginative play essential to the Green Man's rebirth. In many texts, the Green Man is confined to locations in England; Susan Cooper's Caribbean and parallel world settings broaden his role and relevance.

Conclusion

This is an exciting time to be observing the emergence of the Green Man as a new literary God. The tension in many Green Man texts between the cyclic and the apocalyptic may well reflect the perception that global warming is wrenching the seasons out of joint and the only remedy is radical change. 'Think globally, act locally' is the ecological slogan and placing local environmental concerns in the context of global vision should prevent the search for, and invention of, native deities from becoming parochial and inward-looking.

Presenting the Green Man as intervening, globally or in individual lives, can be regarded as circumscribing human autonomy and agency. Some texts present rather earnest didactic models of (usually male) maturation, pressing towards adulthood and not allowing the child to be a child. There is also a risk of perpetuating and recreating patriarchy when the Green masculine is not balanced by the feminine, although each of the three texts that have been discussed above attempts this balance in some way.

The tensions and ideological traps associated with the Green Man in fact serve to provoke very fine, original writing, such the childhood-centred, quest-questioning narratives of *The Stones are Hatching* and *Green Boy*. The Green Man has not yet stabilised into a literary convention, and I hope that he will not but will continue to be depicted with imaginative diversity.

Note: this article is an edited extract of a longer chapter on Herne and the Green Man *to appear in Peter Bramwell,* Studies of Pagan Themes in Modern Children's Fiction. *Lichfield: Pied Piper, forthcoming.*

REFERENCES

Susan Cooper, *Green Boy*. London: Bodley Head, 2002.

Vivianne Crowley, *Principles of Paganism*. London: Thorson, 1996.

Peter Hollindale, *Signs of Childness in Children's Books*. Stroud: Thimble, 1997.

Gordon Jarvie (Ed), *Scottish Folk and Fairy Tales*. Harmondsworth: Penguin, 1992.

J. E. Lovelock, *Gaia: A new look at life on earth*. Oxford: Oxford University Press, 1979.

Geraldine McCaughrean, *The Stones are Hatching*. Oxford: Oxford University Press, 1999.

Bel Mooney and Helen Cann, *The Green Man*. Bath: Barefoot Books, 1997.

Friedrich Nietzsche, *Beyond Good and Evil*. Leipzig, 1886.

Jacqueline Simpson and Stephen Roud, *A Dictionary of English Folklore*. Oxford: Oxford University Press, 2000.

Lemony Snicket [Daniel Handler], *A Series of Unfortunate Events Book the Tenth: The Slippery Slope*, London: Egmont, 2004.

Madelyn Travis

Journey to the Self: Feminine Symbols and Archetypes in Lloyd Alexander's *'The Chronicles of Prydain'* and Susan Cooper's *'The Dark is Rising'* Sequence

Lloyd Alexander's *'The Chronicles of Prydain'* (1964-1968) and Susan Cooper's *'The Dark is Rising'* sequence (1965-1977) are five-volume romance-quests incorporating elements of Welsh myth and legend. Their use of the quest framework in the series has led many scholars to accuse the two authors of adopting patriarchal values, or at least of accepting them without question. Yet both Alexander and Cooper were fascinated by Robert Graves's *The White Goddess: A Historical Grammar of Poetic Myth* (1948), which expands upon the theory that Celtic culture was originally matriarchal and had a Triple Goddess as its deity. Both, too, were strongly affected by the experiences they endured during the Second World War. I suggest that these factors point to an alternative reading of the texts in which the masculine quest structure is subtly undermined from within.

Through an examination of the psychological relationship between masculine and feminine in *'The Chronicles of Prydain'* and *'The Dark is Rising'*, I aim to demonstrate that the use of symbols and motifs from matriarchal myth in these narratives privileges the feminine and contributes to a reading in which feminine and masculine are brought into balance in the inner world of the psyche, as represented by the text. In my particular Jungian reading, the mythological figures within each text may be interpreted as archetypal images within an individuating psyche which is dealing with the adverse effects of war.

The hero of *'The Chronicles of Prydain'*, Taran, is an orphan. Although he yearns to be a hero, Taran seems doomed to endure a lifelong career as assistant pig-keeper at the home of the enchanter Dallben. In the first volume, *The Book of Three* (1964), Taran and his friend Princess Eilonwy join Prince Gwydion in the fight against Arawn, ruler of the underworld, and his henchman, the Horned King. The second volume, *The Black Cauldron*, sees Taran and Princess Eilonwy join Prince Gwydion in a bid to recover a magic cauldron stolen by Arawn. In *The Castle of Llyr*, Eilonwy is forced to travel to her ancestral island to learn to be a lady. She is kidnapped by the wicked queen, Achren, who hopes to use Eilonwy's powers as an enchantress for her own purposes. *Taran Wanderer* is a coming-of-age story in which the pig-keeper

goes in search of his parentage. The final battle between good and evil takes place in The High King. In *'The Chronicles of Prydain'*, Taran is the character most obviously read as the ego of the text.

Susan Cooper wrote *Over Sea, Under Stone*, (1965) as a standalone book, although it subsequently became the first in *'The Dark is Rising'* sequence. The novel introduces Simon, Jane and Barney Drew and their mysterious great-uncle, Merriman Lyon, who, it transpires, is none other than Merlin. The scope and scale of the narrative begin to take shape in the next book, *The Dark is Rising*, in which Will Stanton discovers that he is an immortal Old One and undertakes a quest for the six signs crucial to the Light's fight against the Dark. In *Greenwitch*, Jane Drew is instrumental in recovering a manuscript that holds the key to translating a prophecy written on the side of the Grail. *The Grey King* sees the introduction of the orphan boy Bran Davies, who is the son of King Arthur and Queen Guinevere. All of the children play a role in the climactic conflict between Light and Dark in *Silver on the Tree*. The complex structure of *'The Dark is Rising'* gives rise to a number of ways in which the ego can be read. In view of my emphasis on the importance of the feminine, I will focus on a reading of Jane Drew as ego.

Susan Cooper makes no secret of her admiration of Jung and admits that 'it is quite possible that I need these archetypes, not just as an artist, but personally'. (1996: 63). Cooper believes that American children have no mythical heroes of their own. She cites the link that Joseph Campbell makes between a lack of mythological foundation in society and 'the violence of a cultural chaos' (61) that leads to thousands of deaths a year by handgun in the United States. Cooper lived through war, but had mythology to help her make sense of it; she believes that American children living with the threat of violence do not. Whether or not one accepts her argument, it is unsurprising, given her beliefs, that she hopes that fantasy can help American children to create 'patterns for the future [...] from the mythic echoes of the past' (68).

Cooper likens *'The Dark is Rising'* sequence to a symphony 'in which each movement is different, and yet they all link together' (194). The analogy is apt, for like a symphony, Cooper's narrative moves both 'vertically' and 'horizontally', with each book both an entity unto itself and part of a greater work. The 'vertical' reading of each text can be interpreted as a representation of the individuation process – or partial process – of a character read as ego. Each text contains its own archetypal images within the unconscious of this ego. In the 'horizontal' story, though, the characters function as archetypes to an ego that is outside the text. Put another way, each book can be read as a narrative of the personal unconscious, while the series as a whole invokes archetypal images of the collective unconscious. The vertical and horizontal narratives join in the last book and proceed together to the conclusion.

In a vertical reading of *The Dark is Rising*, for example, Will is likely to be identified as the ego of the text, while in the linear reading he may be read as the archetypal Wise Old Man. In *The Grey King*, Bran may be interpreted as the conscious ego, but in the series as a whole he is imaged as the archetypal Divine Child. The characters' functions as archetypes in the linear, overarching narrative accounts not only for their unorthodox developmental paths in the narrative as a whole, but also for the fact that they fulfil shifting and sometimes multiple roles. This both explains and justifies what Plante criticises as the sequence's emphasis on 'fate mixed with intuition and ritual' (38), which is indeed true in a 'horizontal' reading of the text, although not in a 'vertical' one.

Given her interest in Jungian psychology, it is possible that Cooper deliberately created a work in which the ego of the narrative is located with her readers outside the text rather than within it. She may have used mythical images in order to introduce the archetypes of the collective unconscious to a new generation. Her own acknowledged 'need' for archetypes may be present as well, adding yet another level to this already multi-layered work. It is possible, too, that Jane may be read as a version of Cooper herself: 'I can still feel what it was like to be that child of the 1940s from inside; I am still the same mixture of insecurity and determination, shyness and arrogance, curiosity and fear. I write for her, for that child...' (1996: 131). Could Cooper be attempting through her writing to heal not only the psyches of her child readers, but also – perhaps unconsciously – the trauma she herself suffered as a child in wartime? It is an intriguing possibility.

Read as the conscious female ego of *'The Dark is Rising'*, Jane is initially portrayed as one-sidedly feminine. When her mother is absent, Jane tries to assume her role, protecting her brothers Simon and Barney and worrying about tidiness and cleanliness: '"Barney," Jane squeaked. "Wipe your hand. You'll eat all sorts of germs and get typhoid or – or rabies or something. Here, have my handkerchief."' (1968: 24). Jane's image of 'Mother' is based on her experience of a mother as someone whose role is to nurture others and provide them with food. In this text, the female ego identifies too closely with the personal mother and displays stereotypically 'feminine' characteristics as a result of its inability to acknowledge the masculine elements in the unconscious. Before it can begin to do this, though, the ego must first separate from the mother. This ego has yet to achieve this separation.

Archetypal images change according to what an ego requires at any given time; therefore, the animus takes different forms as necessary. As conscious ego in the early stages of development, Jane is unready to meet the animus in its final form. Young-Eisendrath and Wiedemann suggest that the female ego typically contacts the animus first as alien other, then as father-god or patriarch, then as youth, hero or lover and finally as the partner within (Rowland: 53). Here the ego progresses through these stages in a slightly different order. The animus is initially contacted in the form of the paternal authority figure, imaged as Great-Uncle Merriman Lyon – Merlin. Merriman protects Jane from the dangers of the outside world: 'The Dark will not touch any of you [...] There will be protection. Don't worry. I promise you that' (Cooper, 1977a: 13). Although the animus functions as father-protector, it also helps the ego to access alternative images of the feminine, thereby separating from the mother.

Merriman does this by involving Jane and her brothers in a quest for the Grail, which Cooper depicts as a pre-Christian symbol akin to the cauldron, the precursor of the Holy Grail of medieval Arthurian romance. The Grail, one of a number of vessels symbolising an aspect of femininity, is associated with breasts and nourishment (Neumann: 47). It is Jane who realises that the Grail is located in a cave, a symbol of the womb (Knapp: 16). The link to the uterus is made explicit in Cooper's description of the cave as 'narrow and triangular' (Cooper, 1968: 178). Jung's imagery associated with the underworld realm of the mother is generally negative, producing hellish images of stifling chthonic prisons to be encountered as in a nightmare. In contrast, Cooper's underground topography is generally depicted in positive terms, representing feminine depths and the unconscious, to be recognised and welcomed. At this stage, though, the ego is unready to explore its feminine depths. Jane refuses to enter the cave to retrieve the grail: 'It gives me the creeps. We can't go in there.' (178).

The Grail, which is found and then stolen, is in any case of little use on its own without its accompanying manuscript, which enables its crucial text to be deciphered. The manuscript's connection with words suggests that it is a symbol of Jung's concept of Logos. Its phallic case further suggests that it is a symbol of masculinity, although as it and the Grail come as a pair, the two together represent the union of masculine and feminine in the psyche. Unfortunately, the case has been lost beneath the sea.

Before the ego can start to contact the inner masculine it must access the inner feminine rather than the outer, 'shadow', feminine. Jane attends a women-only harvest ritual: the making of the Greenwitch, a fertility figure of primordial power. She is initially frightened of the Greenwitch, for its power challenges her limited perception of femininity:

> There was something menacing in its broad squat shape. Yet it was hypnotic too; she could barely take her eyes off it. It. She had always thought of witches as being female, but she could feel no she quality in the Greenwitch. It was unclassifiable, like a rock or a tree (1977a: 39).

Yet Jane's feelings quickly turn to awe; the image of the Greenwitch has unlocked the ego's growing awareness of the unlimited potential of the feminine, which is experienced first through empathy for the creature and later expressed in a wish for its happiness.

As Jane considers for the first time possibilities of feminine power, her need to rely on a father figure diminishes. After her encounter with the Greenwitch, she sees Merriman in a crowd, 'but ma[kes] no attempt to reach him' (43). Instead, the ego encounters the animus as youth. The animus is imaged as Will, a boy of Jane's own age who 'remind[s] her oddly of Merriman' (45). Though still a child, he is a substitute authority figure. Indeed, Jane tells him 'you're like a grown-up sometimes' (112).

Soon after the Greenwitch ceremony, Jane explores the feminine within. She dives off a cliff in a storm: 'she was still falling, falling slowly, floating down through the green underwater [...] And before her she saw the Greenwitch [...] The huge leafy head turned towards her, and without a voice the Greenwitch spoke, spoke into her mind'. (56-58). Jane dives into the watery underworld depths of the powerful Earth Mother (Neumann: 47-48); the ego makes a psychological journey into the unconscious, the 'inner ocean' (Knapp: xv).

Jane has a conversation with the Greenwitch, who reveals that it has a secret: it is guarding the manuscript case. The case is 'a small bright shining thing, lying within the cleft in the rock, on the white sand; it was like a small glowing stick' (Cooper 1977a: 58). The imagery associated with the sexual union of male and female, together with Jane's desire to possess the case, suggests that the female ego is now ready to take steps to contact its inner masculine. The transformative effect of the meeting with the primordial feminine is one which occurs commonly among female characters in women's literature, according to Pratt: 'at the core of their quest [they] often encounter a powerful integrative mother figure who offers regeneration' (105). The conversation with the Greenwitch occurs while Jane is asleep; the dream world, intimately connected with the unconscious, is no less real than the waking one.

The Greenwitch, provoked to a rare display of anger by the Dark, unleashes the terrifying 'Wild Magic' on the village, but the ego has now assimilated atavistic, empowering feminine images into the psyche and is no longer afraid. The Greenwitch recalls Jane's empathetic wish for its happiness, and gives her the manuscript case. The girl wakes up with it in her hand. The developing ego has come a long way, from an early need to hide behind a motherly persona, through encounters with the powerful archetypal feminine, to the acknowledgement of masculine elements in the unconscious. The conscious ego needs, then, to assimilate aspects of the masculine, including assertiveness and anger. Jane's discovery not of the missing Grail, but of its masculine partner – the Logos that unlocks the prophetic words engraved on the side of the mother vessel – is the next step in the individuation of the text. As ego, Jane has encountered the animus as patriarch-father, alien-other and youth. She remains attracted to Will: 'She grinned at him. "I said I hoped we should see you again someday. Didn't I?" Will grinned back, and Jane remembered the way his smile had always transformed his rather solemn face' (Cooper 1979: 74). An image of the animus as partner appears to the ego in the form of Bran Davies, whose quest for the crystal sword is the final one in the battle between Light and Dark. The ego is not yet ready to recognise this animus image. It is Will's role to support Bran in his quest, and Jane resents this, seeing in Bran a rival for Will's attention. 'She felt a vague formless resentment of the way his presence somehow complicated their relationship with Will: *it's not just us any more*, she thought, *the way it was last time...*' (88). Her brother asks what the problem is. 'It's not a *problem*. It's that Bran. It's just – oh dear, you wouldn't understand' (91). Bran's presence is the catalyst that enables Jane to access her 'masculine' anger. She confronts him.

> *Bran turned to go after [Will]. But Jane was in his way. She stood there, breathing unevenly, looking coolly at them both in a way Will did not recognize [sic] [...] Watching Jane, Will felt suddenly that he was seeing someone he had never met before. Her face was drawn into furious lines of emotion that seemed to belong to someone else. 'You!' Jane said to Bran, pushing her hands fiercely into her pockets. 'You, you think you're so special, don't you, with the white hair and the difference, and the eyes behind those silly glasses. Super-different. You can tell us what we ought to do, you think you're even more special than Will. But who are you, anyway?'* (93).

This is the first time Jane has been bold enough to initiate a confrontation, let alone stand her ground in one. It is an unpleasant experience, but a necessary one. The suppressed aspects of the masculine unconscious are finally assimilated into the conscious ego. Even while undergoing the process, Jane as ego has an inkling of its importance: 'This was a strangeness she could not define, had never known before. A restlessness, a half-fearful anticipation of something part of her seemed to understand and part not...'

(98). Bran represents a strong animus; he is unfazed when Jane is angry and engages with her argument.

The animus as partner is associated with romantic and sexual potential. Bran notes that a girl who throws a rose at Will is 'Not so pretty as Jane, that one…' 'As who?' Will said. 'Jane Drew. Don't you think she's pretty, then?' (181). Yet the ego is still unready to recognise the animus in this mature form; psychic integration begins to seem possible, but remains uncertain.

An image or images of the Self usually appear once an ego has assimilated the contrasexual aspects of the psyche. The Self-image takes the form of the Lady – the Goddess – who passes on a vital message through Jane: 'It was intended, from the beginning, that you should carry the last message […] Remember, my daughter. And be brave, Jane' (100-101). A clear relationship is established between Self-image and ego, yet the ego does *not* realise the Self; the text does not individuate. This is not entirely surprising, for in Jungian psychology, as in contemporary society, the range of positive feminine images available to women is, at present, still more limited than the positive images available to men. The ego's failure to individuate is a reflection of the lower status of the feminine in patriarchal society.

The linear reading proceeds to its predictable conclusion. The archetypal Wise Old Men, imaged as Will and Merriman, the Lady, the Divine Child, imaged as Bran, his father, King Arthur, and the mortals join forces to defeat the Dark. Merriman departs for paradise with the Lady and King Arthur.

But the aftermath of the quest is a disappointment for many readers, for the conclusion is unexpectedly downbeat. It is consistent, though, with the return to the vertical narrative in which individuation of the text does not occur. In the end, Jane and Bran fail to depart for paradise in triumph after the completion of the quest. Their memories of the experience will disappear, as Merriman tells them, 'into the hidden places of your minds, and you will never again know any hint of it except in dreams' (283). Furthermore, although the Dark has been defeated, the world will never be free of conflict: 'Good men will still be killed by bad, or sometimes by other good men, and there will still be pain and disease and famine, anger and hate' (282-283). Cooper, a woman who gave up Christianity at the age of 16 (1996: 146), is unable even to offer readers the reassuring image of a transcendent God. With the departure of King Arthur, Merriman tells the children: 'you may not lie idly expecting the second coming of anybody now, because the world is yours and it is up to you' (Cooper 1979: 282).

This lack of closure, even if unsatisfying, is a fitting conclusion to the series, for contemporary readers live in a world in which war and terrorism are facts of everyday life. Rowland points out that the goal of Jungian Goddess feminism is 'the healing not of individuals, but of the cosmos' (67). Although the text reveals possibilities for encounters with an array of positive feminine images in the psyche, the incomplete individuation process, with its failure to reconcile masculine and feminine, suggests that the attainment of the wider goal poses an even greater challenge.

And although the ending is inconclusive, it is not without hope. There is no psychic resolution for Jane as ego, but another Self-symbol appears in the final lines: a stone, a symbol of totality which 'transcends of the problem of the opposites and thus succeeds in uniting them' (Jung and von Franz: 217-218). This particular stone helped Bran, as ego in *The Grey King*, to come to terms with the Mother image in the psyche and subsequently to realise the Self. For Jane as ego, therefore, the stone has weighty symbolic significance, suggesting the connection between ego and animus as well as the union of conscious and unconscious, masculine and feminine. Bran holds out the stone and says: 'Found this in my pocket [...] You want it, Jenny-oh?' (Cooper 1979: 284). Does she take it? The reader never finds out.

Yet some possibilities are hinted at. Shortly before this moment a new Self-image appears, yet remains unexplored within the text: 'Will saw again the tawny eyes of Herne the Hunter in Bran's face… He blinked, wondering' (279). Herne the Hunter, also known as Cernunnos, is a pagan symbol of male fertility and the partner of the Goddess (French: 28). As the Goddess, the Lady is maiden, mother and wise old woman. She may be interpreted as a Self-image not only of Jane as ego, but of author as ego or author-as-reader as ego, with Herne the Hunter the animus of this ego. The partnership of Herne the Hunter and the Lady represents the unity of male and female and posits an immanent, dual-gendered deity image in the place of the transcendent male God. Through the image of a Goddess united with her Greenworld lover, the text suggests the possibility of a future in which the earth and its inhabitants live in harmony and in which the psyche of a society damaged by war is healed.

As in *'The Dark is Rising'*, the unsettling and, at times, frightening modern world underlies the fantasy world in *'The Chronicles of Prydain'*, which, as a representation of the individuation of a psyche, follows a fairly straightforward path. Taran, read as the conscious ego of the text, is at first a 'macho' male, eager to go to war, interested only in the company of other potential heroes. Having fought in World War II, the author experienced first-hand the psychological effects of war on those who serve in the armed forces: '[I]t damages you, it damages everybody who fights in it. You've seen and done bad things. This applies to both sides. Nobody comes out of it innocent' (Alexander, 2005b). After World War II, though, instead of pursuing policies of peace, the United States became embroiled in the Cold War and wars in Korea, Vietnam and Iraq. If Alexander is consciously exploring the effects of war in his books, he may also unconsciously be attempting to come to terms with the rift between his personal unconscious and the American collective unconscious – the conflict between his own pacifism and a national psyche that is widely viewed as excessively aggressive.

A male ego needs to assimilate Mother images in the unconscious before it can integrate the anima and realise the Self. But although Taran, an orphan, takes a great interest in his paternal lineage, he has no curiosity about his personal mother. As Rowland points out, the male ego is 'particularly liable to suppress the feminine anima-soul' (77). A developing ego encounters Mother images in the unconscious, which often take the form of the 'Terrible Mother': 'goddesses of the underworld and the dead, witches, Furies, negatively demonic figures' (Neumann: 80). As the developing male ego, Taran adopts a persona of stereotypical, exaggeratedly 'masculine' behaviour and encounters in his unconscious the Terrible Mother, imaged as Achren, the wicked former queen of the underworld.

Pratt describes the queen of the underworld as 'an inhabitant of the feminine labyrinths so dreaded by Jung and the heroes of the romance quest' (114). Some Goddess feminists revision the Terrible Mother as the repressed, misunderstood mythical Goddess of the underworld. Perera images her as the Goddess Inanna, who is forced into the underworld, where she becomes the 'Terrible Mother' Erishkigal, queen of the dead. Inanna is eventually reborn 'loathsome, and claims her right to survive. She is not a beautiful maid, daughter of the fathers, but ugly, selfish, ruthless, willing to be very negative, willing not to care' (177). This description is a fitting one for Achren, a deposed queen who rises from the underworld as a woman attempting to reassert her power in patriarchal society. It is no wonder that a patriarchal male ego finds the image a nightmarish one. Both attracted to and repelled by feminine images, Taran is at first willing to be convinced that Achren is a 'Good Mother':

> At the pressure of her fingers, a comforting warmth filled Taran's aching body... a delicious sensation of repose came over him, repose as he remembered it in days long forgotten in Caer Dallben, the warm bed of his childhood, drowsy summer afternoons.
> 'How do you come here?' she asked quietly.
> 'We crossed Great Avren,' Taran began. 'You see, what had happened...'
> 'Silence!' Gwydion's voice rang out. 'She is Achren! She sets a trap for you!'
> Taran gasped. For an instant he could not believe such beauty concealed the evil of which he had been warned (Alexander, 2004a: 54).

Following this encounter, Taran is imprisoned in the dungeon of Achren's home, Spiral Castle, a name which, according to Robert Graves, refers to a place of death (99). The ego at this stage associates 'Mother' with death and underground prisons; therefore, when it encounters the anima as partner within, imaged as Princess Eilonwy, it continues to see feminine images as negative: '...he wondered how much he could count on this scatterbrained girl [...] [S]he might betray him to Achren. It might be another trap, a new torment that promised him freedom only to snatch it away...' (Alexander, 2004a: 68).

Eilonwy, though, helps him to escape via a tunnel, an image which suggests the process of birth, thus releasing the ego from its paralysing fear of the Terrible Mother. Leaving the castle, they discover a jewelled sword, Dyrnwyn, which Eilonwy carries for the impetuous Taran's own safety. Eilonwy represents a function of the anima which 'furthers the process of individuation' (Jung and von Franz: 178-179). Eilonwy rides a white horse, symbolising 'unconscious powers at the disposal of the consciousness' (von Franz, 1996: 152) and carries a golden bauble, a symbol of the Self (von Franz, 1993: 23). The association of these symbols with Eilonwy suggests that this anima image will be the catalyst for the ego's realisation of the Self.

Taran comes to understand that Eilonwy is not evil; the feminine images encountered by the ego become ambivalent rather than wholly negative:

> 'Gird [the sword] on me – I mean, if you please. Say you will. I want you to be the one to do it.'
> Eilonwy turned to him in surprise. 'Yes, of course,' she said, blushing, 'if you really...'
> 'I do!' cried Taran. 'After all,' he added, 'you're the only girl in Caer Dallben' (Alexander, 2004b: 26).

Taran's quest involves the recovery of a cauldron, a 'Mother' symbol of transformation (Jung, 1991: 109-110). The evil lord of the underworld is using the vessel to give dead warriors 'life' as mute bringers of death. The cauldron's true owners are three witches, Orwen, Orddu and Orgoch. Manifestations of primordial feminine power, they are 'neither good nor evil. We're simply interested in things as they are'. (Alexander, 2004b: 150). The three sisters are representations of the Triple Goddess, the Mother in both benign and devouring forms – literally in the case of Orgoch, who is constantly hungry for human flesh. Taran, who initially fears them, trades a precious brooch, which gives him insight and wisdom, for the cauldron. For the first time, he confronts the feminine unconscious: 'Taran lifted his head and his eyes met Orddu's. For that instant it seemed to him they were quite alone [...] "The [cauldron] is ours," he said, looking Orddu full in the face' (159). The incident is a turning point, for after this encounter with the feminine, Taran weeps. Shortly afterwards, the ego integrates the Shadow and the macho persona is discarded.

Traditional Jungian analysts believe that the developing masculine ego needs to overcome the Mother, and that this act leads to increased masculinisation, which in turn leads to the anima (Neumann: 38). This narrative as a representation of a psychological process suggests, alternatively, that it is the negative *image* of the Mother which must be overcome rather than the Mother herself. Jungians such as Whitmont believe that societies which tend too much towards the masculine need feminine symbols 'in order to achieve psychological resolution' (Rowland: 59). Indeed, Taran as ego begins to develop significantly only when he acquires the cauldron and begins to acknowledge aspects of the feminine in the psyche.

After it is able to meet the primordial feminine without being overwhelmed by terror, the ego is ready to encounter the anima. Lloyd Alexander admits that the character of Eilonwy is based on women he knows, and says, 'I wonder if this is a kind of idealization or dream realization of my ideal woman or some such thing.' (Naranjo: 154). Alexander seems to acknowledge that Eilonwy may be a textual manifestation of his own anima. The character was created within the context of the author's own personal and socio-historical background, and the logical, argumentative, spirited and active princess certainly does not correspond to Jung's rigid views of femininity.

Although the ego of the text is ready to contact the anima, it remains out of reach. The princess is kidnapped and held captive by Achren. Taran journeys to rescue her, and in a dark cavern uses Eilonwy's bauble to light up the dark:

> ... his mind turned from his own plight to thoughts of Eilonwy [...] He was about to return the bauble to his jacket, but stopped short and stared at his hand. A point of light had begun to flicker in the depths of the sphere. As he watched, not daring to breathe, it blossomed and shimmered' (Alexander, 2005a: 100-101).

Instead of 'overcom[ing] the monster of darkness: the long-hoped-for and expected triumph of consciousness over the unconscious', (Jung, 1961: 118-119), the ego 'sees the light' of the feminine unconscious. Taran has been occupied only with himself; it is when he thinks of Eilonwy that, as ego, he is ready to integrate the feminine unconscious and to realise the Self.

Caer Colur, the castle in which Eilonwy is imprisoned, is on an island; to reach it Taran must cross deep water, a symbol of the Mother and the unconscious (Jung, 1995: 219). The princess is kept in a tower, whose walls he climbs to reach her. According to Jung, the anima is so far above male consciousness 'that the hero has to climb up to it with considerable effort' (1972: 117). When he reaches her, though, Eilonwy is bewitched and semi-conscious, wondering what has become of an assistant pig-keeper she has met in her dreams. '"He is here now," Taran said quietly. "He has long sought you and in ways even he himself did not know"' (Alexander, 2005a: 163). The ego has recognised the anima in the unconscious and integrated it into its consciousness.

The young man initiates a rescue attempt; he confronts the evil queen and recalls 'the nightmare memory of another day when he had stood in terror before Achren' (168). Although some vestige of fear of the Terrible Mother remains, the ego has moved a long way towards psychic wholeness and the connection to the anima is strong. Eilonwy is rescued, and the princess and Taran become engaged.

From this point on, the ego no longer struggles with Mother images in the unconscious, so perceptions of 'Mother' become positive – even Achren has now assumed the role of 'Good Mother' and is to be seen 'tend[ing] the cooking fire' (Alexander, 1999a: 4). At this stage of psychological development, Mother symbols stand for 'the unconscious as the creative matrix of the future' (Jung, 1995: 301).

Once the developing ego has integrated the anima in the psyche, the image of the Self emerges. As ego, Taran undertakes an extended search for the Self. He seeks his vocation, spending time apprenticed to a female weaver and to Annlaw, a potter who makes 'Mother' vessels – goblets and vases. Finally, he sees his true identity – his own reflection – in the Mirror of Llunet, a pool of water in a cave. The feminine unconscious, the water, reveals a Self-image that is immanent rather than transcendent, suggesting that responsibility for the future lies with humanity on earth rather than God in heaven. Yet although the image of the Self has appeared, the textual process of individuation is as yet incomplete.

Taran's final task is to recover the sword Dyrnwyn, which has been stolen. In order to do so he must travel to Annuvin, the realm of the death lord, but much of the overland route is blocked by Arawn's armies. Taran carries with him a talisman, a fragment from a 'Mother' pot made by Annlaw. As the process of psychological development nears its end, the ego continues to encounter positive feminine images in the unconscious. Taran travels underground to Annuvin, and is given safe passage through Fair Folk mines. Where once the feminine underworld was imaged as chthonic dungeons and death, the ego now sees the underground world as a place of protection. The cavernous mines are a type of space positively associated with 'reservoirs of untold fertility – passageways to unknown worlds' (Knapp: xvi). The chambers are rich with 'jewels of bright red and brilliant green, with gems clear as water or, in their glittering depths, flecked with gold and silver' (Alexander, 1999b: 157). Travelling through the tunnel, a symbol of rebirth, 'the jewels seemed to grow more plentiful' (157). Emerging above ground, the friends see Arawn's warriors. They thaw a frozen river; the 'rushing waters' (179) gush down a ravine to deluge the camp, leaving only 'dark water' (179).

Taran reaches the gates to the underworld, the place where the hero traditionally overcomes the chthonic Terrible Mother (Neumann: 157). This underworld, though, is no longer the domain of the Mother, but of a war-mongering male. It is the war lord, who has subverted the natural cycle of life and brought death and destruction to Prydain, who must be overcome. Masculine and feminine unite to accomplish the task: Taran discovers the sword nestling in a uterine hollow, while Achren delivers Arawn to Taran, who kills him.

The once frightening witches appear in their 'true' form – that of beautiful Goddesses – to give Taran the tapestry they have been weaving. "'But here… it is unfinished." "Naturally," said Orddu. "You must still choose the pattern […] as long as thread remains to be woven"' (Alexander, 1999b: 234). Taran chooses to remain in Prydain, a decision which leads to his coronation as High King, and he and Eilonwy marry. The Self is higher than the 'Self-image', for the king is the common man who follows his own path to Self-hood, even if both process and outcome diverge from his culture's requisite masculine persona. The 'dormant, inherent possibility' (von Franz, 1993: 22) of the Self is realised within the individuated psyche of the text.

The conclusion, although optimistic, is not a traditional fairytale ending in which evil is defeated for all time. It is rather more sobering, for as in *'The Dark is Rising'*, the fantasy world, like the real one, is one in which 'men still hate and slay each other when greed and anger goad them' (Alexander, 1999b: 245). Both Lloyd Alexander and Susan Cooper lived through the uncertainties and dangers of a world at war. Contemporary readers will have to find their own ways to live in a world that confronts them with a war in Iraq or bombings on tube trains or 9/11.

Taran may be read not just as an individual ego, but as the psyche of the American male, the narrative itself as a psychological fantasy of a masculine American society which comes to accept its inner feminine and is thereby able to reassess its tendency to war. As Rowland points out, Jungians such as Whitmont cite 'narratives of feminine reincorporation' (2002: 59) as essential for a 'spiritual and social' (59) psychological resolution of society.

In my reading of Jane as the ego of *'The Dark is Rising'*, Susan Cooper's text underlines the challenges faced by a woman in a society in which the feminine is devalued and the masculine is associated with war. It explores how, through accessing powerful images of the feminine in the psyche and coming to terms with its masculine elements, young women can begin to find new and positive ways to express both their masculinity and femininity in the modern world. Cooper hopes that, through fantasy, authors can 'drop into the shadowy pool of [readers'] unconscious minds a few images that – perhaps, with luck – will echo through their lives and help them understand and even improve their world, our world' (1996: 70).

REFERENCES

L. Alexander (2004a). *The Book of Three*. London: Usborne. (first published New York: Henry Holt and Company, 1964).

L. Alexander (2004b). *The Black Cauldron*. London: Usborne. (first published New York: Henry Holt and Company, 1965).

L. Alexander (2005a). *The Castle of Llyr*. London: Usborne. (first published New York: Henry Holt and Company, 1966).

L. Alexander (1999a). *Taran Wanderer*. New York: Henry Holt and Company, 1967.

L. Alexander (1999b). *The High King*. New York: Henry Holt and Company, 1968,

L. Alexander (2005b). Telephone interview with M Travis, 8 April 2005.

S. Cooper, *Over Sea, Under Stone*. London: Puffin Books, 1968. (first published London: Jonathan Cape, 1965).

S. Cooper, *The Dark is Rising*. London: Puffin Books, 1976. (first published London: Chatto and Windus, 1973).

S. Cooper, *Greenwitch*. London: Puffin Books, 1977a. (first published London: Chatto and Windus in 1974.]

S. Cooper, *The Grey King*. London: Puffin Books, 1977b. (first published, London: Chatto and Windus, 1975).

S. Cooper, *Silver on the Tree*. London: Puffin Books, 1979. (first published, London: Chatto and Windus, 1977).

S. Cooper, *Dreams and Wishes: Essays on Writing for Children*. New York: Margaret K. McElderry Books, 1996.

M-L. von Franz, *The Feminine in Fairy Tales*. Boston and London: Shambhala, 1993. (first published 1972).

M-L. von Franz, *The Interpretation of Fairy Tales*. Boston and London: Shambala, 1996. (first published 1970).

C. French, *The Celtic Goddess: Great Queen or Demon Witch?* Edinburgh: Floris Books, 2001.

R. Graves, *The White Goddess: A Historical Grammar of Poetic Myth*. G. Lindop (ed.). London: Faber and Faber, 1999. (first published 1948).

C.G. Jung, tr. R. F. C. Hull, *Four Archetypes: Mother, Rebirth, Spirit, Trickster*. London: Routledge and Kegan Paul, 1972.

C.G. Jung, tr. R. F. C. Hull, *The Collected Works of CG Jung – Vol 9, Part 1: The Archetypes and the Collective Unconscious*. London: Routledge, 1990. (first published London: Routledge & Kegan Paul, 1959).

C.G. Jung, tr. R. F. C. Hull, *Aspects of the Feminine*. London: Ark, 1992. (first published: Princeton University Press, 1982).

C.G. Jung, tr. R. F. C. Hull, *The Collected works of CG Jung – Vol 5: Symbols of Transformation*. London: Routledge, 1995. (first published London: Routledge & Kegan Paul, 1956).

E. Jung, *Jung: His Life and Works, an Autobiographical Memoir*. Shambhala, 1991.

E. Jung, *Animus and Anima*. Dallas: Spring Publications, 1985. (first English translation published: Analytical Psychology Club of New York, 1957).

E. Jung and M-L. von Franz, tr. A. Dykes. *The Grail Legend*. Princeton: Princeton University Press, 1998. (first published by the CG Jung Foundation for Analytical Psychology, 1970).

B. Knapp, *Women, Myth and the Feminine Principle*. Albany: State University of New York Press, 1998.

C. Naranjo, *The Divine Child and the Hero: Inner Meaning in Children's Literature*. Nevada City, California: Gateways/IDHHB, 1999. (first published in Spanish by Editions Sirio under the title *El Nino Divino y El Heroe*, 1993)

E. Neumann, tr R. Mannheim, *The Great Mother: An Analysis of the Archetype*. London: Routledge & Kegan Paul, 1955.

S. Brinton Perera, 'The Descent of Inanna: Myth and Therapy' in Lauter, E. and C. Schreier Rupprecht (eds.). *Feminist Archetypal Theory: Interdisciplinary Re-Visions of Jungian Thought*. Knoxville: The University of Tennessee Press. pp. 137-186, 1985.

R. L. Plante, 'Object and Character in *The Dark is Rising.*' *Children's Literature Association Quarterly*. Spring 1986, Vol. 11, No. 1, pp. 37-41, 1986.

A. Pratt, *Archetypal Patterns in Women's Fiction*. Bloomington: Indiana University Press, 1981.

S. Rowland, *Jung: A Feminist Revision*. Cambridge: Polity Press, 2002.

A. Samuels, *The Plural Psyche: Personality, Morality and the Father.* London and New York: Tavistock/Routledge, 1996. (first published by Routledge, 1989).

P. Young-Eisendrath, 'Gender, Animus, and Related Topics' in N. Schwartz-Salant, and M. Stein (eds.) *Gender and Soul in Psychotherapy*. Wilmette: Chiron. pp. 151-177, 1992.

See Rowland, Chapter 3, for a summary of the ideas of the main proponents of Jungian Goddess feminism.

John Burton

Pattern-Matching and Childhood Stories

I HAVE BEEN enchanted with the timeless Sufi stories of the Mullah Nasrudin since I first heard them a few years ago. One story comes to mind – a tale that has been retold as a joke many times in differing cultures and languages. It has more to do with perception than position.

The Mullah Nasrudin was enjoying a rest by the shores of a wide river. The splendour and magnificence of the slowly moving body of water caught his imagination, as he lay daydreaming by the water's edge. Suddenly he heard a man shouting from across the river, 'Mullah, tell me how you get to the other side of the river', asked the man. The Mullah looked up from his rest and answered, 'You're already on the other side!'

I have wondered how this story and its message of relativity and viewpoint has found its way into modern narratives. Some stories never go away – often they are reconfigured into new systems and analogues with the same essential meaning. I am often amazed that my children return from school singing the same rhymes and telling the same jokes that were told in my playground, stories I can remember my father telling me were told in his day.

Why do some stories remain? What is the psychological need for such stories, and what is their impact? Is there really something magical that happens when those spell-binding words of 'once upon a time' are mentioned?

In this paper I shall explore the question of how childhood stories can shape and inform us, and why stories are critical to our ability to gain a sense of self.

Firstly I would like to address the issue of pattern matching, the taste we all share for metaphor. Work done by S. Walker and later picked up by Joe Griffin and Ivan Tyrrell explores fascinating observations of birds in their nest-making behaviour. It was noted that birds' brains are programmed with an instinct to seasonally gather twigs to construct a nest, and then to gather soft lining material with which to furnish it. However, this instinctive behaviour is far from simple. Birds – even those of the same species – are known to vary widely in the style, size, location and composition of their nests. It is thus determined that the instinctive drive must be strong enough to prompt action, yet flexible enough to allow for differing conditions, locations and the range of building materials available. This flexibility allows the bird to gather anything that is 'twig-like', and to line the nest with foam, moss, scraps of cloth, and so forth.

It has likewise been noted that a newborn baby is happy to accept anything nipple-like in order to suckle. The inner pattern laid down in instinct for a nipple must allow for all the variations of human anatomy. The variations in facial features of the mother, the range of tones of the human voice, the colour of skin, the language spoken, all must be accommodated in the patterns laid down by nature in the baby's brain. Clearly such flexibility in accommodating all the variations of life and one's surroundings are essential to survival, and once extrapolated, this flexibility of instinctive drive, of matching our internal patterns or expectations with the outside world, can be applied to every behaviour in which the essential nature of an organism is called upon.

And, as the complexity of the organism increases, from birds to mammals to humans, so do the complexities of these inner patterns, and the flexibility of such patterns. In this sense, the brain becomes a large pattern-matching machine, searching to complete and fulfil the instinctive or learned patterns laid down in the mind, with those in the outside world. This complexity and flexibility in pattern matching, which as babies allows us to recognise a nipple or a teat, in adulthood allows us to recognise a chair or a table – we instantly match up what we see before us with what learned patterns we have in store, and a measure of flexibility in order to allow for variations in colour or design.

In this sense, our consciousness is based on metaphor, understanding that one thing can represent another. This pattern-matching or metaphorical compromise is used in building language, as a word doesn't really constitute a thing, but represents it. It is used in building our understanding of the world, and can sometimes lead us awry.

Research psychologist Joe Griffin has used the example of the ethnologist Konrad Lorenz, who was filmed being followed around everywhere by a family of young goslings. The pattern laid down by nature in the hatchlings is to bond with the first largest moving thing you see – in this case Lorenz's boot. They followed him around with great devotion, displaying real distress when he left them, and ran to him when they were frightened.

Many mental problems exhibited in humans can be traced to an incorrect pattern-match. For example, a person may be unable to enjoy a relationship because a learned internal pattern of abuse is being completed in the image of the genuine lover. Such examples are too many to mention, but each, when examined in light of this understanding how the mind seeks for internal patterns to be completed, can be traced back to a false or inappropriate match made at some point, usually during a state of high emotional arousal. It must be remembered that when a pattern is laid, there is always a measure of flexibility inbuilt. This is both life-saving, and in some cases, damning.

This takes us into a little digression as to why some forms of counselling, in which the patient is asked to go back and revisit past traumatic events, seem to serve only to further embed the unhelpful pattern that, for example, all men are abusive, or that the world is hostile and unforgiving. Such a pattern can easily be completed and thus strengthened daily, if the predisposition is there. Directly revisiting the traumatic event will undoubtedly trigger all the attendant emotional responses, and only strengthen the pattern, rather than challenge it.

New therapies are taking a differing approach, using the brain's taste for metaphor in order to help patients confront old patterns with new alternatives. Revisiting old patterns, and challenging them metaphorically, is shown to undermine the inappropriate metaphor, allowing fresh ideas – and helpful patterns – to take root. This in turn permits new possibilities of behaviour, as new patterns seek for completion in the external world.

This can be illustrated by the use of storytelling I once used with a patient who suffered from a pronounced fear of social engagements. She came to me asking for help having spent years avoiding social interaction, having failed to develop any lasting friendships and feeling desperately lonely. It emerged that she was bullied at school, an experience that taught her that people were cruel and untrustworthy. She turned her attention inward, and spent most of her time reading books. Of the stories she read, those that appealed to her were the stories of the individual against the masses, the romantic hero, the person of inner resolve who fights against the odds, swimming upstream, counter to society, the revolutionaries, the lone warriors. In such stories she found metaphorical food for her portfolio of patterns, ready examples of how the world is not to be trusted. Her mind soon became adept at taking from stories those aspects that completed her inner patterns. Such stories lived with her in her mind, adding weight to her suspicions. At this point in her life, however, she was feeling the pain of exclusion, as her innate need for sociality remained severely unmet, causing stress and depression.

Rather than using cognitive techniques alone, in which I could undermine such notions directly through questioning, I decided to use Milton Erickson's approach, first reducing her emotional arousal levels using some simple breathing techniques, and then some story-telling. The story is of a lioness who was thirsty, and in need of a drink. And one hot day on the savannah, she approached a pool of water, only to find another lioness staring back. She ran, frightened by the encounter, wanting never to go back. But her thirst drove her onward to another pool, and there she met yet another lioness. Soon she had enough determination within her to decide that, come what may, she would leap into the next pool, and drink. And this she did, only to find the lioness disappear in the ripples of the water.

Such stories help us reframe thinking, and give us a new context for understanding ourselves and the world about us.

Work has been done to incorporate story-telling into therapy by Pat Williams,

Alida Gersie and others. Their work has taken a new path recently, a path which I believe opens up new avenues for discussion and research for those interested in the field of children's stories and the psychological impact of them.

Working over the past thirty years, Pat Williams has compiled a running log of stories told in childhood and the ways in which such stories have played out in the lives of those with whom such stories have struck a chord. In a process she describes as 'Forward Shadowing', she describes how many people, when asked which childhood stories could be described as their personal favourite or which particularly resonated with them, can often come up with stories which can then be shown to have cast surprisingly accurate shadows throughout their lives.

One or two examples of the many hundred she reports:

Spike Milligan reported that his favourite story as a child was *Robinson Crusoe*. One can see the inward, lonely, often depressed or manic character who uses his humour to keep the world at bay.

Karen, a managing director of a human resources company, reported a number of stories, each with a strong female character who had to fight for what she wanted, a pattern of behaviour what has lasted with her.

I suppose I could add a more well-known example of a person who took a story and developed its message to him as a pattern encompassing human desire and motivation – that of Freud and the story of Oedipus.

Steve Davidson has conducted a similar study with prison inmates who reported cases of stories that reverberated throughout their lives. These inmates were able to connect with characters in the stories which echoed their own desire for power, status, or in some cases the darker or dangerous elements of fantasy.

Interestingly, the same story can be seized upon for very different reasons. From the story of 'The Three Little Pigs', one person may connect with the lesson that hard work pays off, while another will respond with sheer panic at the instability of home.

Such stories connect with the pattern-matching processes of consciousness, the drive to complete inner patterns with those in the environment. This places a new significance on our reasons for telling stories to children, and on the impact such stories can have on them.

I wonder which childhood stories have informed your inner patterns? While some may have a ready answer, others may need to contemplate the question; but the chances are that some story from your developmental years has stayed with you as a favourite, particularly seductive or appealing. Your learned patterns about yourself and the world about you permitted you to connect with certain patterns and metaphors played out in the story, a process which is partly responsible for why you and I are here today. This elevates the status of the childhood tale from puerile entertainment to a structural component of the adult psyche. We are hardly bound to live out the lives of those we have connected with in the stories (if only that were true in the case of me and my magic beans!) but we are compelled by the pattern-matching desire of the brain to seek for possible integration through the metaphorical representation of the world.

This has implications, not least for story-tellers, whatever form they may take. It is significant, for example, that people appear to match themselves and their concerns with those elements of a tale that complete some predisposed or learned patterns they possess. Thus we should be wary of reducing our children's literature in its scope, allowing it to reflect a full menu of emotional and psychological problems and resolutions.

David Rudd

Holed and Porous, but not Impossible: Children's Literature, Psychoanalysis, and Constructions of the Child

ON THE SURFACE, a psychoanalytic approach would seem an obvious choice in conducting a critical examination of children's fiction, in that both areas are concerned with the child and his/her experience of the world. However, to talk about 'a psychoanalytic approach' is almost as vague as talking about 'a literary' one. There are all the different schools, from Freud and Jung to object-relations, to structuralist and post-structuralist, aside from the different aspects of the literary work to consider. As Peter Brooks (1994) has delineated, these broadly concentrate on the Author, the Text, or the Reader.

Authorial approaches have been common since Freud tried to read Dostoevsky's work through biographies about the Russian author. An example from children's literature would be J.M. Barrie, whose older brother was killed in a skating accident, allowing critics to argue that Barrie himself never grew up, remaining the child that his mother mourned for, a being sublimated in *Peter Pan*. Clearly, there are problems with this sort of approach, in that literary texts can seem nothing more than symptoms of an unhappy or unresolved psychic life. It also means that we need to know about the 'life' first, in order to explain the work. But where does our knowledge of the life come from, if not other texts (often those by the authors themselves – journals and the like, which are then – for some reason – given priority)?

This being the case, it makes more sense to look at the Text *per se*. However, there are still problems about which aspects to prioritise. Many critics, for instance, simply take the chief characters and sit them on the couch. For instance, Mark West examines Toad in *The Wind in the Willows*, commenting that

> Grahame provides little information about Toad's childhood, but the information he provides suggests that Toad may not have experienced the mirroring process.... Toad's mother may not have been available to help build her son's sense of self (Rollin & West, 1999, p.50).

Aside from the fact that none of the main characters' childhoods is discussed – Toad is not exceptional in this matter – or the presumption that Toad is an adult (there's much to suggest that he is a spoilt child) – there is the more significant point that, unlike real people, most literary characters don't have childhoods: they are textual creations only (as L.C. Knights once famously asked, 'How many children had Lady Macbeth?'). (Having said this, Robert De Board (1998) actually wrote a counselling manual, *Counselling for Toads*, that features Toad as analysand!)

We might argue that these two approaches touch on things that are, at best, unknown; at worst, questionable. So, attending to the Reader might seem a better proposition. We are, each of us, fairly close to at least one exemplar of this figure! Norman Holland is perhaps the most famous exponent of this approach, arguing that our personal psychobiography determines, far more powerfully than the words on the page, how we read; hence, he reasons, we tend to read all texts in a certain way. Bruno Bettelheim might also be included here, although he tends to try and have his cake and eat it (something that is quite permissible in the Unconscious!). Thus, after declaring that 'the fairy tale's deepest meaning will be different for each person' (p. 12), he then states that '[t]he true meaning ... can be appreciated ... only from the story in its original form' (p.19) – by which he means the Grimms' versions, clearly not the originals.

After reviewing these three approaches, Peter Brooks does suggest a more complex version, involving both text and reader, based on the Freudian notion of transference, to which I'll return. But first I want to address a view that uses a psychoanalytical approach to argue against children's literature being worthy (or possible) of analysis in the first place. This is Jacqueline Rose's seminal *The Case of Peter Pan, or The Impossibility of Children's Fiction* (1984). Rose draws on a Lacanian notion of identity being established, tenuously, through language; but an identity that is forever and always subject to disruption, this being the very nature of the Symbolic order. Against this, society has clung to the Imaginary figure of the child as somehow standing outside and prior to language: a satisfactory image of plenitude. Rose, as we know, finds in Barrie's *Peter Pan* the outstanding example of this, exhibiting both the problem of taking up 'a position of identity in language' while also indicating 'its denial' (p.141):

> *The hesitancies of both language and sexuality which have appeared throughout its history cannot be separated from the very force of its image as purity itself, embodied by the eternal child.* Peter Pan *seems to have operated constantly on this edge, as if liable at any one moment to offer its disturbance to view but choosing instead to turn the other face of innocence* (p.141).

However, in order to maintain her position, it is interesting how many works Rose needs to set aside, particularly those that *do* play with language (rather than see it as a transparent window on reality). She maintains, though, that these 'have ... been pushed to the outer limits of children's writing [sic]' – not by herself, but by others – hence they don't trouble her. Likewise she manages to set aside Lear and Lewis Carroll (being seen as 'eccentric') and the whole 'order of folklore, nursery rhyme and nonsense'. It turns out, in fact, that Rose herself has a very particular (and Romantic) notion of children's fiction, and shuts out, or disavows, anything that might pollute it. So when Rose emphatically reiterates "We have been reading the wrong Freud to children … We have been reading the wrong Freud to children" [sic] (12-13), I would say that, regardless of Freud, she might have been reading the wrong children's literature.

Karín Lesnik-Oberstein's work has a similar problem, ironically, in that, by arguing that the child is constructed by adults and is thereby voiceless, the child is inadvertently separated out as a special being. Lesnik-Oberstein also creates for herself the equally problematic issue of how (and when) this voiceless being then turns into an adult with a voice. For Lesnik-Oberstein, the only possibility of an honest and open encounter with a child is in a psychoanalytical context – never in children's literature (which already presumes to know the child).

I think she has some insight here, but only insofar as our engagement with all narrative can be likened to the psychoanalytic 'talking cure'. That is, in engaging with a text we experience a desire for plenitude: to know the whole story. This process is heightened by the way our desires are played with in what Barthes calls the 'dilatory space' of the text, where the eventual outcome is deferred, where separate events start to bind together in what we call plot (*sjuzet*), in order that we can finally make sense of the underlying story (*fabula*). This is a very brief outline of Brooks' transferential notion of reading, where we experience the fore-pleasure of deferred gratification while hoping, eventually, to experience a sense of mastery as the *fabula* is realised. Fore-pleasure is thus experienced as the eventual death of narrative ('the end') is fended off – albeit we also experience a competing desire to acquire total knowledge; in short, texts stage desire (or lack) on our behalf.

In the remainder of this paper I'll use Louis Sachar's *Holes* to explore this approach, showing how we move from a state of lack (being full of 'holes') to a state of knowledge, of fulfilment (a 'whole'). *Holes* is also a text that demonstrates the problem that Freud and Breuer originally identified in hysterics: that they 'suffer mainly from reminiscences' (1895, p.58), which Freud was later to develop in his paper 'Remembering, Repeating and Working Through' (1914). People, he argued, become trapped in compulsive, repetitive patterns that stop them remembering properly, so they cannot move on. For transference to be successful, a place (or space) has to be found where the blockage can be undone; Freud describes this place/space as 'a playground in which it is expected to display …everything' (p.154) – which, of course, is what both characters and readers of this novel experience.

It is not, then, for nothing that young Stanley Yelnats is Stanley Yelnats IV: for the whole family is trapped at a point back in their history, with Stanley compulsively repeating the mantra that 'his no-good-dirty-rotten-pig-stealing-great-great-grandfather' (p.7) is responsible for his sense of failure. The fact

that Stanley's name is a palindrome reinforces this: he seems to be in stasis; in the words of Bob Dylan, he 'ain't goin' nowhere'. Stanley's Symbolic chain fetters him to a fate that seems destined to have him, and his progeny (a possible Yelnats V) forever going round in circles (and there are also hints of Dante's *Inferno* here, with the mindless hole-digging that the correction camp inmates have to endure). As both Stanley and the family in general put it: 'They always seemed to be in the wrong place at the wrong time' (p.8). The Symbolic nature of their chains (what Lacan would call the 'quilting point', around which Stanley makes sense of himself) is early on shown to be out of touch with Stanley's reality, such that he isn't even aware of his body image, hence his being bullied by a smaller child. Stanley acts simply as a functionary of the Symbolic. In Althusser's terms, this is how he has been interpellated, or 'hailed', and he accepts his lot.

All this is to change, though, with what Žižek (1992, pp.3-20) calls an eruption of the Real. In Lacan's terms, the Real is the brute stuff of the universe: that which is not symbolised, therefore that which we cannot comprehend. However, there are times when our Symbolic universe is shattered, often when we are, precisely, rendered speechless. Such a moment occurs for Stanley when Clyde Livingston's trainers come crashing out of the sky and hit him on the head, disrupting his universe and resulting in him being relabelled a criminal. This cause Stanley to confront his Symbolic position, seemingly for the first time; he turns around and asks the Lacanian question – now more associated with Žižek: *Che vuoi?*, 'What do you want with me?', or, as Žižek says elsewhere: 'Why am I what I'm supposed to be, why have I this mandate?' (1994, p.113).

Camp Green Lake turns out to be an excellent place for Stanley to be sent to because it intensifies Stanley's realisation that the Symbolic is flawed, or porous; in essence it consists of empty signifiers, or holes. As Morpheus puts it in *The Matrix*, 'Welcome to the desert of the real!' The props of Stanley's prior, mundane existence are absent in this place that belies its name: not green; no lake. But the same is true of Stanley: he bears a name that has little to do with him, that also reaches back 100 years, to Stanley Yelnats I. From the start Stanley is made unsure of what things mean. 'Be careful,' the bus driver warns him, and Stanley wonders whether he means 'going down the steps' or just 'be careful at Camp Green Lake' (p.11). He encounters a man who wears 'sunglasses and a cowboy hat' even when he's inside; who has a name that is not one – 'Mr Sir' – simply two honorifics that, in emphasising his masculinity, simultaneously render it ironic and excessive.

Another member of staff, Mr Pendanski, is more anxious to sustain the existing symbolic order, planning to have everyone use 'the names their parents gave them – the names that *society will recognize them by* when they return to become useful and hardworking members of society' (pp.18-19). But he is thwarted. It is precisely this order that is being rejected, giving the campers a chance not to be enslaved, or cursed, by their history. Thus they all have nicknames (and it is ironic that Pendanski himself, a staunch believer in patronyms, is emasculated by being nicknamed 'Mom'). Their new names are less arbitrary, relating to their current situation, and to some attribute of the person (seemingly in the Real). So the inmates get very annoyed when traditionally hailed, as Stanley learns early on:

> Theodore whirled and grabbed Stanley by his collar. "My name's not Thee-o-dore," he said. "It's Armpit." He threw Stanley to the ground (p.20).

Stanley's name seems the most arbitrary, being called this simply because 'Everyone in his family had always liked the fact that "Stanley Yelnats" was spelled the same frontward and backward' (p.9); in other words, Stanley is determined by an arrangement of letters. His new name, 'Caveman', though, suggests that he is, indeed, a man (rather than a boy); and that he is not just a name but someone with a body, someone who has a physical presence (Reynolds, 2002). The word 'Caveman' also conjures up notions of a pre-Symbolic, or pre-linguistic existence – of an attempt to get at the Real (which is apparent throughout, with the emphasis on the physicality of things: the senses, the smells, the thirst and pain) – while simultaneously pointing to the impossibility of finding any essence in a mere name (a cave is nothing but a hollow space, although it can be filled with all manner of things).

It is not only the inmates' names that are confounded; the whole place is unpredictable according to traditional notions of signification:

> Stanley took a shower – if you could call it that, ate dinner – if you could call it that, and went to bed – if you could call his smelly and scratchy cot a bed (p.21).

Then there's 'the rec room', which turns out to be the 'WRECK ROOM', as '[n]early everything in the room was broken; the TV, the pinball machine, the furniture' (p.43); and the lizards:

> ...it is kind of odd that scientists named the lizard after its yellow spots. Each lizard has exactly eleven yellow spots, but the spots are hard to see ... The lizard ... has big red eyes. In truth, its eyes are yellow, and it is the skin around the eyes which is red, but everyone speaks of its red eyes. It also has black teeth and a milky white tongue.
> Looking at one, you would have thought that it should have been named a "red-eyed" lizard, or a "black-toothed" lizard, or perhaps a "white-tongued" lizard (p. 41).

It is here that Stanley has a chance to avoid being just a number in a series – that is, part of the succession of Yelnatses differentiated only by Roman numerals. This is where 'plot' is important. Plot, crucially, involves tying events together, giving them some sort of patterning or repetition: of showing how earlier events become meaningful when tied to later ones. As Peter Brooks says, narrative is about repetition, 'a going over again of a ground already covered' (1984, p.97) – which is exactly what Stanley is forced to do, both digging and filling in holes – and thus addressing his position in the

Symbolic. Before this, Stanley never seems to have questioned his existence, whether it's being bullied or having no friends. He is like a robot, a complete functionary of the Symbolic, whereas, as Lacan notes, we are split subjects, existing between the Symbolic and the Real, not quite fitting (there's a hole, or lack, at the centre of our existence). The intrusion of the Real via the trainers, though, shifts Stanley's perception (he starts 'looking awry', as Žižek would say), and the process of dialectizing the signifier, that is, personalising the Otherness of the Symbolic, achieving some sort of narrative coherence – as in transference – begins. Stanley engages with plot (and with plots of land, come to that); and plot, of course, is about repetition, as noted earlier. But not in the compulsive way he has repeated family myths up to now. Stanley has the chance to work properly through the events of the past and thus move the whole family out of its rut.

We should also note, of course, that he is a *Roman* numeral, which are very unwieldy and unproductive numbers: they just go on getting longer and longer, but are very difficult to do any computing with. For the latter you need a zero – which functions as a place-holder, allowing patterns to emerge. Zero's name is of interest, then, not only for its associations with nothingness, and with the holes that feature throughout the text (Pinsent, 2002), but also for the fact that the zero is the most versatile of numbers, providing 'a glimpse of the ineffable and the infinite' as Charles Seife puts it, adding, 'through all its history, despite the rejection and the exile, zero has always defeated those who opposed it'. Robert Kaplan also comments on the bad press that zero has received: 'criminals were the zeroes of society: we still call our losers zeroes' (p.66), and it is particularly fitting that Hector Zero is the most marginal character, having grown up almost completely at odds with the Symbolic: no official papers, illiterate, unschooled, father unknown, mother missing.

In Lacanian terms, this means that Zero does not have a traditional masculine structure; that is, he is not totally subsumed by the symbolic order, alienated by language; rather, he fits more the feminine position (it is of note that it is Zero's *female* ancestry that is continually emphasised). This position points to the lack in the Other, allowing the individual 'to step beyond the boundaries set by language', showing 'that the signifier isn't everything' (Fink, 1995, p.107); in other words, pointing up the holes. Such a being is said to 'ex-sist', being closer to the Real. Zero is also the instigator of the plot; in fact, before Stanley is even aware that there is one (he finds this out retrospectively) – just as Madame Zeroni instigated Elya's story. Thanks to Zero the magical coincidences multiply, as isolated parts of the puzzle start to come together. From a lack of signification we henceforth move towards an excess.

Zero and Stanley are thus both prime candidates to undertake what Žižek, after Lacan, terms 'the act', which 'restructures the very symbolic co-ordinates of the agent's situation: it is an intervention in the course of which the agent's identity itself is radically changed' (Žižek, 2001, p.85). Zero's act occurs when he smacks Pendanski in the face with his shovel; Stanley's shortly thereafter, when he steals and wrecks the water truck. They then journey to God's thumb, which, as others have noted, is overtly phallic. But it is also an example of the Lacanian Thing, something beyond the limits of the possible with its uphill-travelling water. Bruce Fink helpfully traces this 'Thing' back to its Freudian roots, noting its close relation to the sublime, having signifiers in such things as "God"; and 'the finding of the signifier', Fink informs us, 'must be understood as an encounter …that is, as fortuitous in some sense' (Fink, 1995, p.115).

Lacan also notes that when objects are sublimated in this way, there is a sense of transcending death – which Stanley and Zero certainly experience, both for themselves and also in the way that they experience the Lacanian position of being 'between two deaths'. That is, their respective ancestors, though physically dead (in the Real), live on in the Symbolic, waiting to be finally laid to rest in order that the living, too, can move on. In properly working through their situation; or, in earlier terms, in remembering with the proper affect, rather than compulsively repeating family myths, the curse can be lifted.

Using Lacan's vocabulary, this act results in Stanley 'traversing the fantasy', such that reality comes to be seen afresh, as the holed landscape of Camp Green Lake certainly is. Stanley thus subjectifies his Otherness; that is, he takes responsibility for his place in the Symbolic: 'He couldn't blame his no-good-dirty-rotten-pig-stealing-great-great-grandfather this time. This time it was his own fault, one hundred percent' (p.148). Interestingly, this recognition of his position is not pronounced overtly, in what Lacan (1998, p.246) would call 'empty speech' (Stanley has just pinched the water truck and driven it into a hole); rather, it is conveyed in terms of free indirect discourse, suggesting a more thoughtful transference from speaker to reader.

This shift is also eloquently demonstrated in the verse of an old song that the Yelnats family recites. 'If only, if only' is its refrain – a song about longing and regret (or lack), featuring a wolf howling pointlessly at the moon.

> *"If only, if only," the woodpecker sighs.*
> *"The bark on the tree was just a little bit softer."*
> *While the wolf waits below, hungry and lonely,*
> *He cries to the moo-oo-oon,*
> *"If only, if only"* (p.8).

The hard bark suggests an initial resistance, just as Stanley experiences when he first starts digging his holes, trying to get beneath the hard crust. At the very end of the novel, the ensuing verse is sung by Zero's mother (someone even more marginalised in the Symbolic – but who, at this point, manages to speak – indeed, she has the last word).

> *If only, if only, the moon speaks no reply;*

> *Reflecting the sun and all that's gone by.*
> *Be strong my weary wolf, turn around boldly.*
> *Fly high, my baby bird,*
> *My angel, my only* (p.233).

She points to the error of addressing the moon – itself, of course, only a reflector of the sun's light (a bit like passing on information second-hand, or seeing your image as the real 'you'). The wolf is thus shown to have been trapped by an image of 'all that's gone by' (as has the Yelnats family) and is advised to 'turn around boldly' – which is precisely what Stanley has done through his 'act' (significantly undertaken in a place that has no mirrors, either – apart from the one that the Warden has, and she, like her ancestors, is shown to be trapped in an Imaginary past).

The excess of coincidences at the end of the novel has effectively shaken up the symbolic order, giving the reader a sense that things can be otherwise. It also passes the buck back to us: 'You will have to fill in the holes yourself' (p.231), we are told. What is especially apparent is that Stanley is not asserted as a sovereign 'I' at the end; rather, it is Stanley and Zero, an interdependent we. There's also no mention of colour, nor of any discrimination by age.

My reading thus differs from two other critics, Annette Wannamaker and Karen Coats. The former argues that masculinity is championed at the expense of the feminine, with Camp Green Lake itself being a feminine wasteland consisting of 'holes and dried up lake, ruled over by the castrating Warden' (Wannamaker, 2006, pp.29-30). I'd argue, rather, that it is a space where the Real leans more heavily on the Symbolic, showing up the latter's porous nature. Wannamaker particularly draws attention to what she calls the book's 'final scene', where Clyde asks Stanley to cover his wife's mouth, showing the silencing of the feminine, 'the way things "ought to be"' (p.31). But this is not the final scene of the book – which is one I mentioned earlier, where Zero's mother is described, especially with 'her mouth [which] seemed too big for her face' (we had previously been told that her grandmother had 'a very wide mouth' (p.29)). And it is Zero's mother who has the last words: for the first time in the novel she is not silent: she sings.

Karen Coats, on the other hand, addresses the racial issues involved in the novel, arguing that Stanley is 'in denial' about the significance of race, as shown in statements like the following:

> *Stanley was thankful that there were no racial problems. X-Ray, Armpit, and Zero were black. He, Squid, and Zigzag were white. Magnet was Hispanic. On the lake they were all the same reddish brown color – the color of dirt'* (p.84).

Coats argues that 'Stanley is part of a larger conspiracy of white denial of the privilege that comes with being a white male' (p.133), which relates to his Latvian ancestor, Elya, being indebted to Zero's Egyptian forebear, Madame

Zeroni. She writes, 'It is this failure, this erasure or even mere forgetfulness of the debt to the Other for one's position as subject, that haunts Whiteness' (Coats, 2004, pp.133-4).

Elya, she argues, is guilty of 'thinking only of himself and in exercising the privilege of the white male to travel and make his way in the world' and has thus 'failed in his responsibility to the Other' (p.133). Again, this is strange, as we've been clearly told that Madame Zeroni's son had already exercised this privilege in travelling to America (Sachar, p.30). Coats, however, argues that when Zero digs Stanley's hole for him, Stanley starts to become aware of the slave/overseer relationship (with which X-Ray taunts him), and of his need to take responsibility for his white privilege by looking after Zero and fulfilling the original promise that his ancestor had made.

Personally, as I said earlier, I find that the whole order of things is challenged in this holey place, whether it be lizards or race (it doesn't seem irrelevant, for instance, that it is the black X-Ray who is top-dog). We've also witnessed the dangers of loose signification in the Yelnats's family history. For it turns out that Elya never really stole a pig; moreover, Madame Zeroni wasn't 'one-legged', either, but lacked a foot only. Finally it does not say that she was a Gypsy, but Egyptian (29). It is a common fallacy that gypsies originated in Egypt (whence the name 'gypsy' derives). They actually came from India. So, if Madame Zeroni is a gypsy, as her prophetic powers might lead one stereotypically to expect, then she is probably not best described as 'black', any more than the lizards should be described as yellow-spotted. (The question of the racial origins of the Egyptians themselves has been a hotly debated topic since the eighteenth century; see Bernasconi, 2007.)

In short, issues of gender and race – like other harmful discourses from the big Other (the Symbolic) – are queried, or put 'under erasure', at Camp Green Lake. And readers, in traversing the fantasy, in experiencing the transference both to and from the Camp, will also have undergone the joys and delays of plot as it advances and retards understanding, offering anticipatory fore-pleasure, arousing desires, before delivering a final sense of mastery. But we should also have an awareness that, without some way of plotting our stories, our lives can seem empty, tales told by idiots, signifying nothing: zero. And yet our sense of 'wholeness' is often excessive, too, hence suspect: the more we fill in the holes showing how stories and their characters are plotted, the more the porosity, the flaws, become evident. And, finally, this might make us look at how we ourselves are storied, and can be re-storied: how rather than stay re-signed, things can be re-signified.

REFERENCES

Robert Bernasconi (2007) *'Black skin, white skulls: the nineteenth century debate over the racial identity of the Ancient Egyptians'*, Parallax, 13, 2, 6-20

Bruno Bettelheim, *The Uses of Enchantment: The Meaning and Importance of Fairy Tales.* London: Penguin, 1991. First published 1976.

Peter Brooks, *Reading for the Plot: Design and Intention in Narrative.* Oxford: Clarendon Press, 1984

Peter Brooks, *Psychoanalysis and Storytelling.* Oxford: Blackwell, 1994

Karen Coats, 'Blinded by the White: The Responsibilities of Race' in *Looking Glasses and Neverlands: Lacan, Desire and Subjectivity in Children's Literature Iowa*, ILL: Univ. of Iowa Press, 2004

Robert De Board, *Counselling for Toads: A Psychological Adventure.* London & New York: Routledge, 1998

Bruce Fink, *The Lacanian Subject: Between Language and Jouissance.* Princeton, JN: Princeton University Press, 1995

Sigmund Freud, 'Remembering, repeating and working through' in *The Standard Edition of the Complete Psychological Works of Sigmund Freud*, Vol. XII: 1911-13 ..., trans. James Strachey. London: Hogarth Press & Institute of Psycho-Analysis, 1977, pp. 147-56

Robert Kaplan, *The Nothing that Is: A Natural History of Zero.* London: Penguin, 2000

Jacques Lacan, *The Seminar of Jacques Lacan. Book II: The Ego in Freud's Theory and in the Technique of Psychoanalysis, 1954-1955*, ed. Jacques-Alain Miller; trans. Sylvana Tomaselli. Cambridge: Cambridge U.P., 1998

Karín Lesnik-Oberstein, *Children's Literature: criticism and the fictional child.* Oxford: Clarendon Press, 1994

Pat Pinsent, 'Fate and fortune in a modern fairy tale: Louis Sachar's Holes', *Children's Literature in Education*, 33 (3), 2002, pp. 203-12

Kimberley Reynolds, 'Come lads and ladettes: gendering bodies and gendering behaviors' in John Stephens (ed.) *Ways of Being Male: Representing Masculinities in Children's Literature and Film.* London: Routledge 2002, pp. 96-115

Lucy Rollin and Mark I. West, *Psychoanalytic Responses to Children's Literature.* Jefferson, NC & London: McFarland & Co., 1999

Jacqueline Rose, *The Case of Peter Pan, or The Impossibility of children's fiction.* Basingstoke: Macmillan, 1984

Louis Sachar, *Holes*. London: Scholastic, 1998.

Charles Seife, *Zero: The Biography of a Dangerous Idea.* London: Souvenir Press, 2000

Annette Wannamaker, 'Reading in the Gaps and Lacks: (De)Constructing Masculinity in Louis Sachar's *Holes*', *Children's Literature in Education*, 37 (1), 2006, pp. 15-33

Slavoj Žižek, *Looking Awry: An Introduction to Jacques Lacan through Popular Culture.* Cambridge, Mass: MIT Press, 1992

Slavoj Žižek, *The Metastases of Enjoyment: six essays on women and causality.* London: Verso, 1994

Slavoj Žižek, *On Belief*. London: Routledge, 2001

Diane Duncan

Love, Loss and Magic: Connecting Author and Story

The idea for this paper has arisen from the preparation of a book I am writing for Routledge, called *Teaching Children's Literature*. In this book I examine some contemporary and immensely successful children's writers: four of them are: Anthony Browne, Michael Morpurgo, J.K. Rowling and Philip Pullman. Whilst researching the background of each of these authors I have been struck by the close relationship of the authors' biographies with the themes of their writing. Each of these authors has experienced some form of parental loss at a relatively early point in their lives. J.K. Rowling's mother died after a ten year battle with multiple sclerosis when Rowling was twenty-five. Death and loss figure strongly in the Harry Potter series. Anthony Browne watched in horror as his father died in front of him from a heart attack moments after he had returned from watching him play rugby. Browne was only seventeen at the time. Philip Pullman lost his RAF pilot father in an air crash when he was eight years old and Michael Morpurgo's father returned from the Second World War to find his wife had fallen in love with another man. Michael's father, Tony, decided it was best for his two sons if he simply moved away so that his wife could build a new life with Jack Morpurgo who was to become the boys' stepfather. So Tony disappeared from his sons' lives almost before they knew him (Fox, 2004). Michael would have been about five years old at the time.

In the work of many of these writers, love, loss and magic are themes which feature prominently. The way in which these themes occur are, of course, very differently narrated and constructed in the authors' stories. For the purposes of this paper I have chosen to concentrate on two writers, Philip Pullman and Michael Morpurgo. With both of these writers, the author's biography of parental loss powerfully informs their prolific narratives. The trope of the orphaned child or the child with absent parents has long been a familiar theme in children's literature. This paper will examine the way in which Pullman's and Morpurgo's absent fathers and, in the case of Pullman, the ambiguous relationship with his glamorous mother, have influenced and driven the literary architecture of some of their finest writing.

The biographies of Philip Pullman and Michael Morpurgo: similarities and differences

In the tradition of much contemporary ethnographic case study research, biography and research intersect dynamically to enrich and enliven the research story. What follows is the beginning of a literary case study of two authors which has drawn upon a range of documentary sources including biographical, autobiographical and interview material, newspaper articles, web-site sources and photographs. At first sight it might seem that these two writers do not have all that much in common. Their writing is different in style, scope and narrative structure. Morpurgo often writes in both the first and third person; Pullman, nearly always in the third. The books I have chosen to focus upon are Morpurgo's *I Believe in Unicorns* and *The Butterfly Lion* and Pullmans' *His Dark Materials* trilogy. In these, the intellectual scope and range of Pullman's work is vastly different from the much shorter adventure stories which Morpurgo writes. However, the two have much in common with respect to biography, values and most importantly, in their extraordinary abilities as story tellers. Such has been the success of their books that both have had some of their best writing adapted for stage and for film. *Why The Whales Came* was adapted for a film featuring Helen Mirren and Paul Schofield and *His Dark Materials* will be released as a film in December, 2007, entitled *The Golden Compass*, starring Nicole Kidman as Mrs Coulter and Daniel Craig as Lord Asriel.

Both writers were born in the 1940s in the shadow of the Second World War. Both men had high achieving stepfathers who remained at some distance from the lives of their stepsons. For Philip Pullman, the death of his natural father did not, at the time of its happening, have much impact upon him; his father was often away and Philip scarcely knew him. He was more surprised than anything and reported to Ross (2002) in an article in *The Independent* his realisation that he was now 'half an orphan'. Whilst Philip Pullman did not feel any close connection with his father, he has nonetheless written at some length about the impact that the death had upon himself and his literary development.

The events of his childhood would, according to Tucker (2003) eventually lead to a preoccupation in his writing with dead or missing fathers. This is certainly true of the *His Dark Materials* trilogy, where both the young protagonists, Lyra and Will, are in an orphaned or near-orphaned state. In her latest book on the *Dark Materials*, Claire Squires (2006) writes that at the beginning of the trilogy, Lyra thinks she is an orphan, and even when it becomes apparent that both her parents are alive her relationship with Lord Asriel and Mrs Coulter is such that she still functions without parental care and protection. Will's father is missing, presumed dead and his mother is suffering from such severe psychological problems that Will has to become her carer; thus he is, in some senses, doubly abandoned (Rustin & Rustin, 2003b). It is this childhood background which initially unites Lyra and Will in a growing bond of friendship which, by the end of the trilogy, becomes a gradual sexual awakening and love.

Philip Pullman also had an ambivalent relationship with his mother who was both glamorous and distant. Indeed, he describes the lives of both his parents as intensely glamorous. He recalls the smell of his mother's perfume, *Blue Grass*, and the sight of the long, flowery dresses, hats and gloves which his mother and her friends wore. The smell of leather armchairs, pipe tobacco, cigarettes and beer in his father's club are equally glamorous to the young Philip. It is likely that these sensual memories of his parents eventually ignited his imagination in the creation of Lord Asriel and Mrs Coulter in *His Dark Materials* (Squires, 2006). Of profound importance to young Philip was the love for his maternal grandfather whom he describes as strong, wise and kind. His grandfather was a vicar in a small Norfolk village. He was a loving, formative influence in Philip's life, and he had a talent for telling wonderful stories which became a source of inspiration throughout Philip's life as a teacher and later as a full-time writer.

Michael Morpurgo's stepfather was a gifted, ambitious man with an iron discipline and an enormous capacity for hard work, eventually becoming history editor for Penguin Books, Director of the National Book League and Professor of American Literature at Leeds University (Fox, 2004). He had high expectations of his stepson which Michael found very difficult to live up to. Their relationship for most of Michael's life was tense and uneasy, eventually leading to feelings of crippling inadequacy in Michael which took years for him to overcome. Even when Michael was married with children, he continued to feel that he had deeply disappointed his stepfather. A seemingly deliberate distance (perhaps not untypical of many child-parent relationships in the austere 1940s and 1950s) was created between Michael and his parents. He was not, for example, allowed to call his mother, *Mum*, or his stepfather, *Dad*. Michael yearned for a close, tactile, affection from his mother which she was not able to give. Neither was he or his brother allowed to speak of their real father who was therefore not allowed to exist in their lives. His stepfather insisted on giving him books to read by Dickens and Trollope, on which he would later question him. Michael did not enjoy these stories and managed to survive his stepfather's close interrogation about them by the subterfuge of reading comic versions of them in the form of *Classics Illustrated*. He eventually found a story of his own which he loved so much that he read it many times: Robert Louis Stevenson's *Treasure Island*. Michael also recalls vividly the delight and joy he experienced when his mother read him stories at bedtime as a child. He was entranced by the rhythm and cadence in the language of the stories she chose. His mother had been an actress and made the stories come alive with her strong and musical voice. These were for him, magical times which ended all too soon when he was sent away to a boarding school at eight years of age. Not only was he terribly homesick when he was away from his mother, but books at school, became a source of dread and active dislike (Fox, 2004).

Michael Morpurgo's first attempt to write stories of his own was undertaken once he had found Clare, the love of his life and current wife with whom he has had three children. Initially, when he started to write his own stories, he was immensely dissatisfied with them and almost gave up. Fortunately, at this point in his life he met Ted Hughes, who was a neighbour of his in Devon. Ted Hughes gave him his first real encouragement after Michael had shown him *War Horse*. Michael Morpurgo has never forgotten the words of his mentor, and what he said after reading it, helped to shape the rest of his writing life: '*War Horse*'. Michael. I've read it. It's a good book. In fact, it's a very good book. But you're going to do better' (Fox, 2004, p.206). Ted's words gave him a new sense of confidence. Without those words Morpurgo claims that he would not have developed that love of adventure and experiment as a writer which drives him on.

It is not surprising therefore that Michael Morpurgo's stories frequently depict lone male protagonists who are self-reliant and resourceful. They have to find their own way out of danger and fear and in so doing, frequently forge intensely close relationships with older people and animals in whom trust, friendship and loyalty remain central to their relationship, regardless of the great cost and personal sacrifice this often means.

In contrast, the heroes in Philip Pullman's narratives are often fiercely independent girls who are intelligent, remarkably resourceful and with an insatiable appetite for adventure and self knowledge. They come across as indomitable, feisty young women, in fast moving plots in which fear and terror are frequently encountered alongside some achingly painful decisions in the journey towards wisdom and self consciousness.

An important theme and driving force in some of Morpurgo's books is his preoccupation with the First and Second World Wars. This arose from his desire as a young child to know more about his Uncle Peter, who had died at the controls of a badly damaged bomber, and his Uncle Francis, who had led a cell of French Resistance fighters. He often met his disfigured uncle and much of the adult talk at home was about war (Fox, 2004). Morpurgo, as a child, was intensely drawn to the photographs of the dead, young and handsome uniformed officers in his parents' home and longed to find out more about them and the circumstances in which they died. Morpurgo is uncompromising about communicating the stark and horrifying facts of soldiers' experiences in both World Wars in his 'war' stories; his child audiences do not appear to be deterred by this, but rather respect the fact that he never talks down to them or attempts to sanitise the truth. I have witnessed Michael Morpurgo on two occasions giving lectures on his writing to an audience consisting mostly of children and have been amazed at how captivated they were, and how interested in the very depressing and desolate details of some of the harrowing events which occurred in the lives of young soldiers. Given that the World Wars are not part of their experience, even vicariously, it is interesting that large numbers of children continue to be compelled by Morpurgo's war stories.

Loss, love and war are themes which feature strongly in both Pullman's and Morpurgo's writing and both draw imaginatively on their life histories for their fictional narratives. Indeed, according to Morpurgo, his stories only work for him when he connects with his own doubts and fears and engages fully with his own past and present life. Both writers bring a strong moral and ethical dimension to their work which is woven into the fabric of their narrative, often quite didactically. Both writers are intensely interested in and concerned about the natural world. Issues of global warming and potential ecological disaster powerfully enter Pullman's narrative in *His Dark Materials*, particularly in the final volume, *The Amber Spyglass*. A passionate concern for animals and the increasing threat to their natural habitat is a strong theme in Morpurgo's work as illustrated in *Why the Whales Came*, in *Kensuke's Kingdom* and his other Island stories. Both writers have learned how to become master story tellers through teaching children, so it is perhaps not surprising that some degree of didacticism with respect to morality, values and principles, is a strong underlying current in their work.

Magic

I have written in some detail about the way in which love and loss connect both authors with the plot, themes and narrative structure of their work but have not yet discussed the role of magic in their work. Before I look at extracts from a selection from the writing of each, it is important to be clear about the place of magic in Pullman's and Morpurgo's stories, because each of them uses it differently in their narratives.

There are four possible definitions of magic:

A supposed supernatural power that makes impossible things happen, or that gives somebody control over the forces of nature – witchcraft, the occult and the dark arts may be part of this kind of magic.

The practice of magic: the use of supposed natural power to make impossible things happen.

Conjuring tricks and illusions that make apparently impossible things seem to happen.

A special, mysterious, enchanting quality or phenomenon which can be wonderful and beautiful or as pleasing as if it had been made or created by magic.

In the case of Pullman's *His Dark Materials*, it is the first of the two definitions which most closely apply to his cross-over genre of fantasy, crime thriller and science fiction. Whilst Pullman insists that his *His Dark Materials* is a story of stark social realism, the often terrifying reality which both Lyra and Will have to face and suffer unambiguously takes place in a fantasy world of daemons, armoured bears, anthropomorphised dragonflies, angels, witches, the wheeled 'mulefa' and the world of the dead. The alethiometer, or truth measurer, is endowed with a magical power to see into the future; only Lyra knows how to use it, intuitively. The same is true of the 'subtle knife' which has the supernatural power to cut windows into other worlds. The 'amber spyglass', whilst scientifically constructed with intelligence, patience and endeavour by the scientist Mary Malone, has the power to show dust flowing away from the seed pod trees out to the sea. The seed pods are vital to the mulefa who use them as wheels to propel themselves from one place to another. Catastrophically, for these peaceful, talking, horned animals, the trees upon which they depend for their source of seed-pods are dying, and their survival is in jeopardy.

None of these potent objects of mystery and magic are used gratuitously in Pullman's dazzling narrative. Their use is always tempered by careful constraint, intelligence and unflinching responsibility on the part of the protagonists.

In the case of Morpurgo, whilst there are some instances of objects endowed with supernatural powers, as is the case in those of his books which involve a reworking of Arthurian legends, the use of magic has much more to do with the fourth definition, that of the enchantment of story telling and the magical way in which apparently disparate elements come together to form a coherent and powerful story. In writing about his story maker's journey in his book, *Singing for Mrs Pettigrew* (2006) Morpurgo describes the act of writing as 'an art and a craft and a marvellous magic'. In his own words:

> ....*the most important element in the alchemy that produces this creative fusion is the sheer love of doing it, of seeing if you can make magic from an empty page and a pen. The truth is that it is not a trick. ... And I long with every story to understand it better ...* (p.26).

Magic has long been an important motif in fantasy fiction, from the days of Homer's epic tales through to more contemporary authors like C.S. Lewis and J.K. Rowling. In a broad sense, magic can almost be seen as a synonym for fantasy. Objects endowed with supernatural powers, such as the sword in the Arthurian legends, the ring in Tolkien's *Lord of the Rings*, the wardrobe in C.S. Lewis' *The Lion, The Witch and The Wardrobe*, the hidden gateway to the enchanted woods of Narnia, and the wand, broomstick and invisible cloak in the *Harry Potter* series, all have the power to transform and change the fortunes or misfortunes of the protagonists. In some cases magical powers drive the narrative; in others, as is the case in Pullman's *Dark Materials* trilogy, they connect both to drive the plot forward and to increase the powers of Lyra and Will to see beyond their immediate worlds into other, parallel worlds.

The exposure of young children to the role of magic in fantasy and, particularly, in fairy stories is, according to Bettelheim (1991), an essential element in the development of young children's emotional and psychological health and well being. The fairy tale takes the child's inner feelings of loneliness and separation, fear of loss of love, anxiety and jealousy, very seriously, and addresses itself directly to them. Because the child cannot express these feelings in words, the fairy tale offers solutions to these difficulties in ways that the child can grasp on her/his own level of understanding (Bettelheim, 1991). The motifs in the stories of *Little Red Riding Hood*, *Cinderella*, and *Snow White*, for example, have the power to help children's feelings of fear of abandonment, death, disobedience, rage, powerlessness, isolation and hatred, to be understood and appreciated. Fairy tales also help to connect the unconscious with conscious thought, although of course children are not explicitly aware of this. In Bettelheim's words:

> Each fairy tale is a magic mirror which reflects some aspects of our inter world, and of the steps required by our evolution from immaturity to maturity. For those who immerse themselves in what the fairy tale has to communicate, it becomes a deep, quiet pool which at first seems to reflect only our own image; but behind it we soon discover the inner turmoils of our soul – its depth, and ways to gain peace within ourselves and with the world, which is the reward of our struggles (p.309).

Whilst there is much to commend in Bettelheim's thesis with respect to children's psychological need for magic and fantasy, it does not fit entirely with the experience of Pullman's child protagonists in the *Dark Materials* trilogy. Lyra and Will certainly gain wisdom and maturity through their interaction with magical objects and the supernatural worlds of armoured bears, witches, angels and dragonfly protectors. But the turmoils and terrors which they encounter on their journeys through multiple universes, some of them indescribably bleak and agonising, do very little to bring about the inner peace and psychic reward which Bettelheim assures us that children will gain from a reading of fairy tales. However, this is less true of the characters in Morpurgo's stories, where there is more room for optimism and a closer fit with Bettelheim's views on magic and fantasy. In Morpurgo's stories, some of the courageous struggles which his child protagonists endure, often in the teeth of fierce, hostile adult reaction, are rewarded and result in the rescue of lion cubs, adored cats and narwhal whales.

Love, loss and magic; connecting author and story

In order to see how these themes of love, loss and magic feature so prominently and spectacularly in the authors' writing and how, most importantly, they connect in a dynamic synergy, the last part of this paper will focus on an analysis of selected extracts from two of Michael Morpurgo's stories and Philip Pullman's *His Dark Materials*.

Philip Pullman and *His Dark Materials*

In the first book, *Northern Lights*, we meet the glamorous Mrs Coulter at one of her most cruel and ruthless points in her ambition to provide the Church with knowledge about how dust works. The concept of *dust* is central to the

thesis of Pullman's trilogy but its precise meaning is difficult to pin down because he defines it in different ways throughout the work. It is a multifaceted idea being consciousness, wisdom, original sin, dark matter, shadow particles and the thing that made us human in the first place, all at the same time. For a fuller discussion please see Tucker (2003, pp.133-139) and Squires (2003; 2006).

Cutting daemons (the physical manifestation of the human soul taking the shape of an animal form and constant companion/alter ego to their human host) from children releases energy in the form of dust and Mrs Coulter has no scruples in kidnapping young children for this appalling experiment in the Artic wastelands of Bolvanger.

In trying to rescue her close friend Roger from this dreadful severing, Lyra almost experiences the same fate as he. But Mrs Coulter arrives in the nick of time:

"No one's going to harm you, Lyra darling; no one's ever going to hurt you ..."
"But they do it to other children! Why?"
"Ah, my love – "
"It's dust, isn't it?"
"Did they tell you that? Did the doctors say that?"
"The kids know it. All the kids talk about it, but no one knows! And they nearly done it to me – you got to tell me! You got no right to keep it secret, not any more!"
"Lyra ... Lyra, Lyra. Darling, these are big difficult ideas, Dust and so on. It's not something for children to worry about. But the doctors do it for the children's own good, my love. Dust is something bad, something wrong, something evil and wicked.

'Grown-ups and their daemons are infected with Dust so deeply that it's too late for them. They can't be helped...But a quick operation on children means they're safe from it. Dust won't stick to them ever again. They're safe and happy and... " (*Northern Lights*, 1996, pp.283-284).

Not content with having more or less abandoned her daughter and left her to the sporadic care of the scholars and domestic staff of Oxford's Jordan College, Mrs Coulter then almost succeeds in separating Lyra from her daemon, Pantalaimon, in her ruthless ambition to support the political arm of the church in order to free the world of original sin, the source of which is

'Dust'. The church's solution to this is to abduct children, take them to the experimental station at Bolvanger and separate them from their daemons – thus preventing them from growing up (Rustin and Rustin, 2003a). Daemons are inseparable from their human counterparts. They each depend upon each other and neither can live without the other. Separation occurs through an appalling cutting process called 'intercision', which, whilst leaving them both 'alive', renders them incapable of dynamic life. Both the human and his daemon become lifeless, rather like human beings in our world who have been deprived of their sentient life as a result of the brain disease dementia, which progressively robs the afflicted person of vitality, memory and personality. Lyra has two parents who are selfishly and ruthlessly fixated upon their own political ambitions to create new worlds in which children have no part. What more poignant loss could Lyra suffer, given the wilful abnegation of responsibility and love of her parents, than to suffer the separation of her beloved Pantalaimon, who is an inextricable part of her inner life, her soul and closest friend? This unthinkable loss is chillingly rationalised by the callous Mrs Coulter as nothing more than 'a quick operation'.

In the second volume, *The Subtle Knife*, Will gains possession of the knife by fighting a fierce battle with one of the Cittagazze children, Tullio. The consequence of this terrible battle is that Will loses two of his fingers and Tullio is attacked by the Spectres – fearful monsters who suck out the souls of their victims:

> *And Lyra realised with a jolt of sickness what was happening: the man was being attacked by Spectres. Angelica knew it, though she couldn't see them, of course, and little Paolo was crying and striking at the empty air to try and drive them off; but it didn't help, and Tullio was lost. His movements became more and more lethargic, and presently they stopped altogether. Angelica clung to him, shaking and shaking his arm, but nothing woke him; and Paolo was crying his brother's name over and over as if that would bring him back* (The Subtle Knife, 1998, p.188).

In an insightful essay using the concepts of psychological analysis to explore the inner worlds of Lyra and Will, Margaret and Michael Rustin (2003b) make the point that the spectres represent the child's experience of depression, hatred and death whose presence results in the negation of thought and feeling. They describe the conception of the Spectres as 'deeply chilling' and one which represents very potently:

> *every child's nightmare version of an unreachable parent, apparently present but effectively withdrawn and lost to the child. These are the 'spectres of indifference', where meaning and connection have been destroyed* (p.237).

However, whilst loss and separation are inescapable realities for Lyra and Will throughout the trilogy, these are tempered and balanced by acts of warmth, kindness, loyalty and love, the most important of which is the love which

Philip Pullman

The Subtle Knife

"The most ambitious work since Lord of the Rings... as intellectually thrilling as it is magnificently written"
Amanda Craig, THE NEW STATESMAN

slowly develops between Lyra and Will and which is eventually realised towards the end of the final book of the trilogy. In the second book, Will's search for his lost father means having to leave his dependent and mentally-disturbed mother in the care of Mrs Cooper, a friend and his former piano teacher. For some time, Will has had to be carer and parent to his mother. He now desperately wants to find his father, who has disappeared whilst engaged on a scientific mission. In the new world he has stumbled into via a mysterious window, he meets Lyra. They quickly find a common bond. They are both strangers in this new world, both have troubled and fractured family lives, both feel afraid and guilty – Will of possible murder, and Lyra of the unwitting betrayal of Roger, her best friend, which results in his death at the hands of her father, Lord Asriel. All these serve to unite them in a fierce loyalty and friendship which sustains them through some harrowing experiences, despite the power of the magical devices of the subtle knife, the alethiometer and the amber spyglass, which eventually culminate in the release of Dust which pours down from the sky. Both Will and Lyra long for parent figures they can trust and depend upon. Pullman provides 'father' figures in the form of Lee Scoresby, the hot air balloonist, and the magnificently potent armoured bear, Iorek Byrnison. Surrogate 'mother' figures are to be found in the witch, Serafina Pekkala, Ma Costa, the gyptian and Mary Malone, the scientist. These characters, among others, show the constancy of love and loyalty which, for different reasons, both Will and Lyra lack in their family lives. Mary Malone provides a stark contrast to the calculating and self-interested Mrs Coulter. This humane, intelligent and resourceful woman, with her compassionate and scientifically informed concern for the plight of the mulefa as the seed pods so essential to their lives begin to diminish, gives Lyra an important source of mental and emotional comfort which sustains and inspires her. However, even the cruel and ruthless Mrs Coulter is shown by Pullman to be more complex than a woman who merely uses sex to secure her own ends.

In the last novel of the trilogy, *The Amber Spyglass*, she displays and experiences tender feelings of love and maternity towards Lyra as the girl lies drugged and sleeping in a cave; thus she can protect her from the Church's mission to kill and destroy Lyra's prophesied potential to become the new daughter of Eve. Pullman is concerned to show that even though Will and Lyra have, in many senses, lost parental love, they do find trust, love, affection and integrity among other adult figures. Interestingly, almost without exception, the strong, loving 'parent' figures whom Lyra and Will encounter in the trilogy are all empowered with extraordinary skills, knowledge or wisdom of some kind. Lord Asriel and Mrs Coulter are also intelligent, gifted and involved in their respective bold enterprises but their gifts and acumen are directed towards self-seeking omnipotence and the acquisition of power, whilst those of the others are founded upon ethical and moral principles directed towards the care and protection of others. Each of these parent figures also plays a central role in helping Will and Lyra to learn more about themselves, so that they become more mature, wise and resourceful as the story progresses. Pullman's exploration of wisdom and self-consciousness is a strong theme in the development of Will and Lyra as young adolescents. The other kind of love which Pullman provides for his protagonists is, of course, to be found in the intensity of love and affection which Pantalaimon and Lyra have for each other. They can never be apart; their interdependence gives them life; they are two parts of the same person, almost akin to an external 'soul'. Pullman has used this 'narrative device' so successfully, that it is impossible to read the trilogy without longing to possess a daemon of one's own. For this reason, the scene on the jetty before they begin their journey to the suburbs of the dead is one of the most achingly painful and excruciating moments of loss in the entire trilogy. As Will and Lyra step into the boat, the boatman announces with savage ferocity that Lyra's daemon must stay behind and not enter the boat:

> *And she pushed him away, so that he crouched bitter and cold and frightened on the muddy ground.*
> *What animal he was now, Will could hardly tell. He seemed to be so young, a cub, a puppy, something helpless and beaten, a creature so sunk in misery that it was more misery than creature, (The Amber Spyglass, p.298).*

Pullman juxtaposes love with loss throughout the trilogy. Indeed, it is as though one cannot exist without the other. Lyra and her daemon are reunited, Will gets his own daemon and they find love and a sexual awakening in their relationship. For a short time at least, both forget the terrors and exhaustion of the wars, the deaths and the horrors they have encountered. In a lush and beautiful setting they abandon themselves to a tender, adolescent love:

> *They talked, they bathed, they ate, they kissed, they lay in a trance of happiness murmuring words, whose sound was as confused as their sense, and they felt they were melting with love, (The Amber Spyglass, p.509).*

No sooner have they experienced a brief moment of love and longing for each other, however, than they have to agree to go their separate ways back into their different worlds. After all they have suffered and endured together, they have to shut up all the windows the knife has opened, with the exception of one which will be left for the dead to escape through. Because of the people Lyra and Will have become, they make the responsible choice, thus making it inevitable that neither will be able to see the other again. Moral responsibility, maturity and wisdom have been acquired by both Lyra and Will in the course of their epic journey together, but it comes at a high price. Doing the 'right' thing means they must lose the love they have so justly deserved. The ending of *His Dark Materials* is stark and agonisingly painful. Whilst a sentimental ending would not have been fitting for Pullman's dazzlingly written epic, the lack of a more satisfactory resolution is intensely problematic. The question has to be asked whether Pullman's didacticism has played too great a part in the finale of this spectacular and multi-layered quest.

Michael Morpurgo

The story *I Believe in Unicorns* is based upon Morpurgo's own experience of books and reading. Having enjoyed listening to the magic and the music of his mother's voice reading Longfellow, Kipling and Lear to him in bed at night, his experience at primary school and later at boarding school in Sussex could not have proved a starker contrast. The relentless grammar exercises, comprehension, punctuation, dictations, précis, the lines, detentions and punishments that came his way when he did not meet a satisfactory standard, stifled his former love of words and books. The magic he had shared in those quiet, special times with his mother had gone. In Morpurgo's own words, books '...became a source of dread for me, a reminder of my own failure to achieve' (Morpurgo, 2006). The one book he loved with a passion which has lasted all his life was Robert Louis Stevenson's *Treasure Island*. It would be years before he found himself similarly transported and enchanted by another book. As long as he was at school, books made him feel 'frightened and inadequate'. It was this bleak experience which Morpurgo drew upon to write *I Believe in Unicorns*. The protagonist, Tomas Porec, who like Morpurgo, hates school and loathes reading, is one day unwillingly taken to the town library by his mother, where he finds himself inspired by a quiet, smiling librarian who is a passionate story teller. In the library was a model of a unicorn who was lying absolutely still, his feet tucked neatly under him. He was made of carved wood and painted white, but to Tomas, he was so lifelike that he believed him capable of movement. The ritual established by the imaginative, story telling librarian is that she sits on the unicorn to tell one of her stories. After that, any child can volunteer to sit on the unicorn and tell or read his or her own story.

Tomas is entranced, captivated and hooked and each day he longs to sit on the unicorn and tell a story, but he can't find the courage to volunteer. He tells his friends at school about the unicorn lady 'and her amazing stories and the fantastic magical storytelling power of the unicorn', (p.65). One day he is sitting very close to the librarian as she shows the children a charred book which her father has rescued from a fire in a book-burning orgy. The story is Hans Christian Anderson's *The Little Match Girl*. Tomas wants to know why it was burnt and she tells him how there were wicked people in her town who were afraid of the magic of stories and of the power of books. Her father watched the burning of a great pile of books and rushed forward to save one of them, holding on to it whilst the soldiers beat him with sticks but he wouldn't let go. 'It's my favourite book in all the world, Tomas, would you like to come and sit on the unicorn and read it to us?' (p.67). This is Tomas' great moment and as he sits on the unicorn he feels a power and confidence he has never felt before when reading out loud:

> *But now, sitting on the magic unicorn, I heard my voice strong and loud. It was like singing a song. The words danced on the air and everyone listened. That same day I took home my first book from the library, Aesop's Fables, because the unicorn lady had read them to us and I'd loved them. I read them aloud to my mother that night, the first time I'd ever read to her, and I could see she was amazed. I loved amazing my mother, (I Believe in Unicorns, pp.67-68).*

This beautifully crafted story is a clear example of what Morpurgo means when he writes that his stories only work for him when he engages fully with his own past and present life. He has to immerse himself fully in the story and feel that he really knows the people in the story but most importantly:

> *allow the story time to find its own voice to weave itself, to dream itself out in my head so that by the time I set pen to paper, I feel I am living inside that story, (Singing for Mrs Pettigrew, p.26).*

What Morpurgo had lost for large parts of his childhood both at school and at home, with the overbearing academic demands made upon him by his high achieving stepfather, he found again later in his life as a writer. Stories can heal and they can empower; sitting on the unicorn released Tomas from his fear, giving him strength and confidence. Whether you believe the following words to be Tomas as an older man, or Morpurgo himself, is of little consequence:

> *As for me, I'm a writer now, a weaver of tales. And if from time to time I lose the thread of the story, all I have to do is go and sit on the magic unicorn and my story flows again. So believe me, I believe in unicorns, (Singing for Mrs Pettigrew, p.72).*

Strong, resourceful, quiet, listening women, like the story telling librarian, the old lady, Millie, in *The Butterfly Lion*, Michael's sea-faring mother in *Kensuke's Kingdom*, Olly and her veterinary mother in *Dear Olly*, often feature in

Morpurgo's stories. Whilst they are seldom the central characters, they are an important counterweight, serving to balance the narrative and the unfolding plot. There may be resonances here of the role that Morpurgo's mother played in his life and that of his wife, Clare who has, throughout her husband's writing career, tirelessly read and typed up every one of his forty or more books.

In *The Butterfly Lion* Morpurgo weaves personal experience with a close relationship with an orphaned white lion cub encountered by a solitary young boy, who becomes a soldier, is seriously wounded in World War One and is eventually reunited with his lion friend, 'The White Prince'. In a short preface to the story Morpurgo reveals again how his own personal experience connects with a magical and mysterious story of love and war:

> *The Butterfly Lion grew from several magical roots: the memories of a small boy who tried to run away from school a long time ago; a book about a pride of white lions discovered by Chris McBride; a chance meeting in a lift with Virginia McKenna, actress and champion of lions and all creatures born free; a true story of a solider of the First World War who rescued some circus animals in France from certain death* (The Butterfly Lion, preface).

Morpurgo's forlorn, bleak and desperately unhappy time at boarding school, made worse by bullying, the endless detentions, punishments and appalling food are once again drawn upon imaginatively for the beginning of the plot, except that this time it is Morpurgo himself, not a character from his imagination, who sets the story in motion. At the age of ten, he wants more than ever to go home, he has had enough of the misery and hostile environment of boarding school. He decides to escape and make for the train to London. It starts to rain heavily and Michael runs for it. He hears a car slowing down and meets an old lady called Millie with her dog who invites him into her house for tea. Over tea she tells him of the story of her husband, Bertie, and how he found an orphaned white lion cub and lost it to a circus owner in France. In order to save the lion cub from captivity in a circus, Bertie, in desperation, tries to persuade the cub to go back to the wild and live his life in freedom. But the cub does not want to be parted from him. A repeated theme in Morpurgo's stories is the intense relationship that can grow between a lonely young child and an animal. In the following extract we see another of Morpurgo's narratives of intense love and loss:

> "Go back!" Bertie yelled, "you stupid, stupid lion! I hate you! I hate you! Go back!" But the lion kept loping after him whatever he did, whatever he said.
> There was only one thing for it. He didn't want to do it, but he had to. With tears filling his eyes and his mouth, he lifted the rifle to his shoulder and fired over the lion's head. At once the lion scampered away through the veld. Bertie fired again. He watched till he could see him no more, and then turned for home. (*The Butterfly Lion*, pp.49-50).

Millie finishes telling Michael the end of this strange and powerfully moving story. Bertie, having been seriously wounded in the war, finds the place in war-torn France where the circus owner lives and is reunited with 'The White Prince' who recognises him with a soft, rumbling growl. Bertie takes the lion back home to Wiltshire where he and Millie spend the rest of their lives. The lion ages and dies, leaving Bertie bereft and grief-stricken for several months. Solace comes in the form of an idea which will keep the lion alive in their memory for years to come. Bertie and Millie carve the shape of the lion into the chalk hills of Wiltshire near their home. Such was the bond that Bertie had with the White Prince that he and Millie spent the next twenty years on their chalk carving project. When it was finished they noticed that Adonis Blue butterflies came there to drink every summer on the chalk face which is how the White Prince became a butterfly lion, seeming to breathe again with the movement of thousands of blue butterflies.

After Morpurgo has returned to his boarding school having heard the whole of Millie's story, his history teacher tells him that Albert Andrews (Bertie) won a VC and as an old boy of the school, he is told that a memorial plaque is situated in his honour in the school chapel. Apparently the old lady (Millie) had died of a broken heart after she had unveiled it. So perhaps she couldn't have told this story to the young school escapee after all? This is one of Morpurgo's characteristic twists at the end of the story. It closes with Michael sitting alone on the hillside, looking at the butterfly lion, with the voice of Millie in his head exhorting him to "Keep him white for us, there's a dear. We don't want him forgotten, you see," (*The Butterfly Lion*, p.128).

Whilst too much can be made of authors' biographies and their particular psychological connections with loss, death, friendship and love in the stories they write, it is suggested here that the potent family and childhood experiences of both Philip Pullman and Michael Morpurgo are an inextricable part of the themes which drive their remarkable narratives. Love, loss and magic powerfully inform their work in a dynamic synergy with their life histories, and the truth revealed in their stories is as much a part of each man's own personal moral imperative as it is of the characters who live and breathe in the magical worlds of their fictional creations.

REFERENCES

Bruno Bettelheim. *The Uses of Enchantment: The Meaning and Importance of Fairy Tales*, London: Penguin Books Reprint. (First published 1976) 1991.

Geoff Fox. *Dear Mr Morpingo. Inside the World of Michael Morpurgo*, Cambridge: Wizard Books, 2004.

Deborah Ross. 'Soap and the serious writer', *The Independent*, 4th February, 2002.

Margaret Rustin & Michael Rustin. 'Where is home? An essay on Philip Pullman's *Northern Lights*, Volume 1 of *His Dark Materials*', *Journal of Child Psychotherapy*, Vol. 29. No.1. 93-105, 2003a.

Margaret Rustin & Michael Rustin. 'A new kind of friendship – An essay on Philip Pullman's *The Subtle Knife*, Volume 2 of *His Dark Materials*', *Journal of Child Psychotherapy*, Vol. 29. No.2. 227-241, 2003b.

Claire Squires. *Philip Pullman, Master Storyteller. A Guide to the Worlds of* His Dark Materials, London: Continuum, 2006.

Claire Squires. *Philip Pullman's* His Dark Materials *Trilogy: A Reader's Guide*, London: Continuum, 2003.

Nicholas Tucker. *Darkness Visible: Inside the World of Philip Pullman*, Cambridge: Wizard Books, 2003.

Works by Philip Pullman

The Northern Lights. London: Scholastic Ltd, 1996.

The Subtle Knife. London: Scholastic Ltd, 1998.

His Dark Materials III, The Amber Spyglass, London: David Fickling Books, Scholastic Ltd, 2000.

Works by Michael Morpurgo

The Butterfly Lion. London: Collins, 1996.

'I Believe in Unicorns', in *Singing for Mrs Pettigrew: a story-maker's journey*, pp.61-72, London: Walker Books Ltd, 2006

Singing for Mrs Pettigrew: a story-maker's journey, London: Walker Books Ltd, 2006.

Website

www.answers.com/topic/magic/
March 11, 2007

Gerry Byrne

The Evocation of Mystery in the Art of Anthony Browne

Introduction

'Art evokes the mystery without which the world would not exist.' Rene Magritte

We are living in a golden age of children's literature. Authors such as Philip Pullman, J.K. Rowling, and Geraldine McCaughrean have written works that equal and even surpass the acknowledged greats, such as C.S. Lewis, J.R.R. Tolkien, and J.M. Barrie. In addition McCaughrean, through her wonderful, fresh re-telling of myths, legends and the classics, introduces generations of new readers to great literature. However, less attention is paid to literature for children under six and, of course, children at this age are largely dependent upon their parents to choose their books. Not surprisingly, the books that often sell most and are marketed most aggressively are those that appeal to a sentimental and sugar-sweet view of childhood and parenthood. Many of these offer reassurance to parents that their ambivalent feelings about their children need not be attended to and that they can deny their moments of anger, frustration and hate towards their own child. Similarly, they often invite the child to glide over the ambiguities of experience and offer comfort and refuge from their daily battles with parents and siblings.

In contrast to this, Anthony Browne is an author/illustrator who has repeatedly presented to us the world through the eyes of a child, confronting directly the complex and difficult feelings stirred in the child in the course of daily life. Brown's pictures depict real people, often with ambiguous expressions, in contact with a world both real and surreal, and often discomforting. In this paper, I wish to visit the real and surreal worlds intuitively created by Anthony Browne and, drawing from my interview with the author (unpublished) show how they serve to illustrate many of the psychoanalytic concepts of Freud, Klein and Meltzer and the ideas of the great surrealist thinker Rene Magritte.

"Ink drawing my painting is like an iceberg of which only a tenth of its volume is visible ....my exhibitionism masks my true personality" Dali (1974)

Hidden depths / Intolerable mystery

'The mind is like an iceberg, it floats with one seventh of its bulk above water (Sigmund Freud).

The iceberg, (Picture 1) was employed by Freud as a metaphor for the hidden depths of the mind – the conscious mind represented by the visible structure above the water and the structures and primitive processes of the unconscious by the hidden bulk beneath the surface. This photograph, taken from beneath the water while the sun was overhead, by a diver from a ship whose function is to tow icebergs away from shipping lanes, gives a rare and breathtaking view of an entire iceberg. Equally rare (and sometimes breathtaking) are those moments in an analytic therapy in which patient and analyst gain a clear view of the hidden structures and architecture of the unconscious and conscious mind. Dreams are analogous to a nightly dive with a camera beneath the surface, returning with images – negatives, often blurred in their ambiguity, open to many interpretations, and requiring careful development in the darkroom of the therapeutic relationship. The peculiarities of the camera, i.e. the perceptual apparatus of the dreamer, have to be borne in mind in this exacting and delicate work.

It is interesting how often one comes across images or dream sequences involving swimming, diving, and sometimes drowning or fear of drowning, in patients who are embarking on a psychoanalytic therapy. These are often symbolic of the patient's anxiety about what will emerge from beneath the surface. One man in his sixties, who came to analysis late in life to try to get in touch with genuine feelings, dreamt the night before a session that he was writing and indexing a manuscript which gave the design and plan for the building of an underwater sonic detector, to use in deep seas. He linked this with his fear of diving too deeply into his mind, unprotected.

Icebergs also inspired Clive Anderson, journalist and lawyer, to reflect on the mind's tendency to seek what is known when faced with the unknown, when he presented a programme from Greenland called 'Law of the Arctic' on BBC Radio 4. First, he speaks excitedly about his experience of seeing icebergs for the first time.

> *Suddenly I see them, lots of them, they are everywhere, sailing by. Coming down from the Icecap, a slow moving river of ice, the icecap's progeny in the water, icebergs everywhere* (Anderson, 2004).

He marvels at the sheer impossibility of apprehending their beauty. However, by the end of one week he describes something different occurring in his perception.

> *(I) stumbled on a tourist's route....... I'm convinced people are going around shaping these icebergs. Or maybe there is some sort of madness that comes on you if you keep looking at icebergs. There's one I'm looking at, at the moment, there's not very many here, one that looks like it has been shaped into a boat, or you might think it is like shape of a whale, a huge white whale or a huge white boat* (Anderson, 2004).

What is this 'madness' that forces him to fit these previously unknown and fundamentally unknowable shapes into familiar, recognizable forms? Is it madness? Why is it so difficult to tolerate mystery and the Unknown? Keats described the capacity to be 'in uncertainties, Mysteries, doubts without any irritable reaching after fact and reason' as 'Negative Capability', essential to all great writers (Keats, 1817).

The unreliable eye

> *The eye, which sees that which is no longer, the star; on the screen, the image which has disappeared; which does not see that which is too fast, the bullet, that smile; which does not see that which is too slow, grass which is growing, old age; which recognizes a woman and it's another, a cat and it's a shoe, his love and it's emptiness – the freedom of the eye should have put us on our guard long ago* (Paul Nougé, Belgian poet and philosopher and friend of René Magritte,1943).

We do know that even our perceptual apparatus is programmed to match what we see with what we already know. How is it that from the moment of birth the infant strives to assemble the various shapes looming overhead into recognizable contours of a face, although he has never seen a face before? Neurophysiological research shows that pre-natally we are programmed to see faces, to respond to faces and even to endeavour to light up the faces of our mothers (Trevarthen, 1993). Furthermore, perception occurs when an external object or pattern stimulates a pattern of neuronal activation in the brain. The brain searches for a quick and dirty 'good enough' match with a prior pattern of neuronal activation stored in memory.

> *Therefore, the brain automatically processes sensory stimulation, matches patterns and generates perceptions. This is why when you see a cloud you inevitably 'see' objects, fish, boats, etc., as your brain automatically generates perceptions from pattern-matching using the sensory cues of the cloud* (Pally, 2000).

We place great emphasis on 'eye contact' which surely means that at one level we are saying; 'I look at you and know you see me'. Donald Winnicott has described the mother's face as the baby's first mirror, as it is there the baby discovers or encounters evidence of an image of himself as someone beautiful in his mother's eyes (Winnicott,1987). But, as we know, that is not all an infant sees. Melanie Klein, a pioneer of child psychoanalysis, has described how a contented baby who sucks at his mother's breast with enjoyment allays her anxieties while he experiences her joy in feeding and handling him. Difficulties over feeding can arouse a mother's guilt and anxiety and places some strain on both. The infant sees and senses these anxieties and preoccupations in the mother's eyes and face. The mirror of the mother's eyes is clouded. The mirror of her eyes is also clouded by other thoughts and preoccupations too; thoughts of father and of other siblings for example, other relations to the world besides her relation to the baby. The infant becomes aware early on that there is more behind the mirror than his own image. These experiences present the infant with mystery; a mystery that can be borne – or felt to be unbearable, by some.

The rudimentary templates we are born with and into whose familiar recognizable shapes we are driven to mould the external world were called 'preconceptions' by the psychoanalyst W.R. Bion (1962). A preconception is an innate expectation of a reality which when met with the real experience results in the formation of a concept. Therefore a newborn baby joins his preconception/expectation of the breast/milk with the sensory experience/realization of his first feeds developing the concept of the good breast/mother (Klein, 1955). In addition the coming together of this same preconception/expectation with an absent or empty breast may lead to the development of a parallel concept of a bad or denying breast/mother. For a time, it appears, the infant can live in a split world, passionately loving the good breast/mother with wishes and fantasies of incorporation of the breast inside himself and passionately hating the bad breast/mother into which is expelled all adverse experiences of hunger, frustration, lonliness etc. The bad feelings can be temporarily eliminated in fantasies of destruction of the bad breast/mother. Later, the realisation that the good and bad mother are one whole person incites a psychological crisis with feelings of guilt, remorse and concern for the damage he may have caused by his destructive attacks on the mother. Ultimately, if this period of conflict is resolved, the infant can experience love and gratitude towards the mother.

Roger Money-Kyrle, psychoanalyst and thinker, was convinced that man, like any animal, is predisposed to discovering the truth and that from babyhood, is capable of quickly learning to understand the basic structure of all the essential facts of life. Now, by facts of life, Money-Kyrle does not mean knowledge of the mechanics of sex and procreation. He meant something much more fundamental and far reaching. In *the Aim of Psychoanalysis* he described three fundamental facts of life which he felt were essential to growth of the personality:

> *the recognition of the breast as a supremely good object*
> *the recognition of the parent's intercourse as a supremely creative act*
> *the recognition of the inevitability of time and ultimately, death.*

With the recognition of the breast as the supremely good object omnipotent control is relinquished, loss is experienced, and mourning takes place. However, refusal to accept this fact of life and the subsequent replacement of the breast with spurious substitutes constitutes a denial of the loss. If the mother/good breast is internalised through mourning then the parental couple in the mind of the child/adult are capable of a creative intercourse – the source of the creativity of the individual.

Money-Kyrle considered mental illness in its various forms and states of mind as displaying the various means by which these fundamental facts of life are denied and creativitity in the individual is frozen.

The propensity for denial of these facts of life/of reality is always with us, as Clive Anderson discovered. His experience also warns us that when faced with the unknown we need to guard against our tendency to fit it to familiar shapes. This of course, for most if not all parents, applies to that well known iceberg, the baby or toddler, who floats unpredictably in the path of the parent, regularly sinking the grandiose titanic dreams of idealised parenthood. It also applies to the complexity of material children present to us in our clinics and consulting rooms and reminds us of the necessity to struggle to maintain an open mind. We must also remember that young children in particular provoke and re-awaken in their parents unresolved conflicts from their childhoods and their experiences of being parented.

The surrealist eye

Martin Jay has described how until the first world war, sight dominated European thought as the 'noblest of the senses', a 'western ocularcentrism' (Jay, 1991). In the years between the wars a cynical attitude towards visual experience and the 'innocence of the eye' developed and he sees Surrealism as part of this much larger anti-ocularcentric discourse. The poet and founder of Surrealism, André Breton saw Surrealism as dedicated to the liberation of the mind and embraced Freud's findings on the importance of the unconscious mind and its influence on our thoughts and behaviour. Breton located the source of personal freedom in the unconscious mind and believed we were closest to freedom and 'real life' as children.

> *Our brains are dulled by the incurable mania of wanting to make the unknown known, classifiable* (Breton, 1924).

In a sense, Surrealism effectively took the phrase 'seeing is believing' and reversed it; 'believing is seeing'. That is; 'I see that which I believe to be'. In contrast to Renaissance Art in which a painting presented a 'window on reality', surrealist painting sought to question reality, to challenge the viewer to reconsider their trust in the innocence of the eye. Surrealists recognized our fear of mystery, our difficulty in remaining in Keats' state of 'negative capability'. René Magritte, the great surrealist thinker who communicated his thought by painting (this is how he preferred to be described, he refused the name 'artist'), aimed in his paintings to create mystery and stir curiosity, fear and even panic in the spectator. He was particularly interested in the fundamental problem of how we perceive the world and addressed it again and again in many paintings, including the remarkable *La Condition Humaine 1* (*The Human Condition*) 1933 (Picture 2). He wrote of this painting;

> *I placed in front of a window, seen from inside a room, a painting representingthat part of the landscape which was hidden from view by the painting. Therefore, the tree represented in the painting hid from view the tree situated behind it, outside the room. It existed for the spectator, as it were simultaneously in his mind, as both inside the room in the painting, and outside in the real landscape. Which is how we see the world: we see it as being outside ourselves even though it is only a mental representation of it that we experience inside ourselves* (Gablik, 1972).

2

Windows, doors and mirrors/reflections were used frequently by Magritte and the Surrealists and in fact Breton's shift in perspective on reality was inspired by a phrase and image that came suddenly to him; 'knocking at the window' as he put it, of a man cut in two by a window. In surrealist art windows and doors often function to show the transgressible boundary between conscious and unconscious, between reality and imagination, external and internal worlds. Surrealists sought to restore to the object its latent life and Magritte explored the affinities and relationships between objects, and discovered that for any object under his consideration there was 'the thing connected with it in the shadow of my consciousness, and the light wherein that thing would become apparent'. Magritte, like Breton, was inspired by an experience staying in a strange room in which he woke to find that he mistook what he saw and his mind placed an egg in a cage where in actuality a bird resided. He was enchanted by the affinity of the object of the egg to the birdcage which he called a 'poetic secret'. Magritte's treatment of each painting as a problem to be solved in which he seeks to find the poetic secret between an object and its connected other reminds me of the traditional riddle posed by the maiden to the young man, which can be found in an old Irish song called *The Song of Riddles*; 'For my dinner you must give to me a bird without a bone' to which the answer is 'The chicken when it's in the egg it surely has no bone.'

Magritte's choice of objects and how they were positioned was never arbitrary and was usually the result of long periods of research and reflection. His arrival at the choice of an umbrella with a glass of water in *Les vacances de Hegel* (*Hegel's Holiday*) 1958, was arrived at only after 100 to 150 drawings, and further experimenting was needed before he positioned the glass on top of the open umbrella. Thus he created an object that had two opposing functions, at once containing and repelling water.

3

4

Changes

Anthony Browne's illustrations make many references to famous paintings and pay homage to great artists, but particularly to the Surrealists. Browne has said that he was very relieved to learn that others saw the world as he did when, aged twelve or so, he discovered the work of Magritte and Dali. Browne predominantly illustrates and writes for young children and has, in his work, repeatedly presented to us the world through the eyes of a child, depicting the complex and difficult feelings stirred in the child by his experiences. While he is not the only author or illustrator who does so, nonetheless his work challenges the more typical presentation of a sentimental and nostalgic version of childhood in literature for the under-sevens. His work contrasts as starkly with the mainstream as, say, Sally Mann's startling and provocative photographs of her children in *Immediate Family* alongside the saccharine and highly popular images of babies dressed as teddies of Ann Geddes. Janet Malcolm, a psychoanalytic writer and journalist, in her review of Mann's *Immediate Family* writes:

> All happy childhoods are alike: they are the skin that memory has grown over a wound. Children suffer, no matter how lovingly they are brought up. It is in the very nature of upbringing to cause suffering. Sally Mann's project has been to document the anger, disappointment, shame, confusion, insecurity that in every child attach to the twenty-year-long crisis of growing up (Malcolm, 1997).

Parents suffer too. Many parents and children seek appropriate reassurance that their battles and conflicts throughout the day have not damaged their love for each other, in books that celebrate and idealise the love between parents and the child and hopefully are not used as denial of the ambivalent nature of the relationships. A number of books present parents as endlessly patient, always loving, never ambivalent or frustrated by their children and in this way encourage denial of ambivalence or persecute the struggling parent with an ideal that cannot be reached. Some of the latter type address the arrival of a new baby and often suggest that despite initial difficulties in coming to terms with the new rival, the first child is successfully restored to a comfortable position within the family and the parent's mind, and in effect little changes. One such book, in my opinion is the lovely *Rosie's Babies* (Waddell and Dale, 1990).

In *Rosie's Babies* we are presented with what I playfully dubbed earlier the 'grandiose Titanic dreams of idealised parenthood and idealised childhood'. In summary an endlessly patient mother, effortlessly balancing her availability to her young daughter and her baby, listens to her child describe a wonderful imaginary world in which she has, apparently, in identification with an almost perfect mother, two babies of her own. These two babies share a nest Rosie makes for them and we see them being fed simultaneously and happily. Towards the end of the book we see the two babies, cuddling each other blissfully in their nest, while the real baby is put quietly to bed. Finally the mother asks Rosie, 'What will we talk about?' and Rosie replies, while we see them holding and delighting in each other, 'Me.' I think this description of sibling love may be often accurate but it is not the whole story, by any means.

In reality, the birth of a sibling changes life forever within a family. In contrast, Anthony Browne addresses the bewildering experience of the child when faced with the terrible certainty of uncertainty that follows the birth of a sibling in his book, *Changes*.

Changes begins with the words: 'On Thursday morning at a quarter past ten Joseph Kaye noticed something strange about the kettle.' The kettle changes into a cat and as Joseph moves throughout the house and yard outside, more surreal changes of inanimate objects into animals occur.

One is reminded of the Surrealist aim to bring the latent life back into objects. This is indeed what Browne does, both animating an inanimate object and, while transforming it, presenting an in-between period: the two things co-exist in the same new two-but-one object. This new object is then also the original object which is lent symbolic meaning by its transformation into something else, which in itself is a symbol of something else. For example, when Joseph goes outside we see (picture 4) seven images of a football morphing into an egg which, as Joseph kicks, cracks and breaks and from out of which flies a stork. The ball is both ball and egg in the same way that the egg is both egg and latent bird (bird without a bone). Thus we can see that Joseph sees a ball and Browne reveals the egg in the shadow of his unconscious which to Joseph has an affinity to the ball and is symbolic of the imminent arrival of his baby sister. In a talk in Winsconsin (Browne, 2000) Anthony Browne spoke of how *Changes* originated from an image in his head of one thing changing into another;

> I had an image of one thing turning into another. Opposite things turning into another, hard manmade objects, shiny electric kettle. I wondered what it would look like when it was half a kettle and half the opposite and I thought of a cat.

We learn that Joseph's father had said before he left to fetch his mother that things were going to change. Further clues are given that a baby is on the way. We see a picture of Madonna and Child, above Joseph's head as he sits on the sofa, which is changing into a crocodile. On the television screen we see firstly a cuckoo, then a cuckoo's egg in a nest and finally a small mother bird feeding a large cuckoo baby. A pig appears in the family photograph above the television.

It is interesting how many pictures in the book have either a window, or light from a window, mirror or door in them; sixteen out of the twenty-four. Joseph's journey through the surrealist landscape of him mind, projected onto the outside world, takes him from inside the house to the outside through a door, and then he retreats into the darkness of his bedroom. Here, presumably, he has some relief from the endless succession of objects and their associations to the new baby to come, a reality that has still not been accepted nor decoded by his conscious mind. Finally the door opens and his mother, carrying a baby, and his father appear. His mother says, 'Hello, love, this is your sister.' The picture of the baby is ambiguous; the baby looks to be about to cry. In the final picture we see Joseph in a new position in the family, holding his baby sister, a boy-sized mug of tea at his feet, a smaller version of the parents' mugs resting on the floor. To me his father's face bears some concern for his son, and possibly also for his own predicament; another baby in the family; life changes for all.

Cuckoos in the nest

Anthony Browne was inspired to write *Changes* when he heard about his friends' daughter, Anna, who, aged seven, when taken out by her parents for dinner to be told the good news that she would be getting a new baby brother or sister, burst into tears, much to her parents' surprise. The news that a baby is expected confronts the child being told with undeniable evidence about the fundamental facts of life. Namely, that your parents have an exclusive relationship which can create babies; that time passes and change is inevitable, and one cannot possess nor control one's love object. I want to look at some real children for whom siblings represent, at least some of the time, cuckoos rather than welcome bedfellows in the nest.

A baby beheaded

A small boy aged three runs into his parents' bedroom in the middle of the night. Next to the parents' bed is the cot with his new baby sister, Maisy. His father wakes to hear him ask in a panicky voice

> 'Daddy, can we get a new baby?'
> His father answers
> 'We've only just got one, maybe some time in the future.'
> The boy asks again
> 'Daddy, can we get a new baby?'
> This time the father a little more awake asks 'why?'
> The boy says
> 'Because Maisy's head is in the garden. I only touched it and it fell off.'
> Father shows the boy Maisy safe and sound in her cot, head securely on her body, comforts the boy and takes him back to bed.

Fast-forward five years, to the days leading up to the anniversary of the arrival of the cuckoo Maisy in this boy's life, an anniversary the parents insist should be celebrated. He composes an impromptu poem for her on the way home from school. It reads:

> Maisy is nice nicer than ice,
> She does not smell like stinky hell,
> I like Maisy because she's nice and cuddly,
> I like Maisy because she's not muddly,
> Maisy is cute she's not a mute,
> Maisy is nice, not like rotten rice.

This poem is to me a two-in-one object as each time the object of his sister appears it is associated with an unpleasant experience – the thing in the shadow of his unconscious; ice, stinky hell, muddly, mute and rotten rice!

On her birthday he gives her a birthday card he has made for her. It reads;

> Maisy, Maisy doesn't drive me crasy (sic)
> Maisy, Maisy is five
> Thank goodness she is still alive
> Love from your brother.

Maisy, reading the card (picture 5) asks with real wonder

> 'Why should I be dead?'

What Maisy, amazingly, has not quite grasped is just how many times in her brother's unconscious fantasies she has died, was murdered, decapitated at least once. Nor has she grasped that the many bruises, both physical and emotional, she gets regularly from her brother bear witness to his murderousness towards her.

In this instance we see how this boy's dream at age three, and his poem and card at age seven, capture his murderous feelings towards this baby.

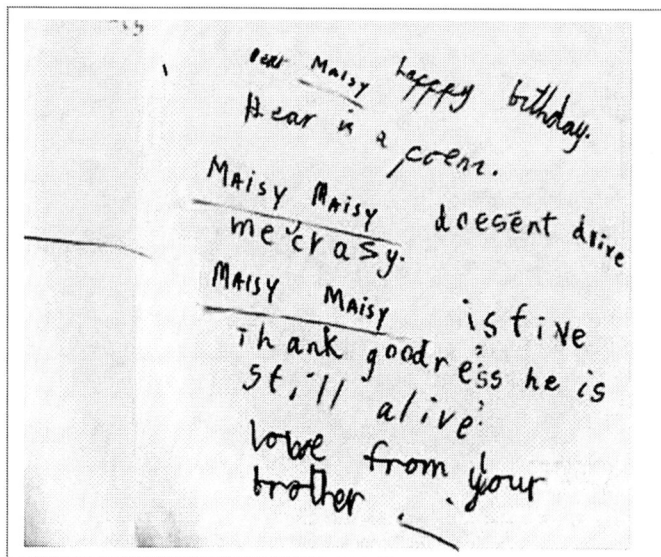

5

How many eggs in your nest?

Barbara Docker-Drysdale, who founded the Mulberry Bush School, recounted the following story which I like to tell as a riddle. One day a small group of children she was with made some nests. She offered them chocolate pieces as eggs for their nests. The first child asked for two eggs, the second for three and so on. One little boy in the group had great difficulties sharing and was also quite greedy. When it came to his turn, Barbara Docker-Drysdale asked him how many eggs he wanted for his nest. What do you think he answered?

He asked for one egg only. Why, when he is so greedy, surely he would want all the chocolate? Because for him the chocolate pieces were no longer chocolate, but held another meaning; as had been suggested, they were eggs. This little boy wanted to be the only egg in the nest.

In my clinical practice as a child psychotherapist I saw a family who attended twice only, and to my delight, both children at one point in the second session began spontaneously making nests out of the plasticine I had provided. The family had come because of concerns about the five year-old boy who was saying, at times, he wanted to die, and on one occasion had gone downstairs and fetched a kitchen knife and threatened to kill himself. The first session focused on him a great deal and his older sister, aged seven, was not present but had been left at home. I asked that she be brought for the follow-up.

The whole family attended the second session and I was struck by her sucking first a lollipop and then just the stick throughout the whole session. When we talked about the boy's wish to kill himself, his sister pointed out that on the occasion when he went downstairs to fetch the knife, he had just woken to discover she was having a cuddle between mummy and daddy in their bed and this had made him angry. When I asked what it made her feel when he said and did such things she said very clearly, 'his worry has got into my head'. I asked if her little brother took up much space and she said with real feeling 'Yes, he even took my space in the womb'. As the session progressed she made a nest of plasticine and filled it with colourful eggs of different sizes (see picture 6). The boy demanded his dad made him a nest, which he did, while the boy rushed to make a lot of eggs for himself. I asked the girl, 'Which egg in your nest is you and which is your brother?' She pointed to the largest egg in the middle for herself, and the smallest on the very edge for her brother. Suddenly her brother dumped his eggs on top of hers and decided he would make a worm out of the nest, again demanding his dad's help. She coped with this sudden intrusion and did some sorting of the eggs.

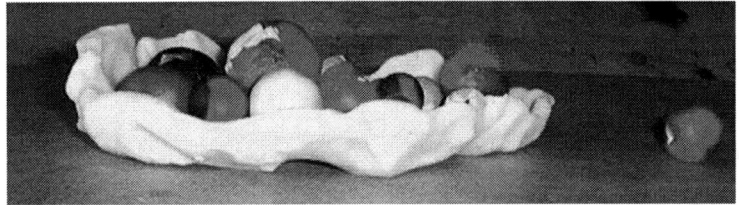

6

At the end of the session, she asked if she could leave the nest and eggs with me and I accepted them. I followed her with my eyes as she slowly walked across the room and placed the nest very carefully on the table. After the family left I went to examine the nest and realised that the egg she signified as her brother was missing. I looked around the table, and then on the floor and under the table beneath the heating lay the little egg. It seemed like some kind of magic trick, this unconscious displacement of the brother-egg.

A gorilla's eyes

There are a number of objects that appeared saturated with meaning for Magritte and appear again and again in his paintings; a jockey, the bowler hat, a pipe, a tuba are well known. In 1928, he painted a disturbing image of a woman whose face is covered by a cloth. She stands behind a table on which stand a tuba and a valise. The painting is entitled *L'histoire centrale (The Heart of the Matter)*. In the same year the image recurs in *Les amants (The Lovers)* (Picture 7), in which the faces of man and a woman who appear to be a couple are similarly covered. Magritte's recollections from childhood were all bizarre, but when he was aged fourteen, his mother apparently committed suicide, throwing herself into the river Sambre. When her body was recovered they found her nightgown wrapped around her face and it was never known whether this was something she had done before jumping or whether the river's currents veiled her face as she drowned. Gablik (*Magritte*, London, 1972) deems it likely that this represents an unconscious memory of his drowned mother.

7

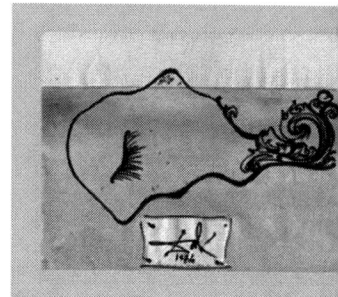

8

Anthony Browne will forever be associated with gorillas as they appear in many of his books, often as central characters. Browne over time has discovered or conceded to himself that the gorilla is associated in his mind with his father. He was a great big man, generous and loving, who encouraged his children's creativity. He had also fought hand-to-hand combat in the Second World War in North Africa. Like many veterans, he never spoke of his experiences but his diaries remain in the family. He was wounded and went missing on the battlefield while his wife was having her first baby, believing her husband was dead. Her husband lived, but the baby died three or four days after a traumatic birth. Browne's father apparently suffered symptoms of post-traumatic stress disorder, in which an individual suffers flashbacks to traumatic experiences, reliving them in the present. Browne recalls that his mother discovered the father wrestling with a vacuum cleaner one night having mistaken it for a German guard. On another occasion, in the middle of the night he similarly mistook his wife for the enemy and attempted to strangle her. Anthony Browne was seventeen when he witnessed his father's tragic death of a massive heart attack; a loss he describes as having a powerful effect upon him (Browne 2002). It is interesting in itself that Anthony Browne initially worked as a medical illustrator but discovered that he could not suppress the animation that appeared in his pictures as images from his internal world emerged as he sketched the internal physical of the body. One must be cautious about ever interpreting any author/illustrator's work but it seems to me that throughout his work, one sees a development akin to the mourning process. In this, initially the father is experienced as lost to the child or as a very ambivalent presence; as a Nazi in *Bear goes to Town*; a remote, unavailable father in *Gorilla*; and a base, ignorant father in *Zoo* are just three examples. Through mourning, which is inevitable if one faces and bears Money-Kyrle's fundamental facts of life, the father is eventually restored, internalised by the mourner. This has culminated in an unashamed outpouring of love for his father in *Dad*, but I believe it is most evident in *Changes*, though in more subtle and unconscious ways.

One of the most striking illustrations in *Changes* – and, I think, in the whole of children's literature – accompanies the words 'Was everything going to change?' (Picture 9). It shows Joseph from behind, looking over the wall of his back yard at two windows in the house opposite. Behind these windows, barred, are the compassionate, sad eyes of a gorilla. The eyes appear to look with sadness on the boy, as if to answer, 'Yes, everything is changing' and yet they also offer containment in their compassion and willingness to face the truth of change and loss. It appears to me that one sees in these gorilla's eyes, not only the compassion and sadness of a father who is unable to prevent his son from suffering the losses entailed in the arrival of a new sibling, but also Anthony Browne's internalised father, who, though unable to spare his son the suffering of his loss, is nonetheless available as an internal object that can help contain his loss and sadness. Thereby, he offers hope and, combined with an internalised mother, remains a source of creativity.

9

I think it is fascinating that like the Surrealists, Browne uses the image of the windows to give the view into the internal world of the child and that the father is portrayed as both present and remote. The father's compassionate gaze envelops the child and the reader, but the father remains mysteriously locked behind the barred windows in the house opposite, a Hitchcockian rear window, able to observe and communicate only when the eyes of his son turn to find him.

I think *Changes* ranks alongside *Where the Wild Things Are* (Sendak, 1963) as a work of genius in modern children's literature. I find that I recommend it more often to parents who have young children than any other book. Some parents understand that it captures something extremely valuable and acts as a container for a small child's anxieties while others appear oblivious, just as they appear oblivious to the depth of their child's distress. However, with these latter families, my belief is that the wonderful illustrations and exquisitely balanced prose in *Changes* offers some containment directly to the child's unconscious anxieties. The work of a child psychotherapist appears to me to be akin to that of the surrealist illustrator or painter. The surrealist painter interprets the latent life of the object to the spectator with a shocking newness of context and the child psychotherapist takes the material (dreams, free associations, play) of the child and, through interpretation, attempts to illuminate the symbolic content, both facilitating insight into the facts of life, inviting the spectator/patient away from self-illusion and delusion, and supporting them to bear the mystery.

REFERENCES

Clive Anderson, *Law of the Arctic*. Radio 4, 2004.

Wilfred Ruprecht Bion, *Learning from Experience*, London: Heinemann, 1962.

André Breton, *Manifestoes of Surrealism*, Ann Arbor Paperbacks, University of Michigan Press, 1972 (originally published 1924).

Anthony Browne, *Changes*, London: Walker Books, 1997.

Anthony Browne, *Let the pictures tell the story*, Lecture. University of Winsconsin, 2000.

Barbara Docker-Drysdale, *Therapy and Consultation in Child Care*. London: Free Association Press, 1993.

Suzi Gablik, *Magritte*. London: Thames and Hudson, 1972.

Martin Jay, "The Disenchantment of the Eye: Surrealism and the Crisis of Ocularcentrism," in *Visual Anthropology Review*, Vol. 7, No. 1, 1991.

John Keats, *Selected Letters of John Keats*. ed Grant Scott. Harvard: 2002 (first published 1817).

Melanie Klein, *Love, Guilt and Reparation*, London: Hogarth Press, 1937.

Melanie Klein, *Envy and Gratitude and Other Works*, London: Hogarth Press, 1955.

René Magritte, quoted in Suzi Gablik's *Magritte*. London: Thames & Hudson, 1972.

Janet Malcolm, *Diana and Nikon*, New York: Aperture, 1997.

Roger Money-Kyrle. *Collected Papers*. London: Karnac Books, 1978.

Paul Nougé, quoted in Suzi Gablik's *Magritte*. London: Thames & Hudson, 1970.

Regina Pally, *The mind-brain relationship*. London: Karnac Books. 2000.

Maurice Sendak, *Where The Wild Things Are*. New York: Harper & Row, 1963.

Colwyn Trevarthen, 'Playing into reality: conversations with the infant communicator', *Winnicott Studies*, No.7 (Spring), 67-84, 1993.

Martin Waddell & Penny Dale, *Rosie's Babies*. London; Walker Books, 1992.

Donald W. Winnicott, *Babies and Their Mothers*. London; Free Association Books, 1987.

Victoria de Rijke & Howard Hollands

The Thing That Is Not There
A Psychoanalytic Reading of Mervyn Peake's *Captain Slaughterboard Drops Anchor*

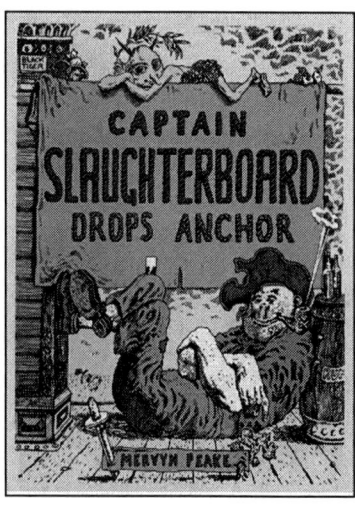 

> Captain Slaughterboard is the most fearsome and wicked pirate you could ever imagine. He likes nothing better than chopping men to bits with his cutlass or making them walk the plank. Then, one day, on a remote and exotic island he spies a strange yellow creature, and from that moment Captain Slaughterboard is a changed man (Book Jacket blurb, London: Walker Books, 2001).

Mervyn Peake, 1911-1968, wrote poetry and plays, was a painter and illustrator and designed theatrical costumes. He is best known for his *Gormangast* Trilogy *Titus Groan*, *Gormangast*, and *Titus Alone*. He also illustrated Carroll's *Alices Adventures in Wonderland* and *The Hunting of the Snark*, Robert Louis Stevenson's *Dr. Jekyll and Mr. Hyde*, and *Treasure Island*, and wrote and/or illustrated a number of collections of poetry.

Peake was born in Kuling, China, in 1911 to English missionary parents. He spent his childhood in Tientsin in the North. China, an ancient country of rich tradition and dense ritual, made a lasting impression on him. At the age of 12 he returned to England with his family (never to return to China) and attended Eltham College in Kent, Croydon School of Art, and, from 1929 to 1933, the Royal Academy Schools. He exhibited his paintings for the first time in 1931. When a former professor from Eltham invited him to join the artists' colony on Sark, a tiny island in the English Channel, Peake promptly moved. He lived and worked there from 1933 to 1935, exhibiting his paintings yearly in London. His early career was as a painter in London, although he exhibited with the Sark artists. In 1936 he began teaching life drawing and in 1937 married painter Maeve Gilmore.

Captain Slaughterboard Drops Anchor was written and illustrated by Peake in 1936, and first published in 1939.

This written piece tries to emulate the dynamic of image/text, deck/page/set/stage relationship present in the picturebook Slaughterboard, and which we tried to recapture in presenting in visual performance. We have attempted to explore the kinds of reading that can be made between image and text, reflecting Peake's prioritising of the pictures over the text. What the reader sees is what was shown at the conference.

We began with a dramatic image of the ship "The Black Tiger" perched upon the wave as claw and Hokusai's woodblock print *"The Great Wave"* facing one another. Though Peake's text reads 'Captain Slaughterboard ruled her-every inch!' in fact the ship is at the mercy of the all-powerful sea; awesome nature personified. The next page zooms in cinematically on the Captain and what is left of his crew, where pistols, pipe, mast, bottles, feather, flag are all at half cock. It can be tempting to do very orthodox Freudian readings of such imagery, as Alice Mills does below:

> *All the pirate's paraphernalia are phallic: they are surrounded by swords, canon, pistols, telescopes, candle, bottles, and barrels of rum and their tobacco pipes emit a foamy white smoke. Some of the crew's noses, the face's equivalent of a penis in a Freudian reading, are remarkably enlarged, bulbous or elongated* (Mills, 2005).

The danger of sticking to fixed reading positions is that sometimes critics themselves become stuck. Peake complicates this because the deliberate 'staging' of masculinity as a performance on board a pirate ship; the crew presented as a 'cast' of characters. Pirates are 'marked' with masculinity so far as to be painted all over. Together with isolation on board, they need socialisation. Pirates are a kind of standing joke about male preference for male company and the need to be socialised out of it. Judith Butler's theory of the performativity of gender suggests a queer reading of *Slaughterboard*, where 'queer' in this sense is less an identity than a critique of (fixed) identity, so that subjectivity is always a role under development, a site of permanent 'becoming'. Butler describes gender as 'a performance of associated acts made up of gestures and desire... marked on the surface of the body' (Butler, 1993). Like Charlie Choke's tattoos.

Timothy Twitch was the most elegant in battle, his left hand especially.

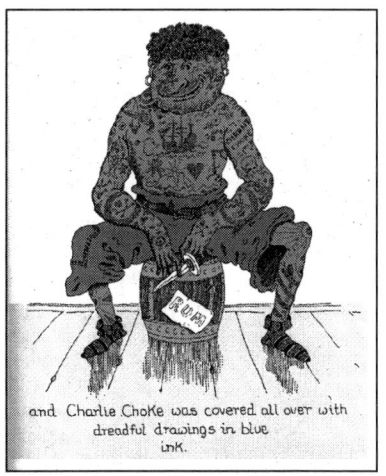

and Charlie Choke was covered all over with dreadful drawings in blue ink.

The Captain first spies the creature through his telescope standing out 'bright as butter' in a pink landscape. Mills reads the Yellow Creature as 'posed behind a tall, thin pile of rocks that he is clasping. The enormous phallic erection rises up between the creature's legs almost as high as the creature himself'. (Mills, 2005) but the image can also be read as looking through a cannon or a porthole, looking into some other, exotic, erotic world. This viewing of the body recalls Laura Mulvey's much-cited 1975 thesis which argued that men are bearers of the gaze and women its objects, but there is much more than narcissistic identification of objectification going on in *Slaughterboard*. Alfred Hitchcock's Peeping Tom film par excellence *Rear Window* is another analogy: about the appetite of the eye, the lust of the eye, audiences haring acts of voyeurism, even scopophilia. As Slavoj Žižek and others ask in the wonderfully titled collection of essays *Everything You Wanted to Know About Lacan, But Were Afraid to Ask Hitchcock,* can a window function as an eye? How can a window gaze at us? And as French filmmaker Jean-Luc Godard said with reference to Hitchcock (Žižek, 1993), it is the gaze that creates fiction. It asks us: what do you want?

Then he took out his telescope and this is what he saw.

"Just exactly the sort I've been wanting", yelled Captain Slaughterboard as he charged over the fruit and turtles that covered the ground. "After him, you dogs!"

The Captain's finger gestures evoke the School of Fontainebleu portrait of the sisters Gabrielle d'Estes and Duchess of Villars but unlike the framed portrait, we are caught in the action of hot pursuit. The Yellow Creature is a

 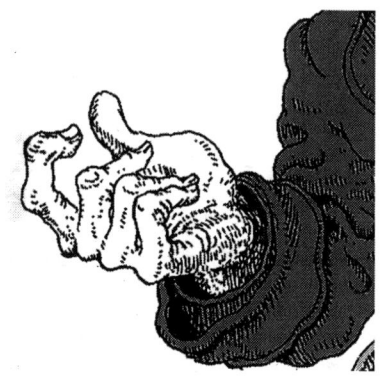

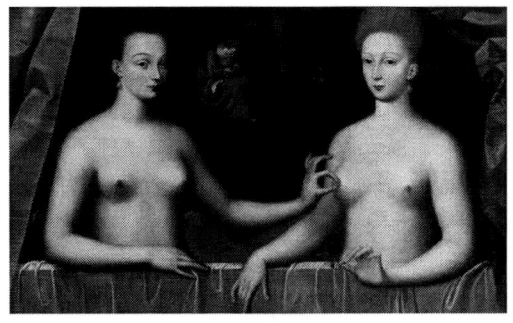

diminutive, almost fetish figure (and in Lacanian terms the fetish creates a substitute for the penis) but the creature has either pan-like hairy pelt, or wears a little apron or adopts other clothes like fancy dress. It does not show its genitals: it could be any sex. Where in this instance, Slaughterboard is as male and rampant as a Greek 6th Century Satyr, The Yellow Creature is as androgynous as Beardsley's faun for *The Yellow Book*. *The Yellow Book* of 1894, an illustrated quarterly, originating from a group of writers and artists that included Aubrey Beardsley, was intended to reflect 'the yellow nineties' when Victorianism gave way to fashionable regency attitudes and an increasing French influence. Yellow was also the colour of the covers of decadent French novels such as J.K. Huysman's *A Rebours* (*Against Nature*).

'Where are the yellow creatures?' cries the Captain, emphasising the piratical association with seeking out treasure made up of precious metals such as gold coins and bullion. 'Yellow' used to mean gold in Old English, and 'a yellow boy' was slang for gold coin in the mid seventeenth century. Yellow was a colour used by Chinese Emperors, is a sea and a river in China, and the 'inscrutable Chinese' were labelled 'the yellow peril', a dated and derogatory term used from 1900 for the supposed danger posed by Asiatic peoples to the rest of the world.

When Peake was recruited to the army, separation from his family took its toll and he was diagnosed as having a nervous breakdown in 1942, invalided out of the army and spent the next 12 years struggling with poor health while doctor after doctor struggled for a diagnosis. In the search for a cure, he underwent electric shock treatments and had an operation on his brain. In fact, he had Parkinson's disease allied with *Encephalitis Lethargica*, or 'sleeping sickness,' which he had contracted in 1911 during the epidemic that had swept the part of China where he was born. In his case it lay dormant for over thirty years. The 'thing' that was not lost. Peake described his own outlook in a radio talk of 1947:

> As I see it, or as I want to see it, the marvels of the visible world are not things in themselves but revelations to stir the imagination - to conduct us to amazing climates of the mind which climates it is for the artist to translate into paint or into words ... whether he can assimilate and build from it an original work of art depends largely on how deeply he is obsessed by his work.

The image of the pirates looking into empty space has Captain Slaughterboard 'lost in thought'. There is something of the Emperor's New Clothes phenomenon here as if the Captain's dreamy believing in The Yellow Creature carries the rest of the crew along: seeing something that is not there. In fact The Yellow Creature is 'on another page, waiting to be written on', in Anna Feinburg's lovely phrase from *Dead Sailors Don't Bite*.

It is important to note that the text in *Slaughterboard* is not type-face, but handwritten, therefore closer to the drawn line. The written text is not as lean as most of the drawing, as if Peake was less sure about how much to leave out. On board deck watching the Yellow Creature 'for hours on end,' the strength of the image is in all the blank space. The first signs of a kind of abandon begin in the Captain, as his shoe is coming off, his hat is off, he's in a smiling reverie, and the crew glance back at him, beginning to worry about the change. The deck here literally becomes the stage with the Yellow Creature out of sight treading the boards meeting the sea. Peake has drawn the boards with the viewer in parallel to the picture plane, like lines in an exercise book, whereas the sea, with little freehand marks, has more texture than the text.

At first scopophiliac, the Captain moves to participation in the dance. Is the Yellow Creature 'das ding': the thing, or whole object that psychoanalysis conceptualised as 'vorstellings representanz', the representation of something deliberately missing that appears as its own repetition; what Žižek calls 'structural duplication'? Dance in the transgressive worlds of pirate ship and Moulin Rouge; back to treading the boards as a means of escape, contact and physical intimacy. Peake uses the boards quite differently here as full of joint action, rather than voyeurism: the medium of mirrored communication; the dance or 'tanz' of 'representanz'.

Psychoanalyst Christopher Bollas used the term the 'unthought known' for what is known but not yet been thought. He argued that psychoanalysis could learn a great deal about this form of knowing from dance, where the dancer expresses the unthought known through body knowledge.

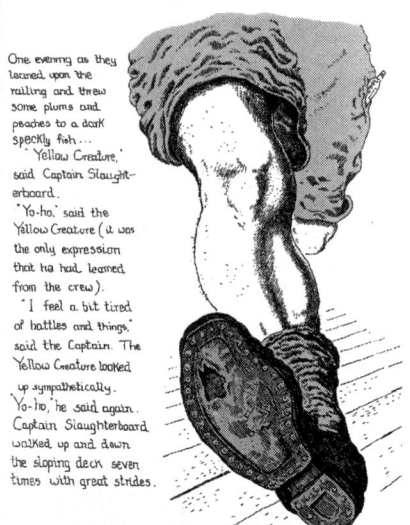

> Dance me to your beauty to a burning violin
> Dance me through the panic till I'm gathered safely in
> Touch me with your naked hand or touch me with your glove
> Dance me to the end of love
> ("Dance Me to the End of Love", Leonard Cohen – 1985)

To see the Yellow Creature as a projection suggests both the idea of it as a fantasy and reading as fantasy. It is open to all kinds of readings to a child or adult, and that gives it a powerful presence. It is not a faun, or pan, or a goblin, or a child, or a spectre, but something brought into existence by the dance and Captain Slaughterboard. In this sense, it is a thing that is not there, yet the most vivid thing in the book.

Manet, back in Paris, has the model as knowing and self-conscious image of modernism. She is part of the feast and her gaze invites us to join at our peril. In Gauguin's *'Woman with Mangoes'* the yellow mangoes are more equivalent to the Yellow Creature than the body of the woman. A table for two is laid under the palms while the Yellow Creature 'makes the most exciting things to eat out of practically nothing', and later they lie blissfully under a palm, feasting on fruit from Captain Slaughterboard's hand and hat.

Captain Slaughterboard finished up all his bullets long ago, but they have both become very good with bows and arrows, and

can hit things a long way off.

But most of the time they are dreadfully lazy and eat fruit.

The following double-page spread demonstrates how inextricably linked the two have become; each lying on a rock (Slaughterboard's coat finally off) his cutlass now blunted as a rod for fishing, his threatening poses replaced by playful ones where their two fishing lines interweave like the patterns on the 'glittering fishes'. No longer the pirate ship but companionship. The non-sexual and the sexual are traversed in both directions, as in play and like the movement of transference and counter-transference in object relations theory. The unthought known expressed in interwoven fishing lines. This works in parallel to the psychoanalytic notion of 'reciprocity', where mutually dependent, complementary interchanges describe reciprocal paths of influence; otherwise called 'libidinal co-excitation'. A little of what you fancy clearly does you good.

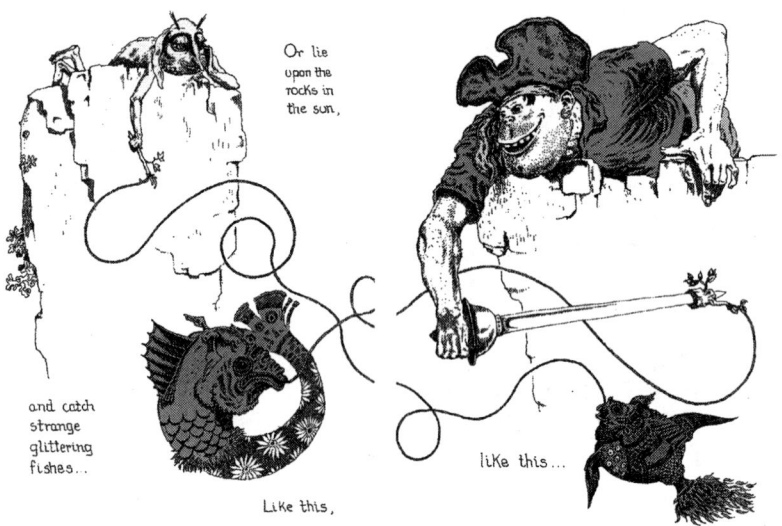

We would like to argue that *Captain Slaughterboard Drops Anchor* found something (that was not lost and has been found time and again in the best artist's picturebooks): the manifestation of a new psychic structure: in this case the Yellow Creature. It is like a revelation. The truth is uncovered and what was hidden is revealed – the work of the creative unconscious- seeing what is there, was there, all along. Is it childhood, the mother country, disease lying dormant? Is it love? Is the Yellow Creature a fantastic projection of the Captain's as an image of his golden self (surely the real quest, never the treasure)? Is it about the rejection of materialism? There is no suggestion of colonising, but living a found life. What does a retired pirate do? Settle down, or return to childhood bliss?

What does a retired pirate do? Drop anchor: literally and figuratively speaking: find security and confidence. 'Anchoring' is also coupling, fitting, making connections, fixing securely; to dwell. This pirate comes to rest, lives in hope, lives in the imagination.

An old and crumbling parapet
Arose out of the dancing sea -
And on its top there sat a flea
For reasons which I quite forget
But as the sun descended, and
The moon uprose across the sky,
We were alone, the flea and I
And so I took it by the hand

And whispered, 'On your parapet
D'you think that there'd be room for me?'
'I cannot say,' replied the flea,
'I'm studying the Alphabet.'

But that was long ago, and saints
Have died since then – and Ogres bled.
And purple tigers flopped down dead
Among the pictures and the paints.

REFERENCES

Christopher Bollas, *The Shadow of the Object: Psychoanalysis of the Unthought Known*, Columbia University Press, 1990.

Lizbeth Goodman, ed, *The Routledge Reader in Gender and Performance*, London: Routledge, 1998.

Alice Mills, *Stuckness in the Fiction of Mervyn Peake*, Amsterdam: Rodopi, 2005

Laura Mulvey, Visual Pleasure and Narrative Cinema. Screen: 16.3, Autumn 1975. (first published London: Country Life, 1939.)

Mervyn Peake, *Captain Slaughterboard Drops Anchor*, Candlewick Press, 2001. (first published London: Country Life, 1939.)

Mervyn Peake, *A Book of Nonsense*, Picador, 1974.
(interviews) http://www.peakestudies.com

Slavoj Žižek, *Everything You Wanted to Know About Lacan, But Were Afraid to Ask Hitchcock*, London: Verso, 1993.

1. Peake, Mervyn *Captain Slaughterboard Drops Anchor* Reprinted from 1939 original by Walker Books, London 2001 (all images in the text apart from those referenced are from this publication)
2. Peake, Mervyn *Self Portrait*
3. Hokusai Katsushika *The Great Wave* (detail) Hakone Museum, Japan 1831
4. Hitchcock, Alfred *Rear Window* Paramount Pictures 1954
5. School of Fontainebleu *Gabrielle D'Estrees and Her Sister, the Duchess of Villars*, 1573-99
6. Cover Design for *The Yellow Book Prospectus* for Vol. V. 1895. Not used in Vol. V. Design was adapted for Smithers Catalogue of Rare Books (Taken from *The Best of Beardsley*, Collected and Edited by R. A. Walker, The Bodley Head, 1948, Great Britain).
7. Greek 6th Century Sculpture of a Satyr, artist unknown.
8. Film poster source unknown
9. Toulouse-Lautrec Henri, *Jane Avril* lithograph 1893
10. Cohen, Leonard *Dance Me to the End of Love* from the album '*Various Positions*' Sony 1985
11. Matisse, Henri *La Danse 2* The State Hermitage Museum, St Petersburg 1910
12. Derain, Andre *La Danse,* Courtauld Institute, London 1906
13. Gauguin, Paul *Woman with Mangoes,* Pushkin Museum Moscow 1896
14. Manet, Edouard *Le Dejeuner Sur L'Herbe* Oil on canvas Musée d'Orsay, Paris 1862-63
15. Peake, Mervyn *An Old and Crumbling Parapet* from '*A Book of Nonsense*', Picador, London 1974

Antony Lishak

The Story of the Story of the Story

What is it that makes a child engage with a story? What transforms page upon page of ink-scratchings into an enticing world of words? How can the worked and re-worked ramblings of old farts like me persuade children to, for a while at least, switch off *Hollyoaks* or swap their Nintendo DS for a handful of paper? I ponder these questions daily. As it happens, as you'll hear, I am in the privileged position of being able to work closely with literally hundreds of different children a week – and I frequently take the opportunity of asking enthusiastic readers (and, I am happy to report, that there are many...) what it is that makes reading some stories so enjoyable, to which I often get an incredulous look that loosely translates to "see, I knew you were a rambling old fart". But sometimes children stoop to indulge me and agree to open up about why they are willing to spend great chunks of their time reading and I have come to the conclusion (and don't hold your breath for any great original idea here...) that either consciously or unconsciously, children look for themselves in what they read – something to identify with. It's how they make sense of a story – how they "get into" it.

Similarly, I believe, children should be encouraged to use themselves and their experiences in what they write. Writing should be much more than just a way of filling up a blank sheet of paper or a way of responding to an array of keywords in order to jump through SATs hoops – it should be a form of self-expression. I strive to help children find their voice on paper by encouraging them to make the link between verbal story telling (the playground story, the joke, the "guess what happened in school today" chat on the way home...) and the written form of story telling. I see it as the duty of facilitators in this area (whether they are people like me or classroom teachers...) to remove the barriers that inhibit children in finding their voices on paper. For me that involves having the confidence of affording the grammatical and structural side of literacy work its proper place – that is being vital tools that will help you say what you want to say – not detached abstract rules that have to be digested and regurgitated in order to get a level 5. One of the phrases I find myself repeating on a daily basis is "we are all authors and we all have stories to tell" – and I firmly believe this to be true.

What is the importance of creative writing? This is the way I try to explain it to children. I haven't found a better way to explain it to adults.

Why bother to do creative writing? What's the point? Anyone can tell a story... but no matter how articulate you are, you've got no more than about a second to work out what you're going to say. But when you speak through your pen and put your voice on paper.... no-one else has to hear it until you're pleased with it.

Write about what you know. Use personal experiences as starting points for stories, then fabricate, elaborate, elucidate – lie!

Row Your Boat

Row your Boat was written when Emily, my oldest daughter was a baby. She loved rocking back and forth to the song and to alleviate my boredom I created my own verses ("Fly, fly, fly, your plane gently in the sky, merrily, merrily, merrily, merrily watch the clouds go by....") purely to amuse myself. Thirty seconds of work – the easiest money I've ever earned!

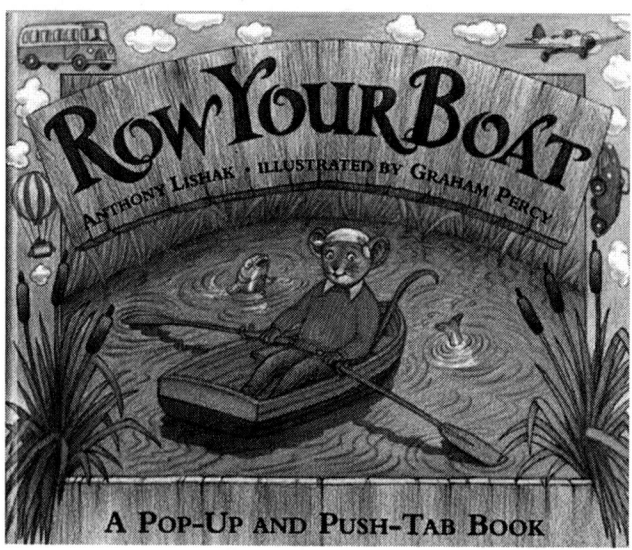

Baby Bear Comes Home

Baby Bear starts;
> Jessica was tired after her first day at school. After tea she went straight to bed.
> "Goodnight mum" – "Sleep well dear."
> Jessica dreamt of all the exciting things that happened to her during the day.
> She didn't hear her two bears talking.
> "We must find baby bear" – "Shush – don't wake Jessica."
> Jessica had left baby bear in school and mother and father bear had to go and find him...

It's true my daughter is called Jessica – the dedication in the book is "To the real Jessica". It's true that as a baby she rarely slept and it's true that school introduced her (and her parents!) to the world of sleep... And it's also true that she left her bear at school on her first day. A few days later it was back in her room – I've no idea how it got there, but two of Jessica's other bears had very muddy paws...

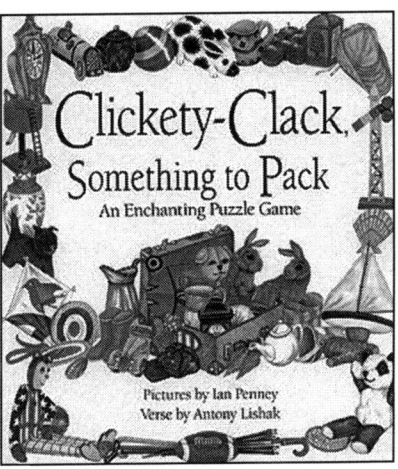

The Story of the Story

How I get kids to do it...

My approach when working with children is to empower them – I want them see themselves as containers of countless stories just waiting to be told, rather than viewing stories as abstract external ideas that simply pop into their heads. One of my mantras is "the one with the pen has the power!"

Drill down into your brain to find the story. It's all to do with asking questions. As long as you don't say I don't know, you have the beginnings of a story.

How about confessional writing? Write about something that has happened to you, that you've always kept quiet about... like this...

The Asparagus Bush

Normally a sensible woman, my mother recklessly planted an asparagus bush in the middle of our garden and, over the years, trimmed it into a dense green lollipop. It stood proud and prominent. My brother and I never played football nearby – damaging it would have meant certain and swift death. But, like Henry, I was a truly useless footballer. My talented older brother refused to waste time playing with me – so I spent many a lonely hour trying to hone my skills alone. It was while attempting to perfect the art of kicking a ball straight that I scored a direct slice on my mother's pride and joy. Rather than panic, my eight-year-old mind whirled into action and hatched a scheme that involved green string binding and a thin stick splint… Within minutes the asparagus bush was upright again; dead, but nonetheless standing. And I said nothing.

Two days later I was looking down from my bedroom window. My brother was playing with his friends at the safe end of the garden while the bush was still how I had left it – although I could notice the hints of brown on its now wilting firs. But as I was watching (who knows – maybe it was the vibrations of my brother and his friends playing football…) the bush chose that moment to fall over. I froze with fear – but then thought "what's it got to do with me? I'm here in my room."

But soon there was an explosion from the kitchen – my mother came out and charged at my brother. Ironically, the crime he was being accused of was probably the only misdemeanour that he didn't actually do and refused to own up to. He was guilty of everything else he denied – in fact getting my brother to own up was a major ambition of my parents. They resolved to make this concealment a point of principle. For two days his life was hell – you name it he was deprived of it. But my brother never owned up to things he did do – there was no chance of him owning up to this.

It was a tribute to the gloss I had managed to work up on my own halo that no one ever suspected me. The truth only came out thirty years later when I was preparing a writing task for some children – I wanted them to use "things-you've-got-away-with" as a starting point for a story and decided to write this all down as an example for them. My brother's son found a copy that weekend and took it home – the ensuing waves of anger from both my mother and brother were only quelled when I bought them each two huge asparagus bushes...

Antony Lishak explains why he advises young authors to tell a few lies...

One teacher I know described trying to get her normally bright 10-year-olds to write a story as like setting fire to a pile of ashes. Why is story writing such a problem? Why are children so keen to spin a yarn in the playground, and so reluctant to do it on paper? Why do so many teachers tell me that when it comes to marking they are likely to pour themselves a stiff drink before embarking on a pile of 30 stories?

I was a primary teacher for 15 years before I left to pursue a career as a children's author. Now I have returned to school as a visiting author invited in to talk to primary children about the process of writing and inspire them to try for themselves. In the past eleven years I have visited almost 1500 schools and have been amazed by the enthusiasm and expertise children can show.

Why do we ask children to write stories? I have often posed this question in staff-rooms. More and more I get asked into schools because "we've got to work on our level 3s" or "OFSTED has identified writing in key stage 2 as a major weakness", or "because they need to do it for SATs". No wonder the results are so uninspiring.

People tell stories because they want others to listen. The purpose of writing a story is the knowledge that someone is going to read it. That is, not just to cast a tired eye over it and litter it with red ticks; I mean react to it, as children are expected to react to the chosen texts in literacy hour.

If you want your pupils to be enthusiastic writers then you must respond to their writing as an enthusiastic reader. Laugh if they have tried to be funny, gasp if they have tried to be shocking, be appalled if they have tried to be revolting. Children have to see that their words can elicit a reaction in their reader. This is even more apparent when a friend reads their work. The approval or constructive criticism of a trusted classmate carries more weight than the response of a teacher.

"Why do you write stories?" I have asked numerous children. "Because we get told to!" they reply. How depressing: "write a story" is code for "fill a page with ink, keep it neat, check your spellings and sprinkle in lots of impressive punctuation". A canny Year 4 child once confided: "I never write more than a page. She always makes you write it out again – it takes ages." Children should be encouraged to draw on their own experiences when writing stories, as authors do. We take familiar events and expand on them. We try to make sense of the world by taking what is normal and distorting it until it becomes remarkable in some way. This is the approach I use in schools. "Think of the things you know about. The things you see or hear every day. The things that get you worked up. The argument you had with your brother, the time your sister hid the remote control. The time you got the blame for something you did not do. Or the time you did something wrong and someone else got the blame." If you want children to write you have to give them confidence to delve into their own lives for ideas.

But (and this is the crucial ingredient) encourage them not to be afraid to make it up. Start from something that has happened to you and then exaggerate, fabricate, invent new outcomes. "They used to call me a tell-tale when I was a child," I say. "What do I do now? I tell tales, I put them in books and they pay me for it." There is nothing more liberating for a child then to be encouraged to lie!

Does it really matter that children are losing the ability to write stories? Yes, it does. Children who are given the time and encouragement to explore their own experiences in their writing start to develop a distinct voice on paper. They become able to express themselves in writing in a far more lucid way than they could orally. They realise that the voice they have on paper is a more considered voice. Writing can be redrafted and revised; it is not restricted by the need to be immediately understood, as speech is. And, used regularly, it becomes a powerful tool of communication. To deny children the opportunity to find their own voice on paper is tantamount to gagging them.

The Cast

In order of appearance:

Rosemary Stones began her career in children's books in the 1970s as a reviewer for *Spare Rib*, *Time Out* and *Race Today* and as a campaigner against racism, sexism and class bias in children's books. She was co-founder of the *Other Award*. In the '80s and '90s she was an Editorial Director at HarperCollins and then at Penguin. She is currently Editor of the review journal *Books for Keeps* and a psychoanalytic psychotherapist

Dr Alison Waller teaches for Bath Spa University and for Study Abroad programmes in Bath. She has published several articles on children's literature, and is currently finishing her book on young adult 'fantastic realism' and the construction of adolescence. She also writes stories and screenplays, and is helping to develop a national creative writing prize for sixth-formers.

Rebecca R. Butler holds a BA in English Literature and an MA in Children's Literature both from Roehampton University. She has published articles in the *Journal of Children's Literature Studies* and the *New Review of Children's Literature and Librarianship*. She spoke on children's literature and the Holocaust at the IBBY conference in 2006. Her research interest is children's literature and disability. She is currently working on a handbook adults can use to help them guide young readers through stories and picture books about disabled characters.

Dr Rebecca-Anne C. Do Rozario teaches fantasy and children's literature at Monash University, Melbourne, Australia. She has published in journals including *Women's Studies in Communication, Femspec, TDR: The Drama Review* and *Journal of Dramatic Theory and Criticism*. Her research interests include musical theatre, animation, fairy tale and fantasy and children's literature.

Dr. Debbie Hindle is the organising tutor of the Clinical Training in Child Psychotherapy at the Scottish Institute of Human Relations in Edinburgh and works with the Looked After and Accommodated Child and Adolescent Mental Health Team in Glasgow. Her Doctorate in Psychoanalytic Psychotherapy (Child) from the Tavistock/University of East London focused on the assessment of siblings in foster care. She also has a particular interest in literature and the arts and psychoanalysis.

Sylvia Wilson has recently retired from her position as Consultant Child and Adolescent Psychotherapist in an NHS CAMHS Team. She continues to teach part-time on the clinical training of child psychotherapists in Scotland. She has a First Class Honours degree in English Literature and since she retired has been enjoying some creative writing courses with the Open University.

Dr Andrea Peterson lectures in English Literature at the University of Birmingham and is a member of the Centre for First World War Studies. She has published various articles on women's writing and the First World War. Her first book, *Self-Portraits: Subjectivity in the Works of Vera Brittain*, was published in 2007. She is currently researching representations of the First World War in children's literature.

Dr Jenny Plastow teaches on EdD and MA programmes at the University of Hertfordshire and has published articles on primary teaching and literacy, and on Modernist Literature and gender studies. She has worked extensively in practical theatre and Shakespeare, and writes stage and radio plays for children and adults.

Dr Pat Pinsent is Senior Research Fellow at Roehampton University, specialising in Children's Literature, the subject matter of most of her twelve books, and supervising MA Children's Literature and PhD students. She researches the diverse ways in which children's literature is currently developing, and the relationship between it and spirituality/religion. She edits three journals.

Jake Hope studied English literature at the University of York where he was supervised by Peter Hollindale (author "*Signs of Childness in Children's Books*"). He studied an MA in International Children's Literature at the University of Reading specialising in constructions of race ideology. He now co-ordinates Lancashire's annual children's book award.

Nick Midgley is a Child and Adolescent Psychotherapist based at the Marlborough Family Service, London and a Clinical Tutor at the Anna Freud Centre/University College London. He is an avid reader of children's fiction and one of the organisers of a series of 'connecting conversations' between psychoanalysts and children's book authors that takes place regularly in London.

Professor Michael Rustin is a Professor of Sociology at the University of East London and a Visiting Professor at the Tavistock Clinic, London.
Margaret Rustin is the Head of Child Psychotherapy training at the Tavistock Clinic, London.
They are joint authors of *Narratives of Love and Loss: Studies in Modern Children's Fiction*, (1987/2002) and *Mirror to Nature: Drama, Psychoanalysis and Society* (2001). They published articles on the three volumes of Philip Pullman's *His Dark Materials* trilogy in the Journal of Child Psychotherapy, Vol. 29, 2003.

Peter Bramwell tutors Language and Education courses for the Open University and contributes to Sunderland's MA in Children's Literature. Since gaining an MA in Children's Literature from Roehampton, he has continued to research and write independently. He is currently working on a book exploring pagan themes in children's fiction.

Madelyn Travis is Features Editor for the Booktrust Children's Books website and Associate Editor of the Journal of Children's Literature Studies. She has contributed to The Horn Book magazine and The Ultimate Book Guide. She has an MA with Distinction in children's literature from the University of Roehampton and is currently researching representations of Jews in contemporary British children's literature for a PhD at Newcastle University.

John Burton is a psychotherapist and an English Literature PhD student at the University of Wales, researching the role of literature in developing a sense of self. As a psychotherapist, he has interests in the use of story-telling as a therapeutic tool, a way of using metaphor in helping clients, especially children, to develop their own personal problem-solving dynamic, which works particularly well with children. As a Renaissance researcher, he is interested in the ways in which the modern concept of self emerged through the new cultural ethos of interiority, and the development of new literatures, particularly the sonnet sequence.

David Rudd teaches Children's Literature in the Department of Cultural & Creative Studies at the University of Bolton, England. He has published some ninety articles on the subject and two books: one on Roald Dahl, *A Communication Studies Approach to Children's Literature* (1992) and one on Blyton, *Enid Blyton and the Mystery of Children's Literature* (2000). He is currently working on the issue of animals and toys in children's books.

Dr Diane Duncan has been a primary head teacher, university lecturer and external examiner. Her academic background is in sociology, psychology and the teaching of English. Research interests include: mature women students in higher education, emotional intelligence and successful female primary head teachers, peer PhD supervision and the teaching of English in primary education. Now a freelance writer/researcher, she works part-time for the University of Hertfordshire. Her life-long interest and passion is the role of children's literature in their education. She is currently writing a book on the teaching of children's literature for Routledge.

Gerry Byrne is a consultant nurse, child and adolescent psychotherapist, and associate clinical director of Specialist CAMHS (OBMH) in Oxford. He is an honorary principal lecturer at Oxford Brookes University and a tutor on the Oxford Psychoanalytic Observational Studies Course. With two colleagues he runs the annual Children in Troubled Worlds conference, now in its seventh year. This conference promotes the contributions psychoanalytic thinking and the arts can make to work with troubled children. Previous speakers from the arts include Philip Pullman, Anthony Browne, Michael Rosen and Geraldine McCaughrean.
Children in Troubled Worlds website: http://childrenintroubledworlds.org/

Dr Victoria de Rijke is Reader in Arts and Education at Middlesex University in North London. Victoria publishes regularly on children's literature, often in collaboration with young readers and colleagues. Victoria and Howard Hollands are interested in projects dealing with Pirate Pedagogies, things that stand for other things and things that do not seem to be there. They have co-written several articles or chapters featuring picturebook artists, such as Max Velthuis's work in "Crocodiles and Naked Pigs" for the book *Studies in Children's Literature*, Ed C. Keenan & M. Shine-Thompson, Four Courts Press, 2004.

Dr Howard Hollands is Principal (Boy) Lecturer in Art and Design Education at Middlesex University. He devotes much of his time to nothing and recently presented papers 'Drawing a Blank: picturing nothing in the gallery and the classroom' at the 2005 Engage international conference and 'Blackboard Singing in the Dead of Night: mourning the loss of a pedagogic palimpsest' at the Irish Museum of Modern Art in 2006. On a good day he can be seen at work with his PGCE Art and Design students, otherwise he can be found at the top of an ivory tower, attempting to recycle institutional constraints into worthwhile projects.

Antony Lishak Between university, where he studied Sociology, and teacher training college, Antony worked in a wine-bottling factory, a DIY warehouse, as an audio-tape salesman in Stockholm, an orange-picker in Israel and an assistant cook on the night shift in a factory kitchen. All his own experiences, and plenty of other people's, are put to use in his cause of inspiring children to creative writing – he visits 150 schools a year, spreading his passionate enthusiasm among children and their teachers.

ACKNOWLEDGMENTS

For the pleasures of our second conference we would like to thank the Fielder Centre for their impeccable hospitality and support. Thanks to Tony McDermott for his design and his enthusiasm, and Lisa Garner for keeping all the plates spinning.

Also thanks:
To Anthony Browne and to Walker Books, for permission to use illustrations from *Changes*.
To Barefoot Books, for the cover image for *The Green Man,* by Bel Mooney, illustrated by Helen McCann.
To David Higham Associates for permission to use illustrations from Mervyn Peake's *Captain Slaughterboard Drops Anchor*.
To Bloomsbury, for permission to publish illustrations from two books by Neil Gaiman – *The Wolves in the Walls* (2003) and *Coraline* (2004). In both cases, the illustrations are by Dave McKean.
To HarperCollins Children's Books, for permission to use illustrations from *Lost and Found* by Oliver Jeffers.
To Random House, for permission to use illustrations from *Katie Morag and the Tiresome Ted* by Mhairi Hedderwick.

An earlier draft of Nick Midgley's paper was presented at a conference on 'Fear and Fiction' organised by the Yale Child Study Centre and the Anna Freud Centre in New York in December 2006, and one section of it was included in the *Psychoanalytic Study of the Child*, Volume 61, as part of their report on that conference. Thanks to the publishers and editors of that journal for permission to use some of that material in the present chapter.

Still available: UH Children's Literature Annual No.1 (2006 Conference)
Email **L.A.Garner@herts.ac.uk** for further information/orders

University of Hertfordshire
School of Education

CHILDREN'S LITERATURE
ANNUAL No. 1

Owners of the means of instruction?

Children's Literature
some Marxist perspectives

papers and presentations from conference 2006

Coming April 2008: book now -

The Sands of Time
Children's Literature, Culture, Politics and Identity

A two-day conference at the University of Hertfordshire's Fielder Centre, Hatfield, Hertfordshire
Thursday 3rd and Friday 4th April 2008

Key speakers include:
Anne Cassidy, Berlie Doherty, Alan Gibbons, Elizabeth Laird, Anthony Lishak, Richard MacSween, Beverley Naidoo and others

For further information:
Tel: Lisa Garner 01707 285695   **E-mail:** L.A.Garner@herts.ac.uk

University of Hertfordshire